Digital Logic Simulation and CPLD Programming

Steve Waterman

DeVry Institute of Technology
DuPage Campus

Prentice Hall

Upper Saddle River, New Jersey   *Columbus, Ohio*

Cover art: John Still/photonica
Editor: Scott Sambucci
Production Editor: Stephen C. Robb
Design Coordinator: Karrie M. Converse-Jones
Cover Designer: Karrie M. Converse-Jones
Production Manager: Patricia A. Tonneman
Marketing Manager: Ben Leonard

This book was set in Times New Roman by Steve Waterman and was printed and bound by Victor Graphics, Inc. The cover was printed by Victor Graphics, Inc.

© 2000 by Prentice-Hall, Inc.
Pearson Education
Upper Saddle River, New Jersey 07458

Printed in the United States of America

10 9 8 7 6 5 4 3 2 1

ISBN: 0-13-084256-7

Prentice-Hall International (UK) Limited, *London*
Prentice-Hall of Australia Pty. Limited, *Sydney*
Prentice-Hall Canada, Inc., *Toronto*
Prentice-Hall Hispanoamericana, S. A., *Mexico*
Prentice-Hall of India Private Limited, *New Dehli*
Prentice-Hall of Japan, Inc., *Tokyo*
Prentice-Hall (Singapore) Pte. Ltd., *Singapore*
Editora Prentice-Hall do Brasil, Ltda., *Rio de Janeiro*

To my wife Betty
and sons
Alexander and Christopher

Table of Contents

Parts list

Max+plus II Version 7.21 Student Edition software by Altera Corporation
(1) Breadboard
(1) 741 Operational amplifier
(1) 555 Timer IC
(10) Light emitting diodes
(1) DAC0808 digital-to-analog convertor (National)
(1) ADC0804 analog-to-digital convertor (National)
(1) 6116 memory chip (2K x 8)
(1) Thermistor
(3) Quad DIP switches (SPDT)
(2) Pushbutton switches (SPDT)
(1) Byte blaster
(1) * Circuit board with the MAX7000S chip

(1) 220-Ω resistor
(10) 1-KΩ resistors
(4) 4.7-KΩ resistors
(3) 10-KΩ resistors
(5) 20-KΩ resistors
(1) 33-KΩ resistor
(2) 47-KΩ resistors
(5) 100-KΩ resistors
(1) 1-KΩ potentiometer PC mount
(1) 10-KΩ potentiometer PC mount
(1) 50-KΩ potentiometer PC mount

(1) 20- μFd capacitor
(1) 1-μFd capacitor
(2) 0.1-μFd capacitors
(2) 0.01-μFd capacitors
(2) 0.001-μFd capacitors
(1) 150-pFd capacitor

* Contact the vendor directly for prices:

University Board from Altera Corporation, 101 Innovation Drive, San Jose, California (408) 544-8274
http://www.altera.com
or
UPXa Board from Intectra, 2629 Terminal Blvd - Mountain View, CA 94043 USA   (650) 967-8818
http://www.intectra.com

Free software: Max+plus II Version 7.12 (or more current version) Student Edition software
Altera Corporation, 101 Innovation Drive, San Jose, California (408) 544-8274

Preface

This lab manual may be used to accompany any well-written digital electronics textbook to teach the fundamentals of digital electronics or may be used by professionals to learn how to use the Max+plus II software by Altera Corporation. Altera does have a university board and a Byte Blaster cable that are connected directly to the computer's RS232 port for programming the on-board CPLDs (Complex Programmable Logic Devices). Appendix C contains a step-by-step procedure to program the MAX7000S CPLD. Any successfully compiled circuit may be downloaded to the CPLD through a JTAG mounted on the board. Contact Altera Corporation at http://www.altera.com for additional information on their University Program and support literature. Other vendors also support the JTAG programmable MAX7000S chip using the Max+plus II software.

The sequence of the labs may be altered; however, a software feature described in a lower numbered lab will not be described in supplemental labs. This may pose a problem for students unless the software features used in a lab are discussed in class.

The Max+plus II software has large libraries of digital devices commonly found in data books, however, your application may require the CPLD to be interfaced to other devices like a microprocessor, microcontroller, memory, and A/D or D/A convertors. If using the university board by Altera, be very cautious since the I/Os are not buffered and carelessness may cause permanent damage to the CPLD.

Occasionally, the labs make reference to the 74 Series Integrated Circuits. Data sheets to these ICs are available for download from Texas Instruments, at http://www.ti.com. Contents and layouts of home pages periodically change so use Texas Instruments' local search engine to locate the specific data sheets.

All data sheets from the Texas Instruments home page are in Adobe format, requiring Adobe Acrobat Reader to read and print the file. The latest version of the Adobe Acrobat Reader is available for download at http://www.adobe.com. Check your computer directories using Windows Explorer for the Acrobat directory. If found, your computer already has the Acrobat Reader.

The lab sequence starts with fundamentals of digital gates and logic control circuits, progresses to MSI devices, to latches and flip-flops and are intended for first-term digital students. These 13 labs introduce the software features needed to master the Graphic and Waveform Editors in the Max+plus II Student Edition V7.21 software by Altera Corporation, as well as implementing digital concepts learned in fundamental digital courses. Subsequent labs are based on clock dependent circuits including counters and registers, memory addressing, and A/D and D/A convertors, some of which will require interfacing the university board to external components on a breadboard. Several labs will focus on the LPM_MACRO functions available (unique) in the software.

Lab 14 may appear to be a duplicate of Lab 13, however, Lab 13 discusses fundamentals of latches and flip-flops with respect to the logic symbols. Lab 14 discusses latches and flip-flops found in integrated circuit form: 7475, 7476, 74LS76, and 74373. If the lab manual is to be used in two sequential courses, the instructor may assign Labs 1 to 13 for the first digital course, then assign the rest of the labs for the second digital course. In this way, Lab 14, of the second course would provide congruency between the two courses.

All circuits the students are asked to build are available to the instructor on CD ROM. Each lab procedure starts with instructions to open the editors and assigning a project name. The file on the CD is named the same as the project name to be assigned and is located in a directory sharing the name of the lab. It is strongly recommended that the students save all working files to his/her floppy disk in Drive A or assigned working directory on the hard drive and save all software generated files to the same directory/drive. Students will quickly fill the FAT (file allocation table) for a diskette, resulting in software crashes. To free up diskette space, delete all files on the diskette except for the .gdf and .scf files. If using networked computers, you may consider assigning a section of the hard drive to each student. Students should avoid using the Maxplus2 directory as his or her working directory.

Students always enjoy getting something for nothing, well almost for nothing. Most students in my classes who have computers at home want their own copy of the software. In this way, they can spend considerable amount of time at home doing their labs and can verify homework assignments using the computer. What a wonderful way to extend lab hours! Of course, the software is free but they will need to obtain the software from Altera. Once the software is installed, the student is directed to Altera's home page where the student fills out a form to get an authorization code necessary to activate the software. Relatively painless! Faculty can send an e-mail request to Altera's University Program asking for XXX student version CD ROMs and they will gladly send them. I normally check these out to students overnight or for a weekend to be installed on their personal PCs.

As with all software, revisions are inevitable. All labs written with student edition V7.21 are upward compatible to the Professional Version 9.0. Only the .gdf and .scf files for each lab appear on the CD ROM. These files may be read with the latest software version, and when compiled the software will generate the necessary files recognized by this version. If someone uses the Professional Version in the lab or at work, then wants to finish a lab at home with the student version, delete all but the .gdf and .scf files on the disk, then read these files with the student edition.

Introduction

Programmable Logic Devices (PLDs) have evolved since the early 1980s from containing a few hundred gates to over a million gates. As the gate density within the devices have grown in excess of 10,000 times, the physical size of the devices have doubled, taking up about the same real estate on a circuit board as two small scale (SSI) or medium scale (MSI) integrated circuits. Three types of programmable logic devices are:

> Simple Programmable Logic Devices (SPLDs),
> Complex Programmable Logic Devices (CPLDs), and
> Field Programmable Gate Arrays (FPGAs)

Simple Programmable Logic Devices

The least-expensive programmable logic devices are Simple Programmable Logic Devices (SPLDs). An SPLD can replace a few 7400-series TTL devices. Most SPLDs are programmed using Boolean-based software, ABEL being one of the most popular. The designer writes a program using a basic text editor, assembles the file into a JEDEC file, then downloads the JEDEC file to the SPLD chip mounted on a programmer unit. SPLDs may be reprogrammed in the engineering lab many times (up to 100 for some devices), making the SPLD ideal for the designer. Several SPLDs that have evolved are:

> PAL (Programmable Array Logic)
> GAL (Generic Array Logic)

PLA (Programmable Logic Array)
PLD (Programmable Logic Device)

Complex Programmable Logic Device

Time to market pressures have increased the demands to making higher density PLDs. Using Complex Programmable Logic Devices (CPLDs) shortens develop times, provides simpler manufacturer development and testing, and supports system upgrades in the field; ISP allows manufacturers to get their product to market quicker. In system programmability, ISP, allow the designer to modify or upgrade the design as needed without altering the circuit card design.

CPLDs have significantly higher gate densities than PLDs. Software enhancements allow the designer more programming techniques than was available for the SPLD. Designs may be graphically entered using symbols based on TTL devices, logic macros designed by the designer, or popular software languages such as VHDL (**V**ery **H**igh Speed Application Specific Integrated Circuit **H**ardware **D**escription **L**anguage). Numerous CPLD manufacturers have proprietary software that may also be used to program their devices.

CPLDs are CMOS logic devices using non-volatile memory cells, using either EPROM, EEPROM, or FLASH technologies. The EPM7128SLC84 is an EEPROM that can be reprogrammed 100 times or so.

Field Programmable Gate Array

Of the three, FPGAs offer the highest logic capacity. The Flex 10K series from Altera is SRAM (Static RAM) based and comes in various pin densities up to 240 pins. Since SRAM is volatile, it is common practice to download the program to ROM memory, which then is automatically loaded into the FPGA when power is applied to the system. FPGAs consist of an array of logic blocks, surrounded by programmable I/O blocks connected together with programmable interconnects. Software places and routes the logic on the device.

The university board by Altera contains the EPM7128SLC84 CPLD and Flex10K FPGA, which exposes students to both technologies. However, the EPM7128SLC84 will suffice for all labs within this manual.

Note to the Instructor

This lab manual is based of the Max+plus II Version 7.21 Student Edition software and the Max7000S family complex programmable logic device (CPLD) by Altera Corporation. The software and university board are available from Altera Corporation, 101 Innovation Drive, San Jose, CA 95134, USA. A lower cost alternative board with fewer bells and whistles is available from Intectra, 2629 Terminal Blvd., Mountain View, CA. 94043. Intectra may be reached at http://www.intectra.com .

All .gdf and .scf files for each lab section appear on the CD ROM supplied with the solutions manual under the directory that matches the lab name. The labs instruct the student to "construct and simulate the circuit in Figure XXX" but you may save the time evaluating labs using the pre-assembled circuit files. Maybe after several labs, you may want to share these circuit files with your students, and they will love you for the rest of the term.

Acknowledgments

I am very grateful to my colleagues, Gary Luechtefeld, Zoran Ulcivich, and J. Samuel Watson, at DeVry DuPage in Addison, Illinois, for their patience, advice, moral support, and willingness to assign the labs in rough draft to their students as the labs were being developed.

I gratefully acknowledge the following reviewers for their insightful suggestions:

* ★ Dan Black, DeVry Institute of Technology, Phoenix, Arizona
* ★ Marco D'Onofrio, Santa Marta's University
* ★ James Hamblen, Georgia Institute of Technology
* ★ Joe Hanson, Altera Corporation, 101 Innovation Drive, San Jose, California
* ★ John Hull, DeVry Institute of Technology, DuPage campus, Addison, Illinois
* ★ Bill Kleitz, Tompkins Courtland Community College
* ★ Shodi Mazidi, DeVry Institute of Technology - Calgary
* ★ Art Ramirez, DeVry Institute of Technology, DuPage campus, Addison, Illinois
* ★ Guillermo Jaquenod, Calle 24 # 709 - (1900), La Plata, Argentina
* ★ Carlos Puleston, Intectra, 2629 Terminal Blvd., Mountain View, California

Thanks goes to the many students who provided constructive criticisms as they completed each lab during development.

Special thanks to Ellen Framke and John Wright for their help in writing parts of the latches and flip-flops experiment. Both were first-term students who needed to install the Max+plus II software, learn how to use the software on their own, and convert notes into a structured step-by-step procedure.

It is a pleasure working with the people at Prentice Hall, and special thanks to Scott Sambucci, Dave Garza, and Evan Girard for their continued support during the completion of this project.

About the Author

Professor Waterman, MEd, teaches in the Electronics Technician and Telecommunications programs at the DuPage Campus of DeVry Institute of Technology in Addison, Illinois. As the digital/micro/controls sequence chair, Professor Waterman is very active teaching Computer Hardware/Software, Digital Fundamentals, Introduction to Microprocessors, Advanced Microprocessors including the Intel 80xxx assembler or Motorola 68xxx assembler. Courses are Internet based where students can access classroom activities using a Web browser and complete assignments on-line. Professor Waterman is a member of DeVry's National Digital Committee that determines course sequence and content, a member of IEEE, ISA, and local SCUBA diving club.

waterman@dpg.devry.edu
http://www.dpg.devry.edu/~waterman

Lab 1: Logic Gates

Objectives:

1. Learn how to use the Max+plus II^R software to create a schematic, create waveforms, compile, and simulate a circuit
2. Analyze waveforms and develop truth tables for these fundamental logic gates:

AND	OR	NOT	NAND
NOR	XOR	XNOR	

3. (Optional) Program the EPM7128SLC84-7 Programmable Logic Device and verify each gate operation

Materials list:

*   Max+plus II software by Altera Corporation
*   University Board by Altera Corporation (optional)
*   Computer requirements:
    Minimum 486/66 with 8 MB RAM
*   Floppy disk

Discussion:

The symbols for the logic gates discussed in this lab are shown in Figure 1. The **NOT** gate, or the INVERTER, produces an output opposite of the input. The NOT symbol shows an active-HIGH input and an active-LOW output.

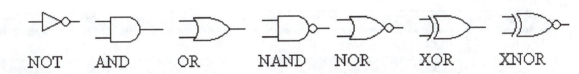

NOT   AND   OR   NAND   NOR   XOR   XNOR

Figure 1

The **AND** gate produces a logic-HIGH output only when ALL inputs to the gate are a logic-HIGH. The AND gate has active-HIGH inputs and an active-HIGH output.

The **OR** gate produces a logic-HIGH output if either or both inputs are a logic-HIGH. The inputs and output are active-HIGH.

The **NAND** gate produces a logic-LOW output only when ALL inputs to the gate are a logic-HIGH. The NAND gate has active-HIGH inputs and an active-LOW output. The NAND gate is derived from inverting the output of the AND gate.

The **NOR** gate is the complement of the OR gate. The **NOR** gate produces a logic-LOW output if either or both inputs are a logic-HIGH. The inputs are active-HIGH whereas the output is active-LOW.

The exclusive OR gate, or **XOR**, produces a logic-HIGH output when either, but not both, input to the gate is a logic-HIGH. Both inputs and the output of the XOR gate are active-HIGH.

If the output of the XOR gate is inverted, you have an **XNOR** function. The XNOR gate produces a logic-HIGH output when both inputs to the gate are the same logic level.

The Draw and Tool Bar icons you will be using in this lab are identified in Figure 2. The tool bar contains buttons such as: New, Open, Save, Print, Cut, Copy, Paste, and Undo. The Font and Point size can be quickly changed using the buttons on the right side of this tool bar. The vertical row of buttons on the left side of the screen contain draw functions such as Select, Text, Line, Diagonal, Arc, Circle, Zoom In, and Zoom Out. Other tool bar buttons will be discussed in the lab where appropriate.

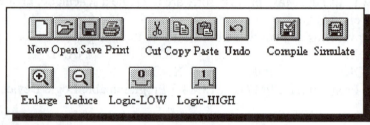

Figure 2

Part 1   Procedure

1.   Open the Max+Plus II 7.21 Student Edition software. From the desktop, select **Start - Programs - Max+plus II - Max+plus II 7.21 Student Edition**.

Once the software opens, you will see a menu bar at the top of the screen with names similar to those you would find in most Windows[R]-based programs, that is, File, Edit, View, Options, Window, and Help.

2.   From the main menu, select **File - Project - Name**. See Figure 3. The Project Name dialog box (see Figure 4) will appear.

Figure 3

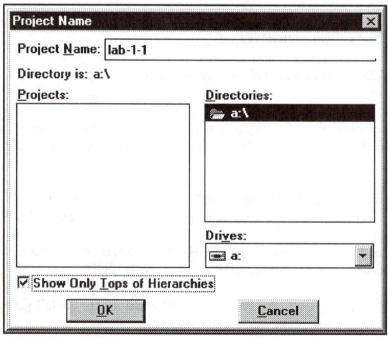

Figure 4

Lab 1: Logic Gates

3.   Insert a diskette into the floppy drive and select the drive letter in the **Drives:** window of the Project Name dialog box. Delete all text in the Project Name window, then type **lab-1-1**. Press **OK**. Every project must have a project name that matches the design file name. Because a project name must be assigned every time the Max+plus II is run, your files must have that same project name.

4.   Select **File - New - Graphic Editor File**. Press **OK**. The Graphic Editor screen will appear with **Untitled1 - Graphic Editor** as the file name.

5.   The student edition allows the programming for a Flex 7000S, 84-pin integrated circuit, and a Flex 10K, 240-pin IC. The IC you will program is the 84-pin EPM7128SLC84-7 IC. To assign this IC, select **Assign - Device**. When the Device dialog box appears (Figure 5), select the MAX7000S device family. Either select Auto or the EPM7128SLC84-7 device. Press **OK**. The device name need only be assigned once, when the software is first opened.

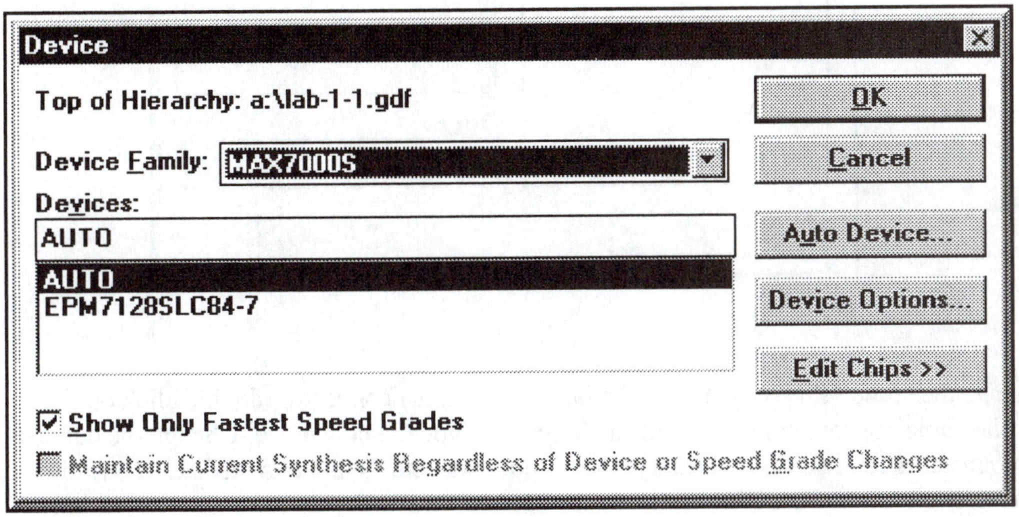

```
Device                                                          [X]

Top of Hierarchy: a:\lab-1-1.gdf                      [    OK    ]

Device Family: [MAX7000S                        ▼]    [  Cancel  ]
Devices:
[AUTO                                              ]  [ Auto Device... ]
┌──────────────────────────────────────────────┐
│ AUTO                                            │  [ Device Options... ]
│ EPM7128SLC84-7                                  │
│                                                │  [ Edit Chips >> ]
└──────────────────────────────────────────────┘

☑ Show Only Fastest Speed Grades
☐ Maintain Current Synthesis Regardless of Device or Speed Grade Changes
```

Figure 5

6.   Now you are ready to enter the logic symbol. Place the cursor (arrow) at the point in the work area where you want to insert a symbol, then click on the left mouse pointer to obtain a flashing square dot. This will be called the "insertion point" throughout this lab. Select **Symbol - Enter Symbol - OK** and the Enter Symbol dialog box appears (Figure 7). Available libraries are the Altera primitives (prim) containing basic logic building blocks, macrofunctions (mf) of the 7400 family logic, LPMs and Megafunctions (mega_lpm) for high-level circuit functions, and the building blocks (edif) for the macrofunctions.

7.   Set the mouse pointer on the **..\maxplus2\max2lib\prim** directory and double click on the left mouse button. Select **and2** in the Symbol Files list and press **OK**. (You could also double click on the symbol name.) The symbol will appear in the Graphic Editor.

8.   Insert the input and output symbols found in the **..\maxplus2\max2lib\prim** directory and position these symbols to create the circuit shown in Figure 6. Single click the left side of each symbol to "click and drag" the symbol to the desired position.

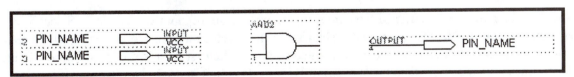

Figure 6

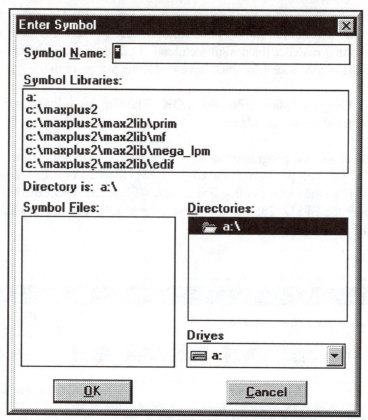

Figure 7

9.   To change the name "PIN_NAME" of the input (or output) connector, double click on the current name. When the name appears in reverse text (highlighted), type the new name. Change the current names of the input connectors to A and B and change the output connector's name to AND2. Your circuit should now look like the circuit in Figure 8.

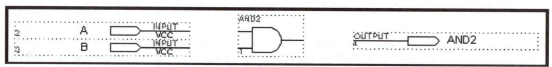

Figure 8

10.   Add lines from each gate terminal to the respective input or output terminal. To make these lines, position the mouse pointer on a gate terminal. When the mouse pointer turns into a cross, click and drag the mouse so that it barely touches the input or output connector lead. Do <u>not</u> drag and release the wire inside a component. The circuit should appear as shown in Figure 9.

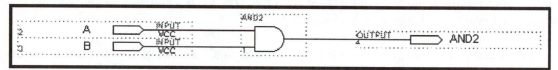

Figure 9

11.   Now that the circuit is constructed, you are ready to create a set of input waveforms.   Select **File - New - Waveform Editor File,** then press **OK**. The Untitled1 Waveform Editor will appear on the screen. An unlimited number of "fields" are below the Name column. The first field is shown in Figure 10, but it does not appear on your screen when the Waveform Editor File is first opened. Don't worry if your scale is different than what is shown in Figure 10.

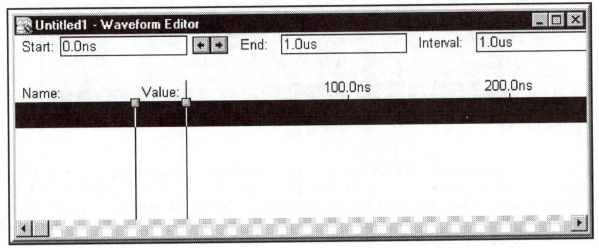

Figure 10

12. Place your mouse pointer in the first field below the Name column, then double click on the left mouse pointer. The Insert Node dialog box will appear. Enter **A** for the Node Name and select **Input Pin** in the **I/O Type** frame. Press **OK**. The input waveform "A" was created with a "value" of "0" from 0 ns to 1 μs.

13. Place your mouse pointer in the first field below Waveform A, then double click on the left mouse pointer. Enter **B** for the Node Name, then press the **OK** button. The input waveform "B" was created with a "value" of "0" from 0 ns to 1 μs.

14. Place your mouse pointer in the first field below Waveform B, then double click on the left mouse pointer. The Insert Node dialog box will appear. Enter **AND2** for the Node Name and select **Output Pin** in the I/O Type frame. Press **OK**. The output waveform "AND2" was created with a "value" of "0" from 0 ns to 1 μs. The Waveform Editor should look like Figure 11.

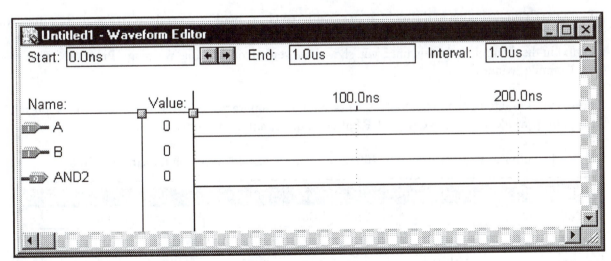

Figure 11

15. Turn on the **Snap to Grid** feature in the Options menu. If this feature already has a checkmark next to it, as shown in Figure 12, the feature is already turned on.

16. Select **Grid Size** (Figure 12) in the Options menu, type **100** in the Grid Size dialog box, then press the Enter key. The Waveform Editor now has vertical timing marks every 100 ns.

Figure 12

17. Highlight the section of Waveform A from 100 ns to 200 ns by clicking and dragging the mouse pointer, starting at the 100 ns marker. Change this highlighted section to a logic-HIGH pulse using the Logic-HIGH pulse button in the Draw tool bar (refer to Figure 2). In a similar manner, change Waveform A, 300 ns to 400 ns, and Waveform B, 200 ns to 400 ns, to a logic-HIGH. Your waveforms should look like those shown in Figure 13.

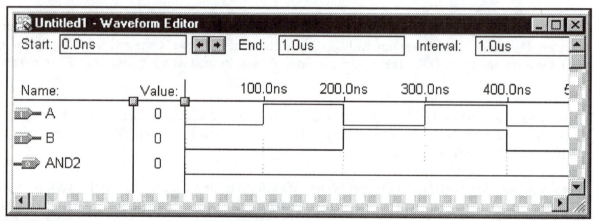

Figure 13

18. Press the Compile button in the tool bar (disk with red check mark). Save the .GDF and .SCF files when the respective Save As dialog boxes appear. You should have zero errors. Press **OK**, then press the Start button in the Compiler. At this time, you should see zero errors and one warning. Press **OK**, then close the Compiler window.

19. Press the Simulate button in the tool bar (disk with blue square wave). Assuming zero errors, press **OK** in the pop-up window, then the **Open SCF** button in the Simulator window.

20. Draw the output waveform from 0 to 400 ns in Figure 14 as displayed on the Graphic Editor.

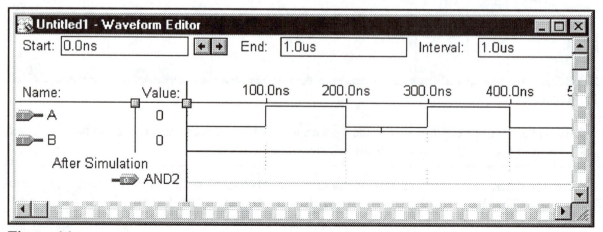

Figure 14

Lab 1: Logic Gates

21. Analyze the waveforms in Figure 14 and complete the function table for the 2 input AND gate.

B	A	X
0	0	
0	1	
1	0	
1	1	

2 input AND gate function table

22. Write the Boolean expression to represent the 2 input AND gate.

X = _____

23. Explain when the output of the AND gate is a logic-HIGH, with respect to inputs A and B.

_____

24. Save the editor files to Drive A as **lab-1-1**, then exit the Graphic and Waveform Editors.

Part 2   Procedure

1. Open the Max+plus II software. Assign the project name **lab-1-2** and assign MAX7000S for the device family.

2. Open a new Graphic Editor file and construct the circuit shown in Figure 15.

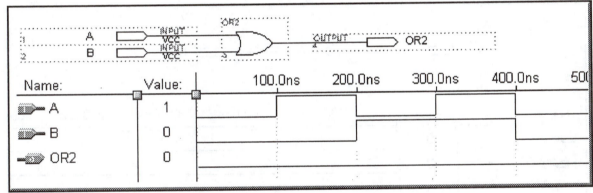

Figure 15

3. Open a new Waveform Editor file, set the Grid Size to 100 ns, and create the waveforms shown in Figure 15.

4. Press the Compile and Simulate buttons. Press **OK** in the Save As dialog boxes. Correct all errors before continuing.

5. Assuming zero errors, draw the output waveform of the 2 input OR gate in Figure 16.

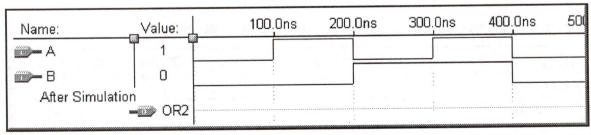

Figure 16

6. Analyze the waveforms in Figure 16 and complete the function table for the 2 input OR gate.

7. Write the Boolean expression to represent the 2 input OR gate.

X = _____

8. Explain when the output of the OR gate is a logic-HIGH, with respect to inputs A and B.

B	A	X
0	0	
0	1	
1	0	
1	1	

2 input OR gate function table

_____

9. Save the editor files to Drive A as **lab-1-2**, then exit the Graphic and Waveform Editors.

Part 3   Procedure

1. Open the Max+plus II software. Assign the project name **lab-1-3** and assign MAX7000S for the device family.

2. Open a new Graphic Editor file and construct the circuit shown in Figure 17.

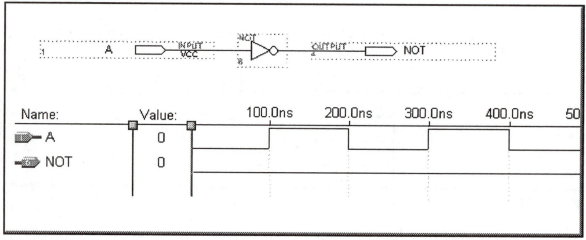

Figure 17

3. Open a new Waveform Editor file, set the Grid Size to 100 ns, and create the circuit and waveforms shown in Figure 17.

4. Press the Compile and Simulate buttons. Press **OK** in the Save As dialog boxes. Correct all errors before continuing.

5. Assuming zero errors, draw the output waveform for the NOT gate in Figure 18.

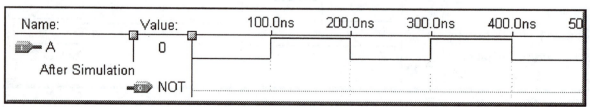

Figure 18

Lab 1: Logic Gates

6. Analyze the waveforms in Figure 18 and complete the function table for the NOT gate.

7. Write the Boolean expression to represent the NOT gate.

X = _____

A	X
0	
1	

NOT gate function table

8. Write a statement explaining output X with respect to input A of the NOT gate.

_____

9. Save the editor files to Drive A as **lab-1-3**, then exit the Graphic and Waveform Editors.

Part 4   Procedure

1. Open the Max+plus II software. Assign the project name **lab-1-4** and assign MAX7000S for the device family.

2. Open a new Graphic Editor file and construct the circuit shown in Figure 19.

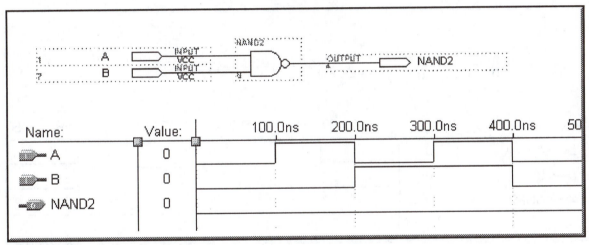

Figure 19

3. Open a new Waveform Editor file, set the Grid Size to 100 ns, and create the circuit and waveforms shown in Figure 19.

4. Press the Compile and Simulate buttons. Correct all errors before continuing.

5. Assuming zero errors, draw the output waveform for the 2 input NAND gate in Figure 20.

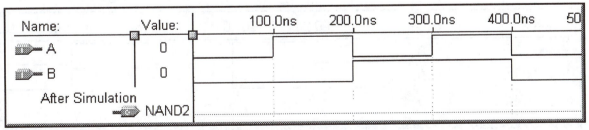

Figure 20

6. Analyze the waveforms in Figure 20 and complete the function table for the 2 input NAND gate.

B	A	X
0	0	
0	1	
1	0	
1	1	

2 input NAND gate function table

7. Write the Boolean expression to represent the NAND gate.
X = ______________

8. Write a statement explaining output X with respect to inputs A and B of the NAND gate.

____

9. Save the editor files to Drive A as **lab-1-4**, then exit the Graphic and Waveform Editors.

Part 5 Procedure

1. Open the Max+plus II software. Assign the project name **lab-1-5** and assign MAX7000S for the device family.

2. Open a new Graphic Editor file and construct the circuit shown in Figure 21.

A
B
INPUT
VCC
INPUT
VCC
NOR2
OUTPUT
NOR2
Name:
Value:
100.0ns
200.0ns
300.0ns
400.0ns
A
B
NOR2
0
0
0

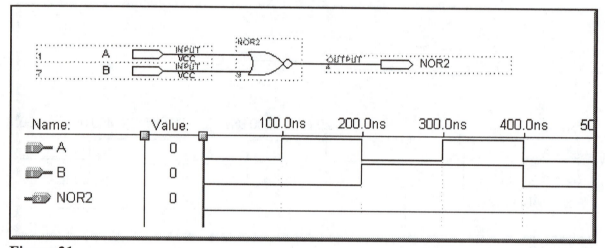

Figure 21

3. Open a new Waveform Editor file, set the Grid Size to 100 ns, and create the waveforms shown in Figure 21.

4. Press the Compile and Simulate buttons. Press **OK** in the Save As dialog boxes. Correct all errors before continuing.

5. Assuming zero errors, draw the output waveform for the 2 input NOR gate in Figure 22.

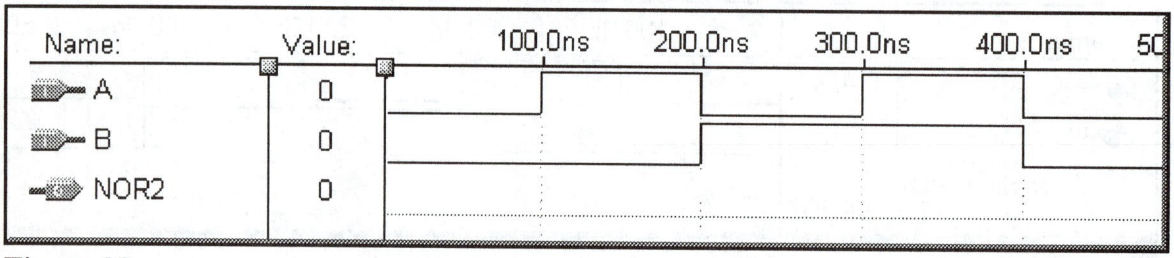

Name:
Value:
100.0ns
200.0ns
300.0ns
400.0ns
A
B
NOR2
0
0
0

Figure 22

6. Analyze the waveforms in Figure 22 and complete the function table for the 2 input NOR gate.

7. Write the Boolean expression to represent the 2 input NOR gate.

   X = _____

B	A	X
0	0	
0	1	
1	0	
1	1	

2 input NOR gate function table

8. Write a statement explaining output X with respect to inputs A and B of the NOR gate.

---

9. Save the editor files to Drive A as **lab-1-5**, then exit the Graphic and Waveform Editors.

Part 6   Procedure

1. Open the Max+plus II software. Assign the project name **lab-1-6** and assign MAX7000S for the device family.

2. Open a new Graphic Editor file and construct the circuit shown in Figure 23.

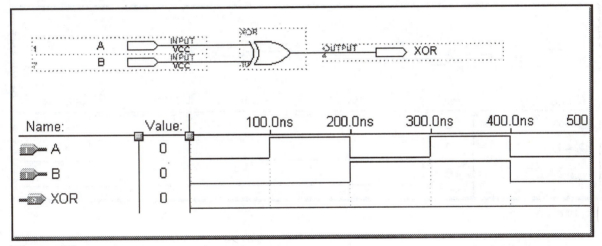

Figure 23

3. Open a new Waveform Editor file and create the circuit and waveforms shown in Figure 23.

4. Press the Compile and Simulate buttons. Press **OK** in the Save As dialog boxes as they appear. Correct all errors before continuing. Assuming zero errors, draw the output waveform for the 2 input XOR gate in Figure 24.

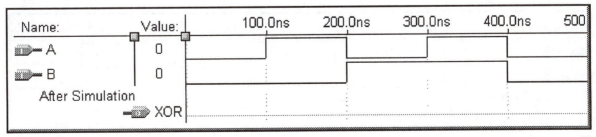

Figure 24

5.   Analyze the waveforms in Figure 22 and complete the function table for the 2 input XOR gate.

6.   Write the Boolean expression to represent the 2 input XOR gate.

X = _____

7.   Write a statement explaining output X with respect to inputs A and B of the XOR gate.

B	A	X
0	0	
0	1	
1	0	
1	1	

2 input XOR gate function table

8.   Save the editor files to Drive A as **lab-1-6** then exit the Graphic and Waveform Editors.

Part 7   Procedure

1.   Open the Max+plus II software. Assign the project name **lab-1-7** and assign MAX7000S as the device family.

2.   Open a new Graphic Editor file and construct the circuit shown in Figure 25.

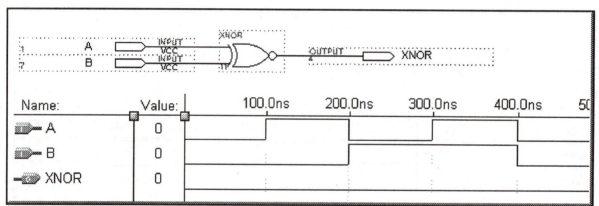

Figure 25

3.   Open a new Waveform Editor file, set the Grid Size to 100 ns, and create the circuit and waveforms shown in Figure 25.

4.   Press the Compile and Simulate buttons. Do save the .GDF and .SCF files when the Save As dialog boxes appear. Correct all errors before continuing.

5.   Assuming zero errors, draw the output waveform of the 2 input XNOR gate in Figure 26.

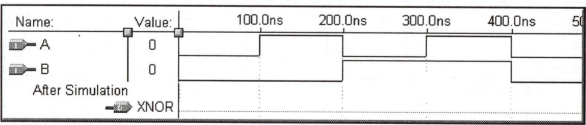

Figure 26

6. Analyze the waveforms in Figure 26 and complete the function table for the 2 input XNOR gate.

7. Write the Boolean expression to represent the 2 input XNOR gate.

   X = _____

B	A	X
0	0	
0	1	
1	0	
1	1	

2 input XNOR gate function table

8. Write a statement explaining output X with respect to inputs A and B of the XNOR gate.

_____

9. Save the editor files to Drive A as **lab-1-7**, then exit the Graphic and Waveform Editors.

Part 8   Procedure

1. Open the Max+plus II software. Assign the project name **lab-1-8** and assign MAX7000S as the device family.

2. Open a new Graphic Editor file and construct the circuit shown in Figure 27.

3. Open a new Waveform Editor file and create the waveforms shown in Figure 27.

4. Compile and simulate the circuit. Save the .GDF and .SCF files when the Save As dialog boxes appear. Assuming no errors and that all output waveforms reflect the proper wave for the corresponding gate, continue with the next step. Correct all errors before continuing.

5. Bring the Graphic Editor to the foreground. Place the mouse pointer in the upper-left side of your figure, then click and drag the mouse to the lower-right side of the figure, highlighting the entire figure. Select **File - Print** from the main menu. In the Pages block, select **Selected Area** and **Fit into 100% of one page**, then press **OK**. This method allows you to print only the selected work area.

6. An alternative method for printing a legible schematic is to select **File - Size**, then set the **Orientation** to Horizontal and select the **Sheet Size** to A: 9×11 in [59 x 77 GUs]. If you receive a "Sheet size is too small for drawing" error message, then select the next paper size listed, B:, C:, and so on. Once the paper size is selected, press the Print icon in the tool bar or select **File - Print** in the main menu.

7. Bring the Waveform Editor to the foreground. Select **File - Print Setup** in the main menu. Check **Landscape** in the Orientation box, then press **OK**. Select **File - Print - OK** from the main menu.

8. Demonstrate the waveforms printed to your instructor. Obtain the signature directly on the answer page for this lab.

9. Save the editor files to Drive A as **lab-1-8**, then exit the Max+plus II software.

10. Create a cover page for the lab in the following format.
    - Name and section in upper-right corner
    - Title of lab centered on page with instructor's name below the title
    - Today's date in the lower-right corner

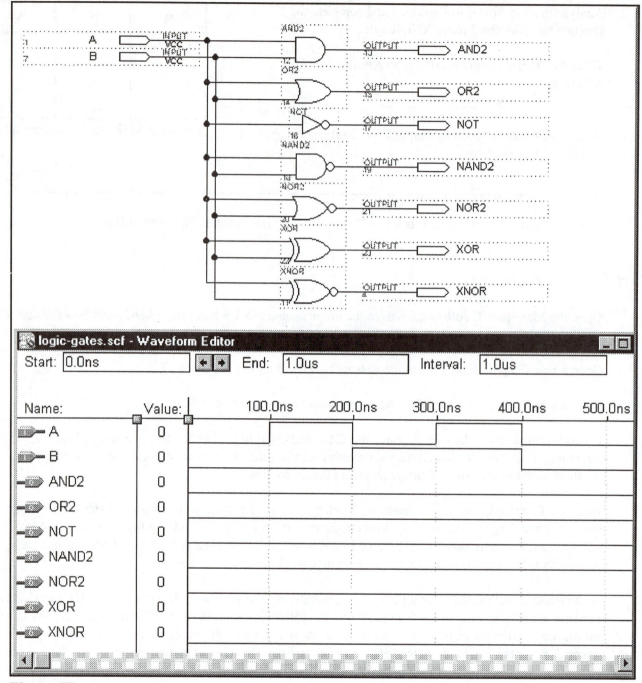

Figure 27

11. Write a one-page summary using Times New Roman 12-point font pertaining to the results obtained from this lab. Include in your summary a single function table with the logic gates AND, OR, NOT A, NAND, NOR, XOR, and XNOR as output column headings.

12. Place all papers for this lab in the following sequence, then submit the lab to your instructor for grading.
    - Cover page
    - Typed summary
    - The completed answer page for this lab
    - The hard copy of the Graphic Editor, **Part 8, Step 5**
    - The hard copy of the Waveform Editor, **Part 8, Step 7**

Lab 1: Logic Gates Answer Page

Name: _____

Part 1

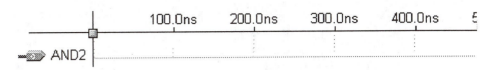

Figure 14

B	A	X
0	0	
0	1	
1	0	
1	1	

2 input AND gate function table

22.   X = _____

23.   _____

       _____

Part 2

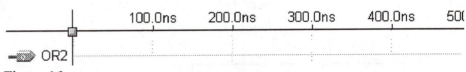

Figure 16

B	A	X
0	0	
0	1	
1	0	
1	1	

2 input OR gate function table

7.   X = _____

8.   _____

      _____

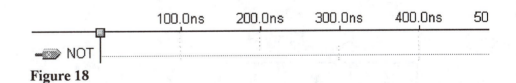

Figure 18

Part 3

7.   X = _____

8.   _____

      _____

A	X
0	
1	

NOT gate function table

Part 4

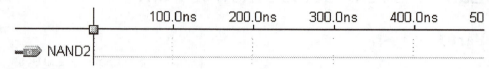

Figure 20

B	A	X
0	0	
0	1	
1	0	
1	1	

2 input NAND gate function table

7.   X = _____

8.   _____

      _____

Part 5

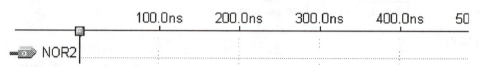

Figure 22

B	A	X
0	0	
0	1	
1	0	
1	1	

2 input NOR gate function table

7.   X = _____

8.   _____

      _____

Part 6

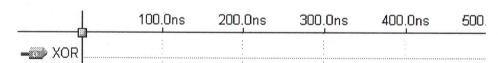

Figure 24

B	A	X
0	0	
0	1	
1	0	
1	1	

2 input XOR gate function table

6.   X = _____

7.   _____

      _____

Part 7

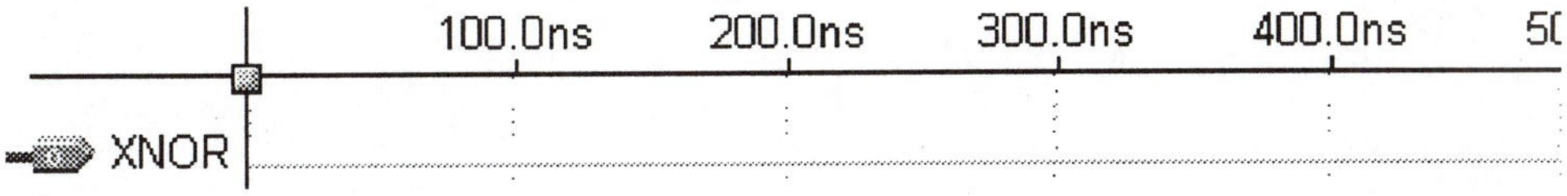

	100.0ns	200.0ns	300.0ns	400.0ns	5(

XNOR

Figure 26

B	A	X
0	0	
0	1	
1	0	
1	1	

2 input XNOR gate function table

7.   X = _____

8.   _____

          _____

Part 8

8.   Demonstrated to: _____ Date: _____

Grade: _____

Lab 2: Boolean: Laws, Principles, and Rules

Objectives:

    1.   Verify Boolean laws using waveform analysis
    2.   Prove the 12 Boolean rules
    3.   Verify DeMorgan's principle
    4.   Demonstrate dual-function gates

Materials List:

    ♦   Max+plus II software by Altera Corporation
    ♦   University Board by Altera Corporation (optional)
    ♦   Computer requirements:
                    Minimum 486/66 with 8 MB RAM
    ♦   Floppy disk

Discussion:

All logic circuits can be expressed mathematically using Boolean equations. Boolean rules, principles, and theorems are used to describe relationships of logic gates and as a means of expressing, analyzing, and simplifying complex logic circuits.

Since the development of sophisticated computer software, analyzing and simplifying circuits becomes easy. You develop the expression for a circuit from a function table or circuit, then let the computer software simplify the circuit logic. Hence, lengthy derivations and complex circuit reduction by paper and pencil are rarely necessary. Standardized circuits become macros placed in libraries used by the design tool.

This lab utilizes the Max+plus II software to illustrate and graphically analyze the following Boolean identities, theorems, and laws.

Commulative law: Rearranging the order of the expression

$$A \cdot B = B \cdot A \qquad \text{and} \qquad A + B = B + A$$

Associative law: Grouping terms or variables using parenthesis.

$$A \cdot B \cdot C = A (B \cdot C) = (A \cdot B)C$$
$$A + B + C = A + (B + C) = (A + B) + C$$

Distributive law: The process of ANDing a single variable over each term of an OR expression or factoring out a common term from an OR expression.

$$A(B + C) = AB + AC$$

The twelve rules of Boolean Algebra are:

$A + 0 = A$	$A \cdot 0 = 0$	$\overline{\overline{A}} = A$
$A + 1 = 1$	$A \cdot 1 = A$	$A + AB = A$
$A + A = A$	$A \cdot A = A$	$(A + B)(A + C) = A + BC$
$A + \overline{A} = 1$	$A \cdot \overline{A} = 0$	$A + \overline{A}B = A + B$

Gate		Double negate	DeMorgans	Statement
OR	$A + B$	$\overline{\overline{A + B}}$	$\overline{\overline{A} \cdot \overline{B}}$	Active-LOW input NAND
NOR	$\overline{A + B}$		$\overline{A} \cdot \overline{B}$	Active-LOW input AND
AND	$A \cdot B$	$\overline{\overline{A \cdot B}}$	$\overline{\overline{A} + \overline{B}}$	Active-LOW input NOR
NAND	$\overline{A \cdot B}$		$\overline{A} + \overline{B}$	Active-LOW input OR

Part 1   Procedure

1. Open the Max+plus II software. Assign the project name **boolean1** and assign EPM7128SLC84-7 as the device.

2. Open a new Graphic Editor file and construct the circuits shown in Figure 1.

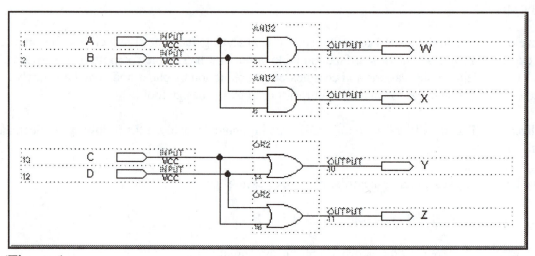

Figure 1

3. Open a new Waveform Editor file and create the waveforms shown in Figure 2.

4. Press the Compile and Simulate buttons. Correct all errors before continuing.

5. Draw output waveforms, W, X, Y, and Z in Figure 3 for Figure 1 that were created by the software.

6. Which law, theorem, or rule is illustrated by the circuits in Figure 1? _____

7. Write the Boolean expression to represent the AND relationship demonstrated in Figure 1.

_____ = _____

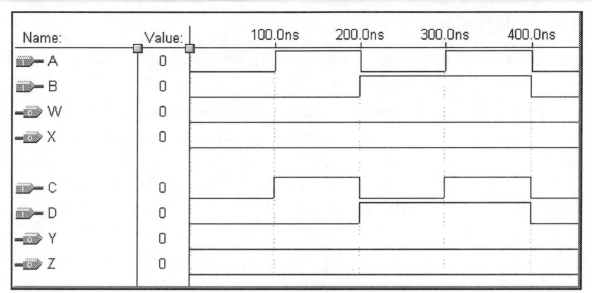

Figure 2

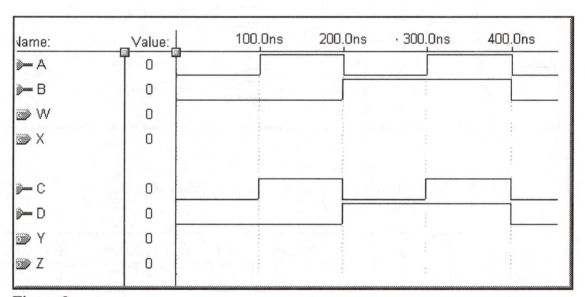

Figure 3

8.   Write the Boolean expression to represent the OR relationship demonstrated in Figure 1.

_____ = _____

9.   Complete the function tables below for outputs W, X, Y, and Z based on Figure 3.

10. Save the editor files to Drive A as **boolean1**, then exit the Graphic and Waveform Editors.

B	A	W	X
0	0		
0	1		
1	0		
1	1		

Table 1

D	C	Y	Z
0	0		
0	1		
1	0		
1	1		

Table 2

Part 2   Procedure

1. Open the Max+plus II software.   Assign the project name as **boolean2** and assign EPM7128SLC84-7 as the device.

2. Open a new Graphic Editor file and construct the circuits shown in Figure 4.

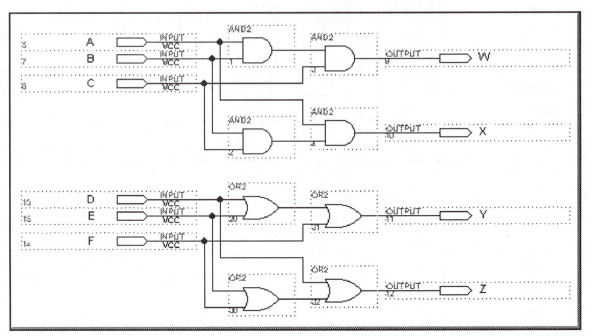

Figure 4

3. Open a new Waveform Editor file and create the waveforms shown in Figure 5.

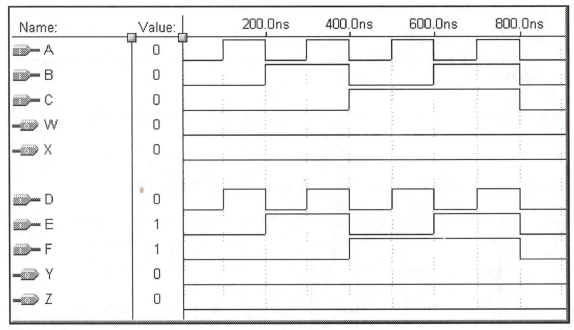

Figure 5

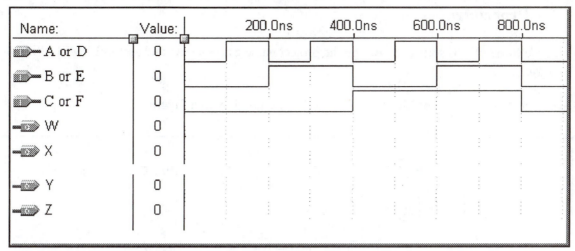

Figure 6

4. Press the Compile and Simulate buttons. Correct all mistakes before continuing.

5. Draw output waveforms W, X, Y, and Z in Figure 6 for Figure 4 that were created by the software.

6. Does output W = output X in Figure 4?   (Yes/No)

7. Does output Y = output Z in Figure 4?   (Yes/No)

8. Which law, theorem, or rule is illustrated by the circuits in Figure 4? _____

9. Write the Boolean identity demonstrated by the AND gates in Figure 4.

    _____ = _____

10. Write the Boolean identity demonstrated by the OR gates in Figure 4.

    _____ = _____

11. Complete the following function tables for outputs W, X, Y, and Z of Figure 4.

12. Save the editor files to Drive A as **boolean2**, then exit the Graphic and Waveform Editors.

C	B	A	W	X
0	0	0		
0	0	1		
0	1	0		
0	1	1		
1	0	0		
1	0	1		
1	1	0		
1	1	1		

Table 3

F	E	D	Y	Z
0	0	0		
0	0	1		
0	1	0		
0	1	1		
1	0	0		
1	0	1		
1	1	0		
1	1	1		

Table 4

Part 3   Procedure

1.   Open the Max+plus II software. Assign the project name as **boolean3** and assign EPM7128SLC84-7 as the device..

2.   Open a new Graphic Editor file and construct the circuits shown in Figure 7.

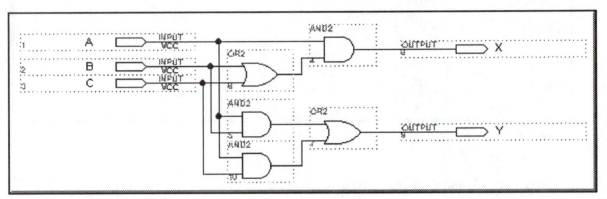

Figure 7

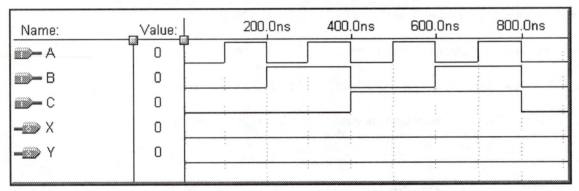

Figure 8

3.   Open a new Waveform Editor file and create the waveforms shown in Figure 8.

4.   Press the Compile and Simulate buttons. Correct all mistakes before continuing.

5.   Draw output waveforms X and Y in Figure 9 for Figure 7 that were created by the software.

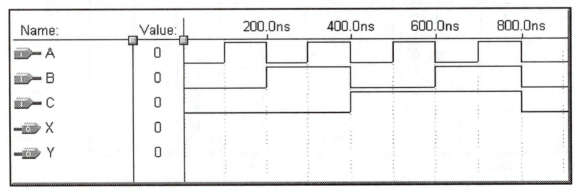

Figure 9

6. Which law, theorem, or rule is illustrated by the circuits in Figure 7? _____

7. Write the Boolean identity demonstrated by the OR gates in Figure 7.

_____ = _____

8. Complete the following function tables for outputs X and Y of Figure 7.

C	B	A	X	Y
0	0	0		
0	0	1		
0	1	0		
0	1	1		

Table 5

C	B	A	X	Y
1	0	0		
1	0	1		
1	1	0		
1	1	1		

Table 6

9. Save the editor files to Drive A as **boolean3**, then exit the Graphic and Waveform Editors.

Part 4   Procedure

1. Open the Max+plus II software. Assign the project name as **boolean4** and assign EPM7128SLC84-7 as the device.

2. Open a new Graphic Editor file and construct the circuits shown in Figure 10.

3. Open a new Waveform Editor file and create the waveforms shown in Figure 11.

4. Press the Compile and Simulate buttons. Correct all mistakes before continuing.

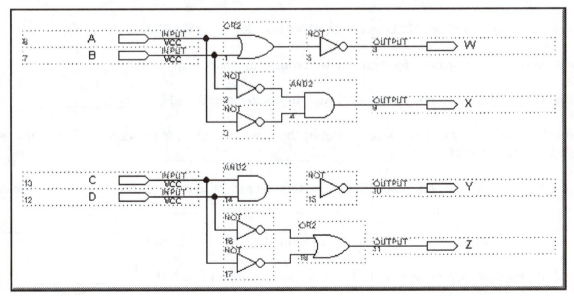

Figure 10

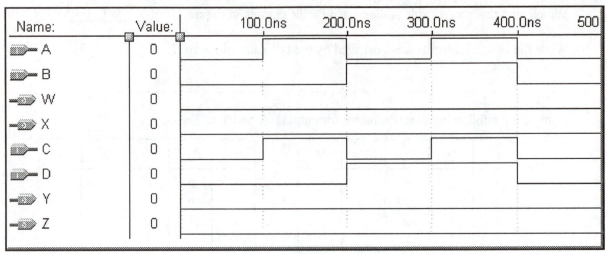

Figure 11

5. Draw output waveforms W and Y in Figure 12 for Figure 10 that were created by the software.

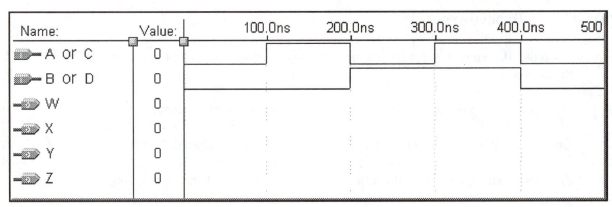

Figure 12

6. Examine waveforms W and X. Does output W = output X?   (Yes/No)

7. Write the Boolean expression for output W with respect to inputs A and B. W = _____

8. Write the Boolean expression for output X with respect to inputs A and B. X = _____

9. What law, theorem, or rule was demonstrated by the circuit consisting of inputs A and B and outputs W and X? (Proper name)   _____

10. Write the Boolean identity illustrated in Figure 10 for outputs W and X with respect to Inputs A and B.
       _____ = _____

11. Examine waveforms Y and Z. Does output Y = output Z?   (Yes/No)

12. Write the Boolean expression for output Y with respect to inputs C and D. Y = _____

13. Write the Boolean expression for output Z with respect to inputs C and D. Z = _____

14. What law, theorem, or rule was demonstrated by the circuit consisting of inputs C and D and outputs Y and Z? (Proper name) _____

15. Write the Boolean identity illustrated in Figure 10 for outputs Y and Z with respect to inputs C and D.
_____ = _____

16. Complete the function tables for the circuits in Figure 10.

B	A	W	X
0	0		
0	1		
1	0		
1	1		

Table 7

D	C	Y	Z
0	0		
0	1		
1	0		
1	1		

Table 8

17. Save the editor files to Drive A as **boolean4**, then exit the Graphic and Waveform Editors.

Part 5   Procedure

1. Open the Max+plus II software.   Assign the project name as **boolean5** and assign EPM7128SLC84-7 as the device.

2. Open a new Graphic Editor file and construct the circuits shown in Figure 13.

3. Open a new Waveform Editor file and create Waveform A but leave Waveform A a logic-LOW.

4. Highlight Waveform A shown in Figure 14 by single clicking on the left mouse button. Set the Grid Size in the **Options** menu to 100 ns.

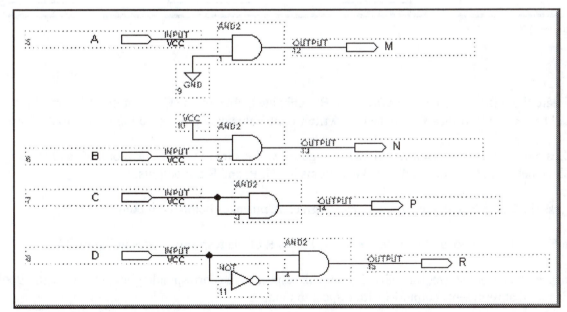

Figure 13

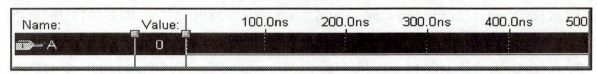

Figure 14

5. Press the "Clock" button in the Draw tool bar. The Clock button is shown in Figure 15 (Right).

Figure 15

6. Note the Overwrite Count Value dialog box (Figure 16) identifies the pulse width as 100 ns (Count Every). Press **OK**. The software generates a square wave from 0.0 ns to 1.0 ns. Figure 17 shows what Waveform A should look like.

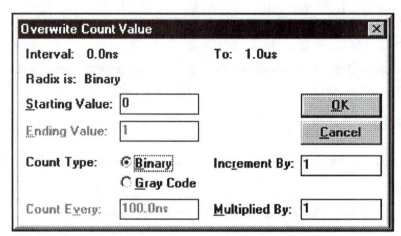

Figure 16

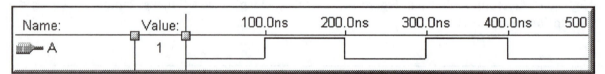

Figure 17

7. Create Waveform B, then with Waveform B highlighted, click on the Clock button (Figure 15) in the Draw tool bar. Set **Multiplied By:** in the Overwrite Count Value dialog box (see Figure 16) to 2. Press **OK**.

8. Create the rest of the waveforms shown in Figure 18. Be sure to create Waveforms C and D using the Clock button in the Draw tool bar. Waveforms M, N, P, and R are outputs.

9. Press the Compile and Simulate buttons. Correct all mistakes before continuing.

10. In Figure 19, draw output waveforms M, N, P, and R of the respective gates in Figure 14.

11. Inspect the output waveforms of each gate with respect to the corresponding inputs. Write the Boolean identity that represents output M with respect to input A.

$$M = \rule{6cm}{0.4pt}$$

Lab 2: Boolean: Laws, Principles, and Rules

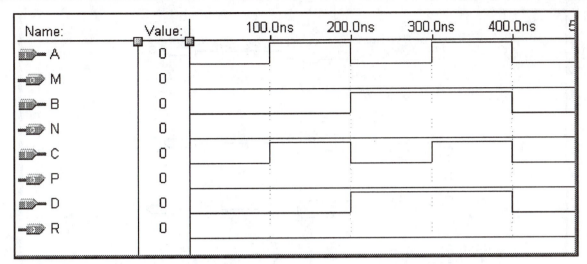

Figure 18

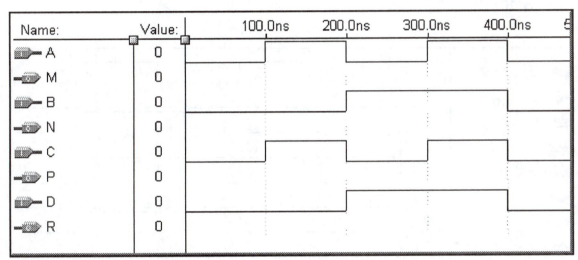

Figure 19

12. Write the Boolean identity that represents output N with respect to input B.   N = _____

13. Write the Boolean identity that represents output P with respect to input C.   P = _____

14. Write the Boolean identity that represents output R with respect to input D.   R = _____

15. Complete the following function tables for the circuits shown in Figure 14.

A	0 v	M
0	0	
1	0	

Table 9

B	5 v	N
0	1	
1	1	

Table 10

C	C	P
0	0	
1	1	

Table 11

D	$\overline{D}$	R
0		
1		

Table 12

16. Add the circuits shown in Figure 20 to your Graphics Editor file aligning input E below input D.

17. Add the waveforms shown in Figure 21 to the Waveform Editor below Waveform R.

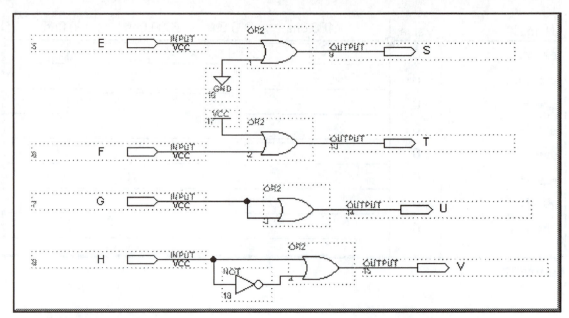

Figure 20

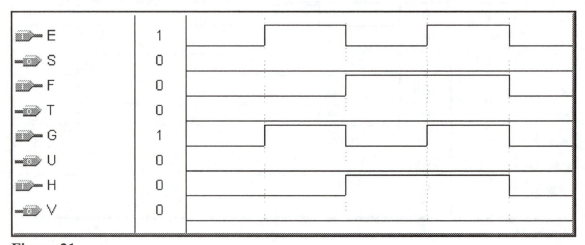

Figure 21

18. Press the Compile and Simulate buttons. Correct all errors before continuing.

19. Draw output waveforms S, T, U, and V in Figure 22 that were generated by the software for Figure 20.

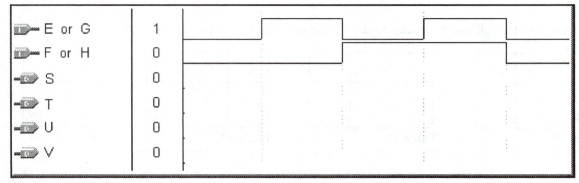

Figure 22

20. Inspect the output waveforms of each gate with respect to the respective inputs. Write the Boolean identity that represents output S with respect to input E.

S = _____

21. Write the Boolean identity that represents output T with respect to input F. T = _____

22. Write the Boolean identity that represents output U with respect to input G. U = _____

23. Write the Boolean identity that represents output V with respect to input H. V = _____

24. Complete the function tables for the circuits shown in Figure 20.

E	0 v	S
0	0	
1	0	

Table 13

F	5 v	T
0	1	
1	1	

Table 14

G	G	U
0	0	
1	1	

Table 15

H	$\overline{H}$	V
0		
1		

Table 16

25. Save the editor files to Drive A as **boolean5**, then exit the Graphic and Waveform Editors.

Part 6   Procedure

1. Open the Max+plus II software. Assign the project name as **boolean6** and assign EPM7128SLC84-7 as the device.

2. Open a new Graphic Editor file and construct the circuits shown in Figure 23.

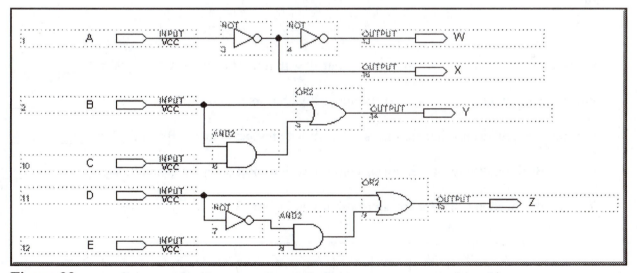

Figure 23

3. Open a new Waveform Editor file and create the waveforms shown in Figure 24.

4. Press the Compile and Simulate buttons. Correct all errors before continuing.

5. For Figure 25, draw the output waveforms W, X, Y, and Z in Figure 23.

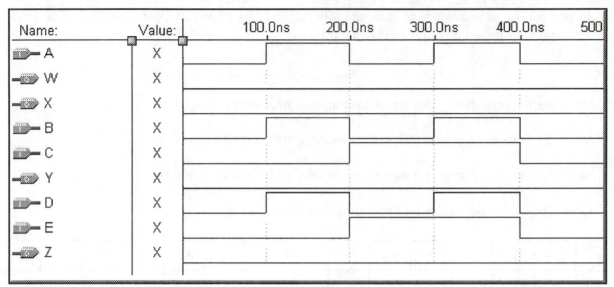

Figure 24

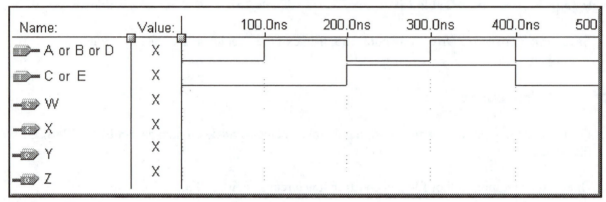

Figure 25

6. Write the Boolean identity that represents output W with respect to input A.   W = _____

7. Write the Boolean identity that represents output X with respect to input A.   X = _____

8. Write the Boolean identity that represents output Y with respect to inputs B and C . Y = _____

9. Write the Boolean identity that represents output Z with respect to inputs D and E. Z = _____

10. Complete the function tables for the circuits shown in Figure 23.

A	X	W
0		
1		

Table 17

B	C	Y
0	0	
0	1	
1	0	
1	1	

Table 18

D	E	Z
0	0	
0	1	
1	0	
1	1	

Table 19

11. Save the editor files to Drive A as **boolean6**, then exit the Graphic and Waveform Editors.

Lab 2: Boolean: Laws, Principles, and Rules

Part 7   Procedure

1.   Open the Max+plus II software. Assign the project name **boolean7** and assign EPM7128SLC84-7 as the device.

2.   Open a new Graphic Editor file and construct the circuit shown in Figure 26 using the BAND2, BNAND2, BOR2, and BNOR2 gate symbols in the **prim** directory.

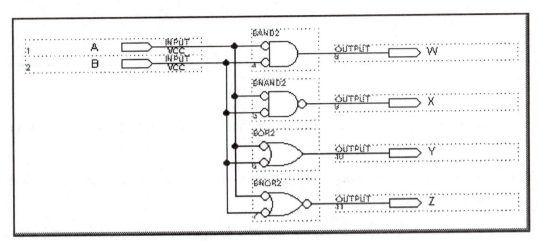

Figure 26

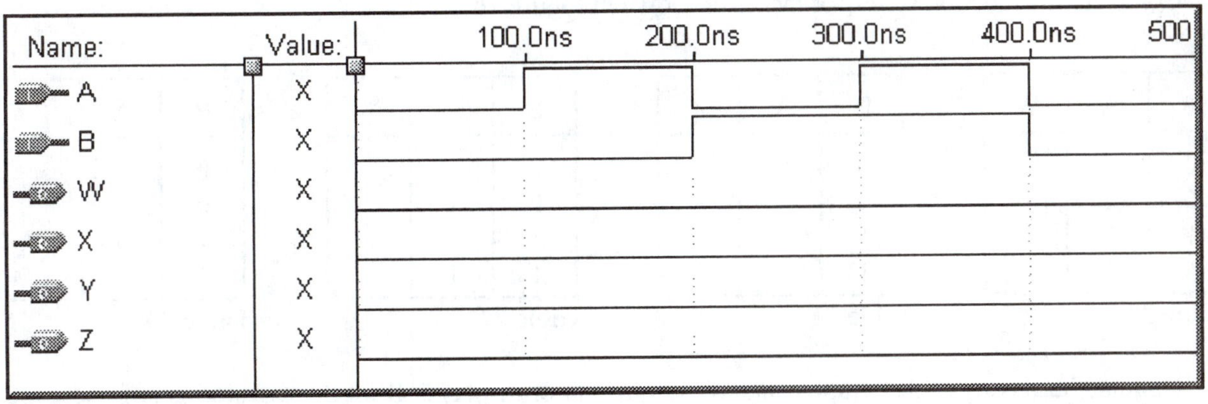

Figure 27

3.   Open a new Waveform Editor file and create the waveforms shown in Figure 27.

4.   Press the Compile and Simulate buttons. Correct all errors before continuing.

5.   In Figure 28, draw the output waveforms W, X, Y, and Z for the circuit in Figure 26.

6.   Examine output W with respect to Inputs A and B. The active-LOW input AND gate is equivalent to what basic logic gate? _____

7.   Examine output X with respect to Inputs A and B. The active-LOW input NAND gate is equivalent to what basic logic gate? _____

> *Note: The active-LOW input NAND gate may also be called the active-LOW input, active-LOW output AND gate.*

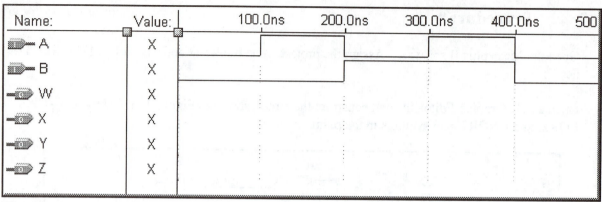

Figure 28

8. Examine output Y with respect to inputs A and B. The active-LOW input OR gate is equivalent to what basic logic gate? _____

9. Examine output Z with respect to inputs A and B. The active-LOW input NOR gate is equivalent to what basic logic gate? _____

> *Note: The active-LOW input NOR gate may also be called the active-LOW input, active-LOW output OR gate.*

10. Complete the function tables for the gates shown in Figure 26.

B	A	W
0	0	
0	1	
1	0	
1	1	

Table 20

B	A	X
0	0	
0	1	
1	0	
1	1	

Table 21

B	A	Y
0	0	
0	1	
1	0	
1	1	

Table 22

B	A	Z
0	0	
0	1	
1	0	
1	1	

Table 23

11. Obtain a hard copy of the Graphic and Waveform Editor displays. Print the waveforms in Landscape mode. Label these hard copies **Part 7, Step 11A** and **Part 7, Step 11B**.

12. Demonstrate the waveforms printed to your instructor. Obtain the signature of approval on the answer page.

13. Save the editor files to Drive A as **boolean7**, then exit the Graphic and Waveform Editors.

14. Create a cover page for the lab in the following format.
    - Name and section in upper-right corner
    - Title of lab centered on the page with instructor's name below the title
    - Today's date in the lower-right corner

15. Write a 1 to 2 page summary pertaining to the results obtained from this lab. Include Figure 26 and Figure 28 (after simulation) as embedded graphics in your summary, basing the written portion of the summary on these two figures.

16. Place all papers for this lab in the following sequence, then submit the lab to your instructor for grading.

- Cover page
- Typed summary
- The completed answer page for this lab
- Hard copy of the Graphic Editor, **Part 7, Step 11A**
- Hard copy of the Waveform Editor, **Part 7, Step 11B**

Part 1

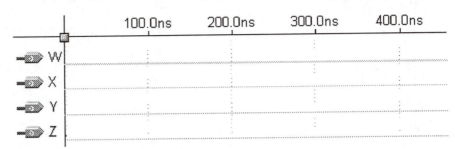

Figure 3

6. _____

7. _____ = _____

8. _____ = _____

B	A	W	X
0	0		
0	1		
1	0		
1	1		

Table 1

D	C	Y	Z
0	0		
0	1		
1	0		
1	1		

Table 2

Part 2

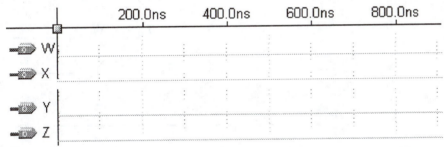

Figure 6

6.   Yes   No

7.   Yes   No

8.   _____

9. _____ = _____   10. _____ = _____

C	B	A	W	X
0	0	0		
0	0	1		
0	1	0		
0	1	1		
1	0	0		
1	0	1		
1	1	0		
1	1	1		

Table 3

F	E	D	Y	Z
0	0	0		
0	0	1		
0	1	0		
0	1	1		
1	0	0		
1	0	1		
1	1	0		
1	1	1		

Table 4

Part 3

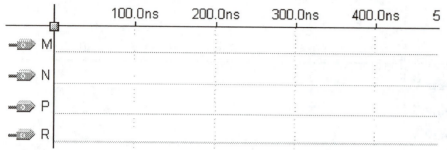

Figure 9

6. _____

7. _____ =

_____

C	B	A	X	Y
0	0	0		
0	0	1		
0	1	0		
0	1	1		

Table 5

C	B	A	X	Y
1	0	0		
1	0	1		
1	1	0		
1	1	1		

Table 6

Part 4

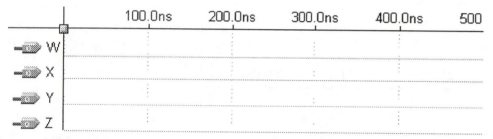

Figure 12

6. (Yes/ No)

7. W = _____

8. X = _____

9. _____   10. _____ = _____

11. (Yes/ No)   12. Y = _____   13. Z = _____

14. _____   15. _____ = _____

B	A	W	X
0	0		
0	1		
1	0		
1	1		

Table 7

D	C	Y	Z
0	0		
0	1		
1	0		
1	1		

Table 8

Part 5

11. M = _____   12. N = _____   13. P = _____

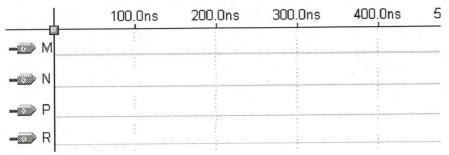

Figure 19

14. R = _____

A	0 v	M
0	0	
1	0	

Table 9

B	5 v	N
0	1	
1	1	

Table 10

C	C	P
0	0	
1	1	

Table 11

D	$\overline{D}$	R
0		
1		

Table 12

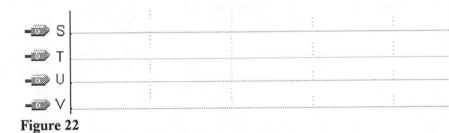

Figure 22

20. S = _____

21. T = _____

22. U = _____

23. V = _____

E	0 v	S
0	0	
1	0	

Table 13

F	5 v	T
0	1	
1	1	

Table 14

G	G	U
0	0	
1	1	

Table 15

H	$\overline{H}$	V
0		
1		

Table 16

Part 6

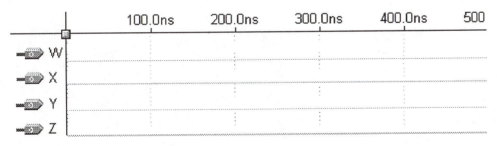

Figure 25

6. W = _____

7. X = _____

8. Y = _____

9. Z = _____

A	X	W
0		
1		

Table 17

B	C	Y
0	0	
0	1	
1	0	
1	1	

Table 18

D	E	Z
0	0	
0	1	
1	0	
1	1	

Table 19

Part 7

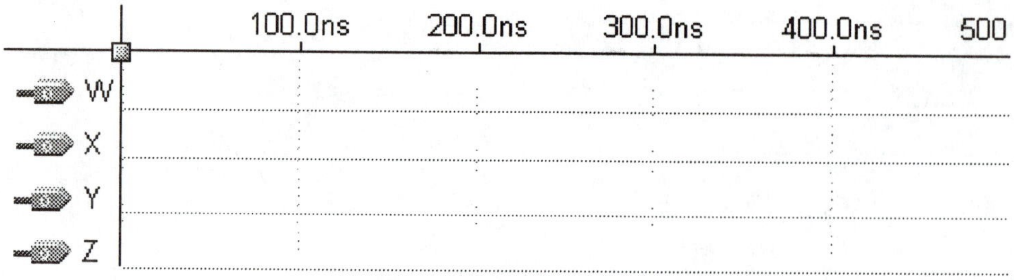

Figure 28

6. _____

7. _____

8. _____

9. _____

B	A	W
0	0	
0	1	
1	0	
1	1	

Table 20

B	A	X
0	0	
0	1	
1	0	
1	1	

Table 21

B	A	Y
0	0	
0	1	
1	0	
1	1	

Table 22

B	A	Z
0	0	
0	1	
1	0	
1	1	

Table 23

16. Demonstrated to: _____ Date: _____

Grade: _____

Lab 3: Combinational Logic Circuits

Objectives:

    1.   Analyze output waveforms of different combinational logic circuits
    2.   Complete function tables for these combinational logic circuits
    3.   Write Boolean expressions for each combinational logic circuit

Materials List:

    ♦   Max+plus II software by Altera Corporation
    ♦   University Board by Altera Corporation (optional)
    ♦   Computer requirements:
                    Minimum 486/66 with 8 MB RAM
    ♦   Floppy disk

Discussion:

All circuits, no matter how complex, will have multiple inputs and at least one output. The inputs and outputs are either "Data" or "Control." The Data is information in binary code, such as the data typed while using a word processor or data that is printed on a page. The Control inputs will direct the data flow through a circuit.

The most fundamental control circuit is the 2 input (AND, OR, NAND, NOR, XOR) gate shown in Figure 1A. The Control input will inhibit the data flow, Figure 1B, or enable the data flow, Figure 1C. As the circuit gets more complex, Figure 1D, the basic function of the control inputs remains the same to control the data flow through the circuit.

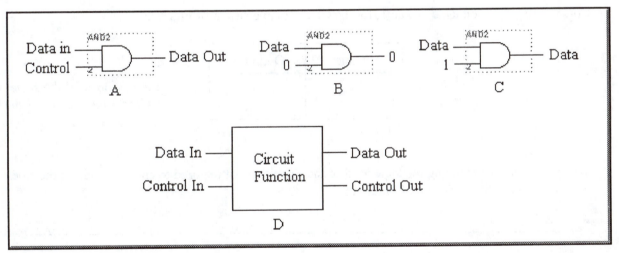

Figure 1

Several commonly used control circuits will be demonstrated in this lab. Each circuit will be constructed and simulated using the Max+plus II software. Waveforms will be analyzed, function tables created, and Boolean expressions will be developed from the circuits in this lab.

Part 1   Procedure

1.   Open the Max+plus II software. Assign the project name **comb1** and MAX7000S as the device family.

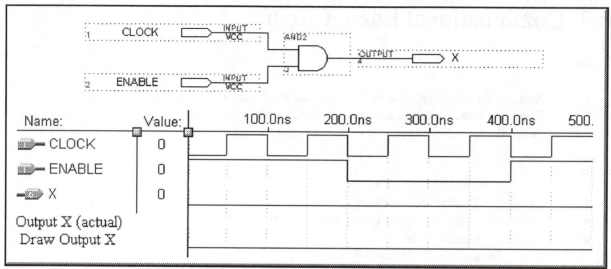

Figure 2

2. Open a new Graphic Editor file and construct the circuit shown in Figure 2.

3. Open a new Waveform Editor file, set the Grid Size in the Options menu to 50 ns, and create the waveforms shown in Figure 2.

4. Press the Compile and Simulate buttons. Correct all errors before continuing.

5. Press the **Open SCF** button in the Simulator dialog box, then draw output X in Figure 2 shown in the Waveform Editor.

6. Complete the function table, Table 1, for the Clock Enable circuit of Figure 2.

Enable	Output X
0	
1	

Table 1

Enter "Clock" if the signal is passed, otherwise enter the logic level for output X.

7. Write a statement describing the logic level of the Enable signal required to enable or inhibit the clock passing through the AND gate of Figure 2.

_____

_____

8. Write the Boolean expression for output X with respect to inputs Clock and Enable in Figure 2.

   X = _____

9. Save all files to Drive A as **comb1**, then exit the Waveform and Graphic Editors.

Part 2   Procedure

1.   Open the Max+plus II software. Assign the project name **comb2** and MAX7000S as the device family.

2.   Open a new Graphic Editor file and construct the circuit shown in Figure 3.

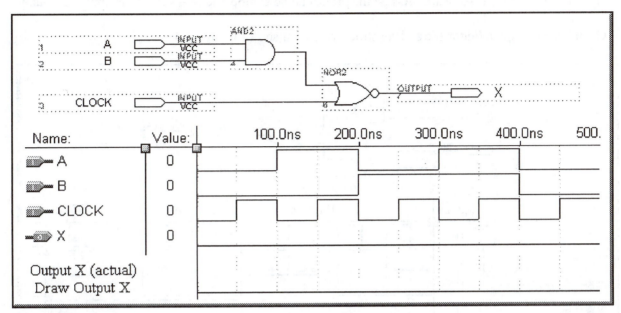

Figure 3

3.   Open a new Waveform Editor file, set the Grid Size under the Options menu to 50 ns, and create the waveforms as shown in Figure 3.

4.   Press the Compile and Simulate buttons. Correct all errors before continuing.

5.   Draw output X in Figure 3 shown in the Waveform Editor.

6.   Complete the function table, Table 2, for the Clock Enable circuit of Figure 3.

B	A	X
0	0	
0	1	
1	0	
1	1	

Enter "Clock" if the signal is passed, otherwise enter the logic level for output X.

Table 2

7.   Write a statement describing the logic level of control signals A and B, required to enable or inhibit the clock passing through the NOR gate of Figure 3.

_____

_____

8.   Write the Boolean expression for output X with respect to inputs A, B, and Clock in Figure 3.

X = _____

9.   Save the files to Drive A as **comb2**, then exit the Waveform and Graphic Editors.

Part 3   Procedure

1.   Open the Max+plus II software. Assign the project name **comb3** and MAX7000S as the device family.

2.   Open a new Graphic Editor file and construct the circuit shown in Figure 4.

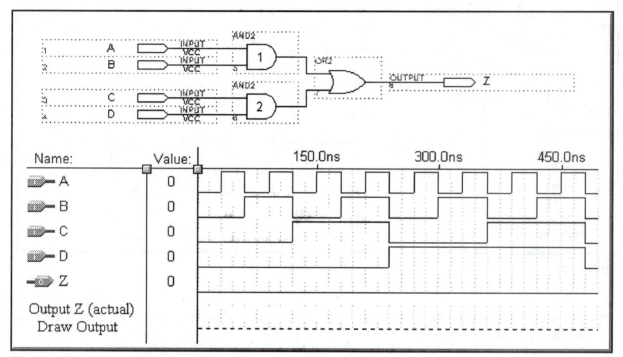

Figure 4

3.   Open a new Waveform Editor file, set the Grid Size under the Options menu to 30 ns, and create the waveforms as shown in Figure 4.

4.   Press the Compile and Simulate buttons. Correct all errors before continuing.

5.   Draw output Z in Figure 4 shown in the Waveform Editor.

6.   Complete the function table, Table 3, for the 2-wide, 2-input, AND OR circuit of Figure 4.

7.   Write the Boolean equation for output Z of the circuit of Figure 4.

Z = _____

D	C	B	A	Z
0	0	0	0	
0	0	0	1	
0	0	1	0	
0	0	1	1	
0	1	0	0	
0	1	0	1	
0	1	1	0	
0	1	1	1	
1	0	0	0	
1	0	0	1	
1	0	1	0	
1	0	1	1	
1	1	0	0	
1	1	0	1	
1	1	1	0	
1	1	1	1	

Table 3

8. Analyze the function table and Boolean expression for Figure 4. Write a statement explaining when output Z is a logic-HIGH.

_____

9. Modify the circuit and waveforms (Grid Size = 20 ns) as shown in Figure 5.

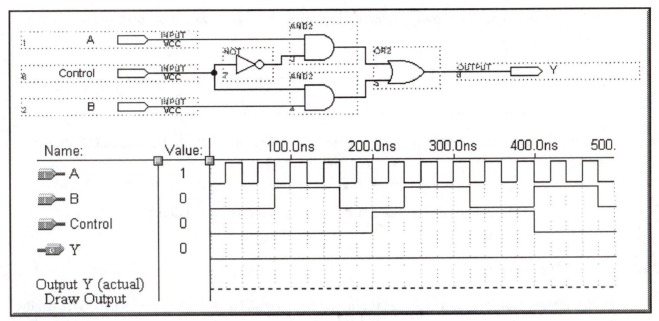

Figure 5

10. Press the Compile and Simulate buttons. Correct all errors before continuing.

11. Press the **Open SCF** button in the Simulator dialog box, then draw output Y in Figure 5 shown in the Waveform Editor.

12. Analyze the waveforms and identify which data waveform, Data A or Data B, appears on output Y when control input C is:

    a logic-LOW _____   a logic-HIGH _____

13. Complete the function table, Table 4, for the AND OR circuit with control input. Note the function table does not show all 8 possible combinations of inputs C, B, and A. Since C is the control input, we are only concerned what data, either Data A or Data B, is passed through the circuit to output Y when the control input is a logic-LOW or a logic-HIGH.

Control	B	A	Y
0	Data B	Data A	_____
1	Data B	Data A	_____

Enter Data A or Data B for output Y.

Table 4

14. Complete Table 5, a simplified version of Table 4, by identifying which data, Data A or Data B, appears on output Y.

Control Input	Output Y
0	_____
1	_____

Enter Data A or Data B
for output Y.

Table 5

15. Write a statement describing how the control signal allows Data A or Data B to appear on output Y in Figure 5.

_____

_____

16. Write the Boolean expression for output Y with respect to the inputs Data A, Data B, and Control in Figure 5.

Y = _____

17. Save the files to Drive A as **comb3**, then exit the Waveform and Graphic Editors.

Part 4   Procedure

1. Open the Max+plus II software. Assign the project name **comb4** and MAX7000S as the device family.

2. Open a new Graphic Editor file and construct the circuit shown in Figure 6.

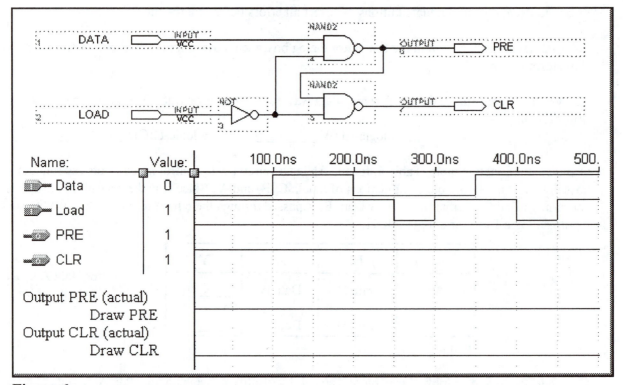

Figure 6

3. Open a new Waveform Editor file, set the Grid Size under the Options menu to 50 ns, and create the circuit and waveforms as shown in Figure 6.

4. Press the Compile and Simulate buttons. Correct all errors before continuing.

5. Draw the PRE and CLR outputs in Figure 6 shown in the Waveform Editor.

6. Complete the function table, Table 6, for the **load-data** circuit of Figure 6.

LOAD	DATA	PRE	CLR
0	0		
0	1		
1	0		
1	1		

Table 6

7. Explain what input conditions to the circuit of Figure 6 will cause the PRE output to be a logic-LOW.

_____

8. Explain what input conditions to the circuit of Figure 6 will cause the CLR output to be a logic-LOW.

_____

9. Write the Boolean expression for the PRE output with respect to the inputs in Figure 6.

PRE = _____

10. Write the Boolean expression for the CLR output with respect to the inputs in Figure 6.

CLR = _____

11. Save the files on Drive A as **comb4**, then exit the Waveform and Graphic Editors.

Part 5   Procedure

1. Open the Max+plus II software. Assign the project name **comb5** and MAX7000S as the device family.

2. Open a new Waveform Editor file and construct the circuit shown in Figure 7.

3. Open a new Waveform Editor file, set the Grid Size under the Options menu to 25 ns, and create the waveforms as shown in Figure 7. Note the CLOCK waveform starts at a logic-HIGH state.

4. Press the Compile and Simulate buttons. Correct all errors before continuing.

5. Complete the function table, Table 7, for the **RCO** circuit of Figure 7.

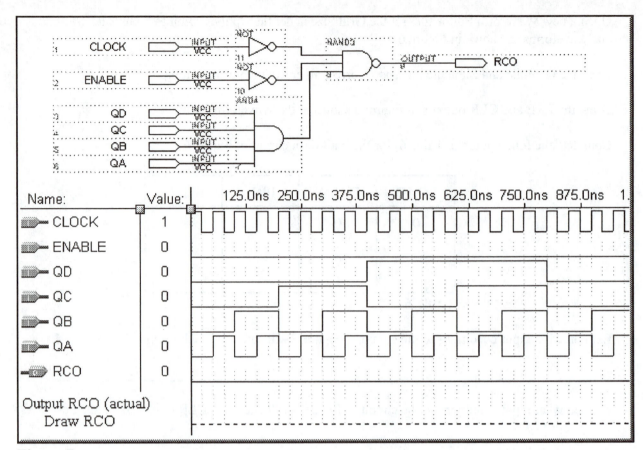

Figure 7

ENABLE	CLOCK	Qd Qc Qb Qa	RCO
1	X	X X X X	
X	1	X X X X	
0	0	0 0 0 0	
0	0	0 0 0 1	
0	0	0 0 1 0	
0	0	0 0 1 1	
0	0	0 1 0 0	
0	0	0 1 0 1	
0	0	0 1 1 0	
0	0	0 1 1 1	
0	0	1 0 0 0	
0	0	1 0 0 1	
0	0	1 0 1 0	
0	0	1 0 1 1	
0	0	1 1 0 0	
0	0	1 1 0 1	
0	0	1 1 1 0	
0	0	1 1 1 1	

Table 7   X is Irrelevant

6.   Explain what input conditions to the circuit of Figure 7 will cause the RCO output to be a logic-LOW.

7.   Write the Boolean expression for the RCO output with respect to the inputs in Figure 7.

RCO = _____

8.   Save the files to Drive A as **comb5**, then exit the Waveform and Graphics Editors.

Part 6   Procedure

1.   Open the Max+plus II software. Assign the project name **comb6** and MAX7000S as the device family.

2.   Open a new Graphic Editor file and construct the circuit shown in Figure 8.

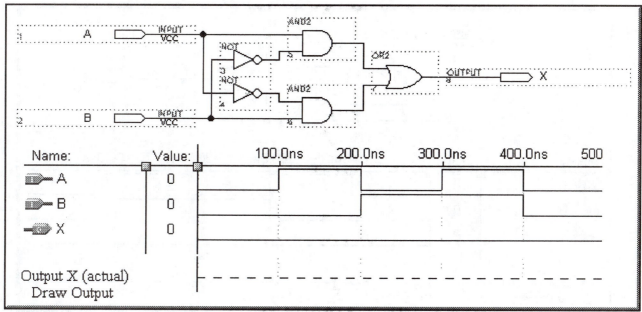

Figure 8

3.   Open a new Graphic Editor file, set Set the Grid Size under the Options menu to 100 ns, and create the circuit and waveforms as shown in Figure 8.

4.   Complete the function table, Table 8, for the circuit in Figure 8.

B	A	X
0	0	
0	1	
1	0	
1	1	

Table 8

5.   Examine the function table and name the basic logic gate. _____

6.   Write the Boolean expression for output X in Figure 8.

X = _____

7.   Write a statement that describes the input conditions that produce a logic-HIGH on output X for Figure 8.

_____

8.   Save the files to Drive A as **comb6**, then exit the Waveform and Graphic Editors.

Part 7   Procedure

1.   Open the Max+plus II software. Assign the project name **comb7** and MAX7000S as the device family.

2.   Open a new Graphic Editor file and construct the waveforms as shown in Figure 9.

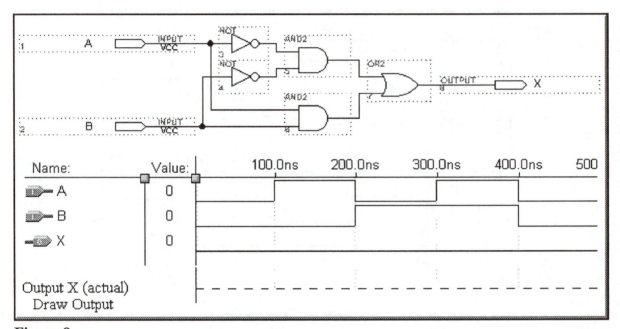

Figure 9

3.   Open a new Waveform Editor file, set the Grid Size under the Options menu to 100 ns, and create the circuit and waveforms as shown in Figure 9.

4.   Complete Table 9 for the circuit in Figure 9.

B	A	X
0	0	
0	1	
1	0	
1	1	

Table 9

5.   Examine the function table and name the basic logic gate. _____

6.   Write the Boolean expression for output X in Figure 9.   X = _____

7. Write a statement that describes the input conditions that produce a logic-HIGH on output X for Figure 9.

_____

8. Obtain a hard copy of the Graphic and Waveform displays. Label these hard copies **Part 7, Step 8a** and **Part 7, Step 8b**, respectively.

9. Demonstrate Figure 9 to your instructor. Obtain the signature on the answer page for this lab.

10. Save the files to Drive A as **comb7**, then exit the Waveform and Graphic Editors.

11. Create a cover page for this lab.

12. Write a 1 to 2 page summary, based on the Combinational Logic Circuits discussed in this lab. Include an embedded schematic and a function table for that schematic along with a technical discussion describing the circuit operation.

13. Staple the pages in the following sequence and submit the completed lab to your professor for review.
    - Cover page
    - Summary
    - Completed answer page for this lab
    - Hard copy **Part 7, Step 8A**
    - Hard copy **Part 7, Step 8B**

Part 1

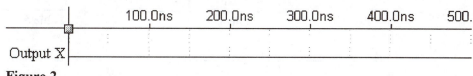

Output X

Figure 2

Enable	Output X
0	
1	

Table 1

7.   _____

8.   X = _____

Part 2

Output X

Figure 3

B	A	X
0	0	
0	1	
1	0	
1	1	

Table 2

7.   _____

      _____

      _____

8.   X = _____

Part 3

A	Z
0	
1	
0	
1	
0	
1	
0	
1	
0	
1	
0	
1	
0	
1	
0	
1	

Table 3

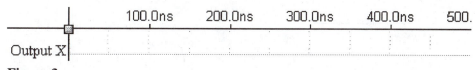

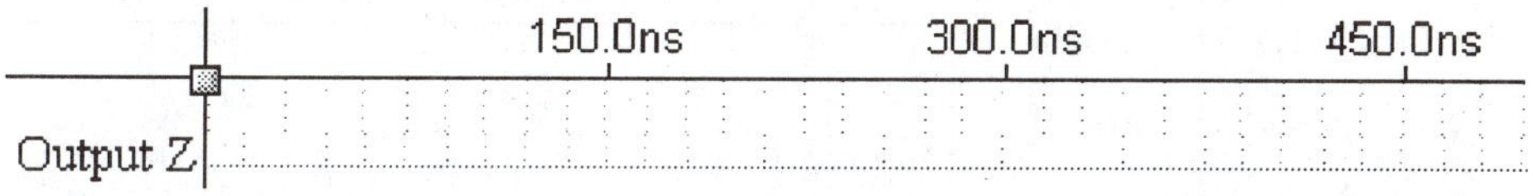

Output Z

Figure 4

7.   Z = _____

8.   _____

12.   a logic-LOW _____   a logic-HIGH _____

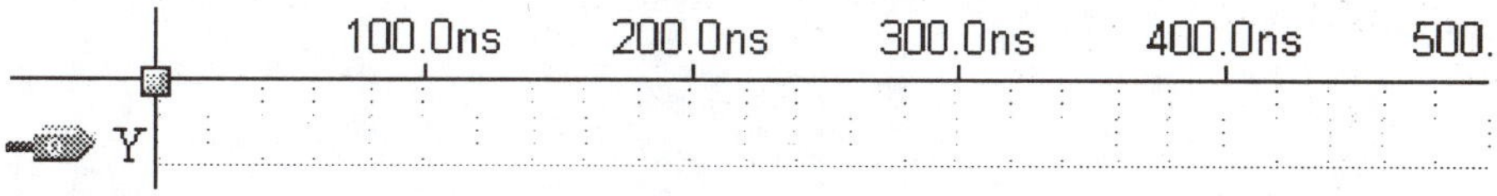

Y

Figure 5

Control	Y
0	_____
1	_____

Table 4

Control Input	Output Y
0	_____
1	_____

Table 5

15. _____

16.   Y = _____

Part 4

PRE	CLR

Table 6

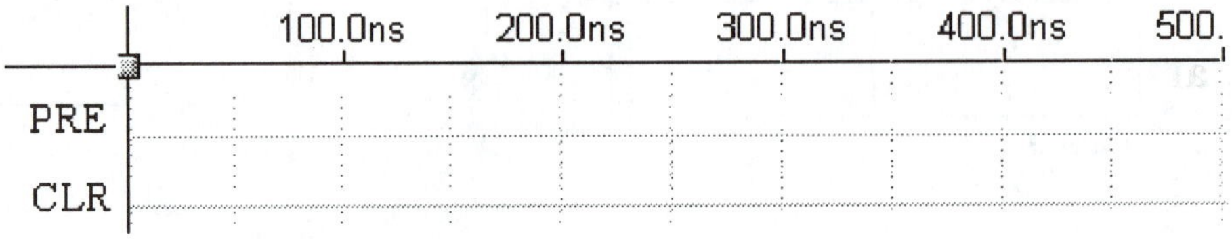

Figure 6

7. _____

8. _____

9.   PRE = _____

10.   CLR = _____

Part 5

Qd Qc Qb Qa	RCO
X X X X	
X X X X	
0 0 0 0	
0 0 0 1	
0 0 1 0	
0 0 1 1	
0 1 0 0	
0 1 0 1	
0 1 1 0	
0 1 1 1	
1 0 0 0	
1 0 0 1	
1 0 1 0	
1 0 1 1	
1 1 0 0	
1 1 0 1	
1 1 1 0	
1 1 1 1	

Table 7 X is Irrelevant

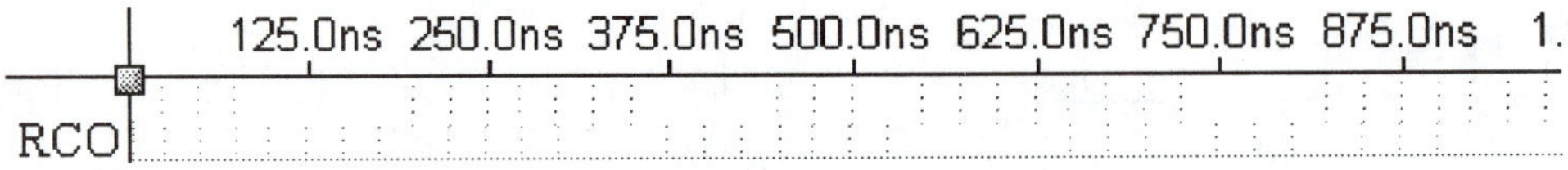

Figure 7

6.   _____

      _____

7.   RCO = _____

Part 6

X

Table 8

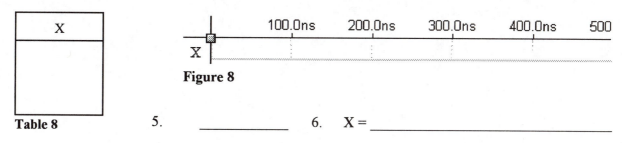

Figure 8

5. _____   6.   X = _____

7. _____

Part 7

X

Table 9

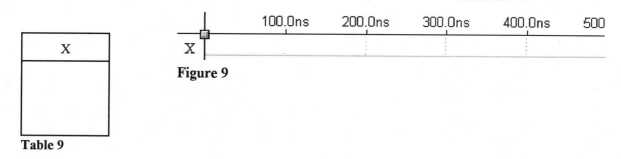

Figure 9

5. _____

6.   X = _____

7. _____

9.   Demonstrated to: _____ Date: _____

Grade: _____

Lab 4: Implementing Logic Designs

Objectives:

    1.   Develop a function table from a statement of conditions
    2.   Extract the Boolean equation from the function table
    3.   Construct the circuit from a Boolean equation
    4.   Verify the circuit constructed matches the function table

Materials List:

    ♦   Max+plus II software by Altera Corporation
    ♦   University Board by Altera Corporation (optional)
    ♦   Computer requirements:
                Minimum 486/66 with 8 MB RAM
    ♦   Floppy disk

Discussion:

Let us assume a circuit is to be designed that produces a logic-HIGH output (X) when one input (B) is a logic-LOW and the other input (A) is a logic-HIGH. The inputs and output are arbitrarily assigned variables such as A, B, and X. Set up a function table to represent the design statement, listing all possible combinations for the input variables, A and B. Show a logic-HIGH output for X that satisfies the statement and a logic-LOW for all other input combinations.

Once a function table has been developed, each logic-HIGH output for a row can be expressed as a multi-input AND gate. The number of inputs to the AND gate is determined by the number of inputs from the logic statement.

B	A	X	
0	0	0	
0	**1**	**1**	⇦
1	0	0	
1	1	0	

Table 1

Start by drawing the two-input AND gate with inputs and output at a logic-HIGH as shown in Figure 1. The output of the AND gate is a logic-HIGH only when all inputs are a logic-HIGH. What must be done to input A to provide a logic-HIGH state? For row 2 of the table, when output X is a logic-HIGH, input A is already a logic-HIGH, so merely wire input A to one of the gate inputs.

However, note input B for row 2 of the table is a logic-LOW. Input B must be inverted before being wired to the AND gate. Output X for row 2 can now be expressed as a function of the inputs. The column equation for the output is derived by ORing the individual row expressions.

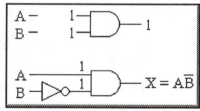

Figure 1

Part 1   Procedure

Statement: The output (X) of a circuit is a logic-HIGH only when inputs A and B are a logic-HIGH, when input C is a logic-LOW, **or** when inputs A and B are a logic-HIGH when input C is a logic-HIGH.

1.   Complete the function table for the logic statement.

2. Write the Boolean expression for each output that is a Logic-HIGH with respect to the corresponding input conditions for that row.

C	B	A	X
0	0	0	
0	0	1	
0	1	0	
0	1	1	
1	0	0	
1	0	1	
1	1	0	
1	1	1	

Table 2

X = _____

X = _____

3. Combine the two expressions from Part 1,Step 2 into a single OR expression to represent the output X column of the function table.

X = _____

4. Using logic gates, draw the circuit to represent output X with respect to inputs A, B, and C.

5. Open the Max+plus II software. Assign the project name **Design1** and MAX7000S as the device family.

6. Open a new Graphic Editor file and construct the circuit you created for Part 1, Step 4.

7. Open a new Waveform Editor file and create the waveforms shown in Figure 2 following these steps:
   ■ Set the grid size to 100 ns
   ■ Set **Multiplied By:** in the Overwrite Count Value for Waveform A to 1.
   ■ Set **Multiplied By:** in the Overwrite Count Value for Waveform B to 2.
   ■ Set **Multiplied By:** in the Overwrite Count Value for Waveform C to 4.

8. At the bottom of Figure 2, draw the output signal created by the software after simulation.

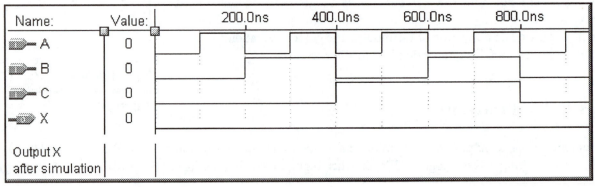

Figure 2

Lab 4: Implementing Logic Designs

9. Examine the simulated output X waveform. Verify that output X is a logic-HIGH only under the two conditions mentioned in the statement. Correct all errors before continuing.

10. Save the files to Drive A as **design1**, then exit the Graphic and Waveform Editors.

Part 2   Procedure

Statement: The output of a circuit is to be a logic-HIGH when the majority of the 3 inputs are logic-LOW.

1. Complete the function table for the logic statement.

2. Write the Boolean expression for each output that is a logic-HIGH with respect to the corresponding input conditions for that row.

    X = _____

    X = _____

    X = _____

    X = _____

C	B	A	X
0	0	0	
0	0	1	
0	1	0	
0	1	1	
1	0	0	
1	0	1	
1	1	0	
1	1	1	

Table 3

3. Combine the four expressions from Part 2, Step 2 into a single OR expression to represent the output X column of the function table.

    X = _____

4. Using logic gates, draw the circuit to represent output X .

5. Open the Max+plus II software. Assign the project name **design2**.

6. Open a new Graphic Editor file and construct the circuit you created for Part 2, Step 4.

7. Open a new Waveform Editor file and create the waveforms shown in Figure 3 following these steps:

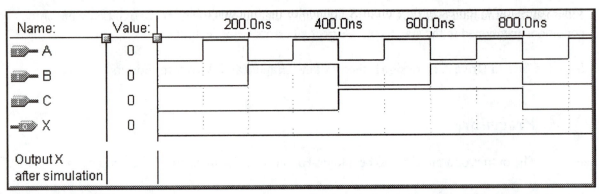

Figure 3

- Set the grid size to 100 ns
- Set **Multiplied By:** in the Overwrite Count Value for Waveform A to 1
- Set **Multiplied By:** in the Overwrite Count Value for Waveform B to 2
- Set **Multiplied By:** in the Overwrite Count Value for Waveform C to 4

8. At the bottom of Figure 3, draw the output signal created by the software after simulation.

9. Examine the simulated output X waveform. Verify that output X is a logic-HIGH only under the conditions mentioned in the statement. Correct all errors before continuing.

10. The Boolean equation may be simplified using Boolean algebra, Karnaugh mapping techniques, or computer software to reduce the number of gates; however, expression simplification is not the objective of this lab.

11. Save the files to Drive A as **design2**, then exit the Graphic and Waveform Editors.

Part 3   Procedure

Statement: A circuit with four variables will produce a logic-HIGH output only when three or four of the four variables are a logic-HIGH.

1. Complete the function table for the logic statement.

2. Write the Boolean expression for each output that is a logic-HIGH with respect to the corresponding input conditions for that row.

D	C	B	A	X
0	0	0	0	
0	0	0	1	
0	0	1	0	
0	0	1	1	
0	1	0	0	
0	1	0	1	
0	1	1	0	
0	1	1	1	
1	0	0	0	
1	0	0	1	
1	0	1	0	
1	0	1	1	
1	1	0	0	
1	1	0	1	
1	1	1	0	
1	1	1	1	

Table 4

X = _____

X = _____

X = _____

X = _____

X = _____

3. Combine the five expressions from Part 3, Step 2 into a single

OR expression to represent the output X column of the function table.

X = _____

4.   Using logic gates, draw the circuit to represent output X.

5.   Open the Max+plus II software. Assign the project name **design3**.

6.   Open a new Graphic Editor file and construct the circuit you created for Part 3, Step 4.

7.   Open a new Waveform Editor file and create the waveforms shown in Figure 4 following these steps:
- ■   Set the grid size to 100 ns
- ■   Set **Multiplied By:** in the Overwrite Count Value for Waveform A to 1
- ■   Set **Multiplied By:** in the Overwrite Count Value for Waveform B to 2
- ■   Set **Multiplied By:** in the Overwrite Count Value for Waveform C to 4

8.   At the bottom of Figure 4, draw the output signal created by the software after simulation.

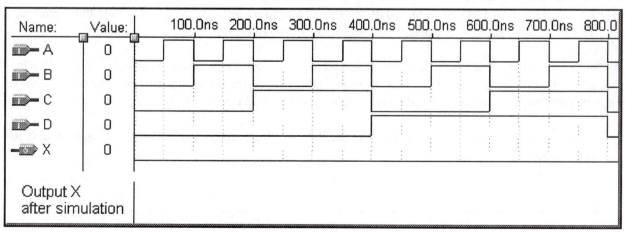

Figure 4

9. Examine the simulated output X waveform. Verify that output X is a logic-HIGH only under the two conditions mentioned in the statement. Correct all errors before continuing.

10. Save the files to Drive A as **design3**, then exit the Graphics and Waveform Editors.

Part 4   Procedure

Statement: The function table for a circuit to drive a common anode seven-segment display is shown in Table 5. A logic-LOW on the **g, f, e, d, c, b,** and **a** outputs will cause the segment to light. For instance, if the MNOP inputs are 0000_2, the low states on **f, e, d, c, b,** and **a** will cause the corresponding segments to light, displaying a zero.

Symbol	M N O P	Shape	$\bar{g}\,\bar{f}\,\bar{e}\,\bar{d}\,\bar{c}\,\bar{b}\,\bar{a}$
0	0 0 0 0	0	1 0 0 0 0 0 0
1	0 0 0 1	1	1 1 1 1 0 0 1
2	0 0 1 0	2	0 1 0 0 1 0 0
3	0 0 1 1	3	0 1 1 0 0 0 0
4	0 1 0 0	4	0 0 1 1 0 0 0
5	0 1 0 1	5	0 0 1 0 0 1 0
6	0 1 1 0	6	0 0 0 0 0 1 0
7	0 1 1 1	7	1 1 1 1 0 0 0
8	1 0 0 0	8	0 0 0 0 0 0 0
9	1 0 0 1	9	0 0 1 1 0 0 0
A	1 0 1 0	A	0 0 0 1 0 0 0
B	1 0 1 1	b	0 0 0 0 0 1 1
C	1 1 0 0	C	1 0 0 0 1 1 0
D	1 1 0 1	d	0 1 0 0 0 0 1
E	1 1 1 0	E	0 0 0 0 1 1 0
F	1 1 1 1	F	0 0 0 1 1 1 0

Table 5

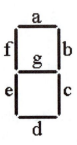

When developing a circuit from the function table, either the Sum of Products (SOP) method based on logic-HIGHs or the Product of Sums (POS) method based on logic-LOWs may be used since both methods will yield equivalent expressions. Table 5 shows 34 output logic-HIGHs and 78 output logic-LOWs. When driving the segments, a logic-LOW will turn the segment on, making these outputs active-LOW.

For the following example, use the Sum of Products method to extract the expressions based on logic-HIGHs, then when constructing the circuit, use NOR gates instead of OR gates on the final output stage. For instance, to find $\bar{g}$, write a sum expression based on the DCBA codes 0000_2, 0001_2, 0111_2, and 1100_2.

1. Write the product terms as a sum of products (SOP) Boolean expression based on the logic-HIGHs for each output, $\bar{g}$ to $\bar{a}$.

$\bar{g} =$ _____

$\overline{f} =$ _____

$\overline{e} =$ _____

$\overline{d} =$ _____

$\overline{c} =$ _____

$\overline{b} =$ _____

$\overline{a} =$ _____

2. Using logic gates, draw the circuit to represent outputs $\overline{a}$, $\overline{b}$, $\overline{c}$, $\overline{d}$, $\overline{e}$, $\overline{f}$, and $\overline{g}$ based on the Sum of Products developed for Step 1.

3.   Open the Max+plus II software. Assign the project name **design4**.

4.   Open a new Graphic Editor file and construct the circuit you created for Part 4, Step 2.

5.   Open a new Waveform Editor file and create the waveforms shown in Figure 5 following these steps:
   - Set the grid size to 50 ns
   - Set **Multiplied By:** in the Overwrite Count Value for Waveform P to 1.
   - Set **Multiplied By:** in the Overwrite Count Value for Waveform O to 2.
   - Set **Multiplied By:** in the Overwrite Count Value for Waveform N to 4.
   - Set **Multiplied By:** in the Overwrite Count Value for Waveform M to 8.

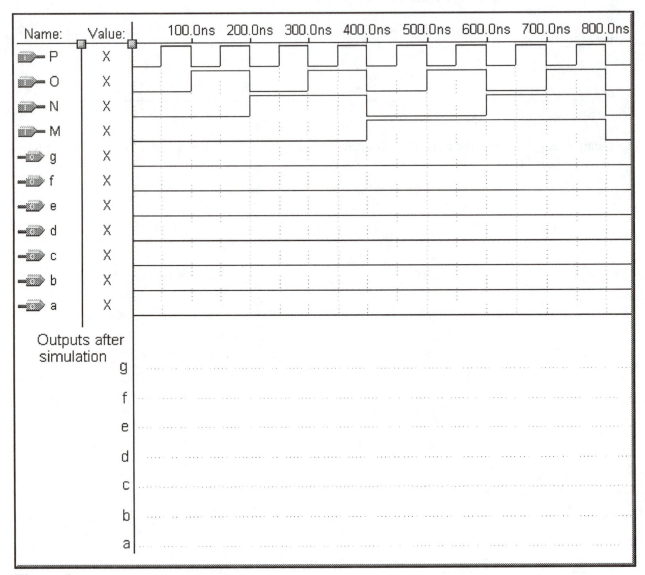

Figure 5

6.   At the bottom of Figure 5, draw the output signal created by the software after simulation.

7.   Examine the simulated output X waveform. Verify that output X is a logic-HIGH only under the two conditions mentioned in the statement. Correct all errors before continuing.

8.   Obtain hard copies of the Graphic and Waveform Editors. Mark these pages **Part 4, Step 8A** and **Part 4, Step 8B**, respectively.

9. Demonstrate the Graphic and Waveform Editor files to the instructor. Obtain the signature of approval on the answer page.

10. Save the files to Drive A as **design4**, then exit the Graphics and Waveform Editors.

11. Two integrated circuits may be used to drive the seven-segment display devices. The 7447 may be used to drive a common anode display. The outputs are active-LOW and require resistors in series between the chip and the display inputs. The 7448 outputs are active-HIGH and may drive common cathode displays. External resistors are not necessary since the 7448 has internal pull-up resistors.

12. Create a cover page and write a 1 to 2 page summary pertaining to the results obtained from this lab. Your typed summary must include Table 4 from Part 4, the sum of product expressions for outputs **g** through **a**, and a discussion explaining how the equations were extracted from the table. Use the apostrophe, ', to indicate the NOT function in your equations; that is: M'N'O'P' represents 0000_2.

13. Place all papers for this lab in the following sequence, then submit the lab to your instructor for grading.

- Cover page
- Typed summary
- The completed lab
- Printout of the Graphics Editor, **Part 4, Step 8A**
- Printout of the Waveform Editor, **Part 4, Step 8B**

Name: _____

Part 1

2.   X = _____

      X = _____

3.   X = _____

4.

C	B	A		X
0	0	0		
0	0	1		
0	1	0		
0	1	1		
1	0	0		
1	0	1		
1	1	0		
1	1	1		

Table 2

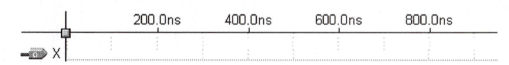

Figure 2

Part 2

2.   X = _____

      X = _____

      X = _____

      X = _____

C	B	A		X
0	0	0		
0	0	1		
0	1	0		
0	1	1		
1	0	0		
1	0	1		
1	1	0		
1	1	1		

Table 3

3.   X = _____

4.

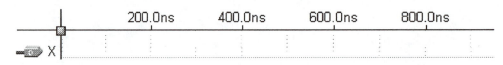

Figure 3

Part 3

2.   X = _____

        X = _____

        X = _____

        X = _____

        X = _____

3.   X = _____

        _____

        _____

        _____

D	C	B	A		X
0	0	0	0		
0	0	0	1		
0	0	1	0		
0	0	1	1		
0	1	0	0		
0	1	0	1		
0	1	1	0		
0	1	1	1		
1	0	0	0		
1	0	0	1		
1	0	1	0		
1	0	1	1		
1	1	0	0		
1	1	0	1		
1	1	1	0		
1	1	1	1		

Table 4

4.

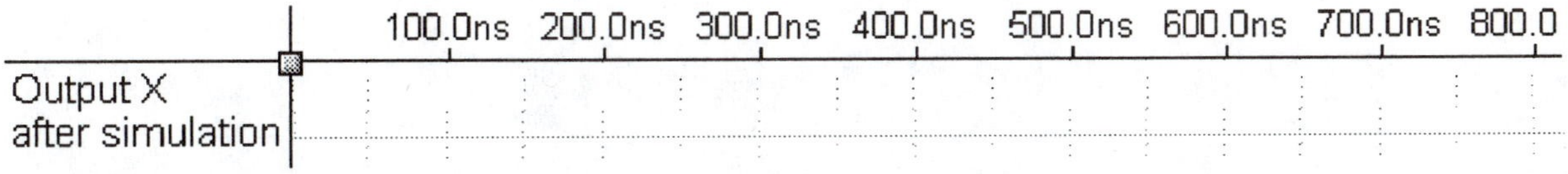

| | 100.0ns | 200.0ns | 300.0ns | 400.0ns | 500.0ns | 600.0ns | 700.0ns | 800.0 |

Output X
after simulation

Figure 4

Part 4

$\overline{g} =$ _____

$\overline{f} =$ _____

$\overline{e} =$ _____

$\overline{d} =$ _____

$\overline{c} =$ _____

$\overline{b} =$ _____

$\overline{a} =$ _____

9.   Demonstrated to: _____ Date: _____

Grade: _____

Lab 5: Adders

Objectives:

1. Design a half adder by extracting the Boolean equation from a function table
2. Design a full adder by extracting the Boolean equation from a function table
3. Construct the half adder and full adder circuits from a Boolean equation
4. Verify the half adder and full adder circuits constructed match the function table
5. Construct and demonstrate adder circuits using the 7483 integrated circuit

Materials List:

- Max+plus II software by Altera Corporation
- Circuit card containing the EPM7128SLC84 chip
- Computer requirements:
    - Minimum 486/66 with 8 MB RAM
- Floppy disk

- (9) 1 K resistors
- (9) LEDs
- 8 STDP switches
- 5-V DC power supply

Discussion:

Digital Electronics is based on 2 logic states, a logic-HIGH and a logic-LOW. As a result, the number system of choice is base 2, using the symbols 1 and 0 to represent the two logic states. When applied to adders, $5 + 7 = 12$, right? No! The correct answer is C. The computer or microprocessor that handles the math treats all data (5 and 7) as binary numbers, performs binary addition, and gives a binary answer. For $5 + 7$, the computer will add 0101_2 + 0111_2 to get 1100_2. The nibbles 5 and 7 are treated by the computer as hexadecimal symbols.

It is left up to the computer engineer or software programmer to convert the binary answer to proper form for display. This lab will treat all numbers as hex, require hex-to-binary conversions, perform all math in binary, and require binary-to-hex conversions for answers.

The fundamental building block of addition is the half adder, whose function table is shown to the right. By observation, you may recognize the Carry output is the AND gate with respect to inputs A and B. The Sum output is the exclusive OR gate with respect to inputs A and B.

B	A	Carry	Sum
0	0	0	0
0	1	0	1
1	0	0	1
1	1	1	0

Half adder function table

The full adder is a circuit with three inputs, A, B, and C_{IN}, and two outputs, Sum and Carry. The function table for the full adder is shown below.

Cin	B	A	Carry	Sum
0	0	0	0	0
0	0	1	0	1
0	1	0	0	1
0	1	1	1	0
1	0	0	0	1
1	0	1	1	0
1	1	0	1	0
1	1	1	1	1

Full adder function table

The half adder is used to add the units column bits of a multi-digit number. Full adders are used to add bits in the twos column, fours column and eights column of a nibble of data.

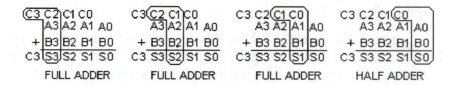

C3 C2 C1 C0	C3 C2 C1 C0	C3 C2 C1 C0	C3 C2 C1 C0
A3 A2 A1 A0	A3 A2 A1 A0	A3 A2 A1 A0	A3 A2 A1 A0
+ B3 B2 B1 B0	+ B3 B2 B1 B0	+ B3 B2 B1 B0	+ B3 B2 B1 B0
C3 S3 S2 S1 S0	C3 S3 S2 S1 S0	C3 S3 S2 S1 S0	C3 S3 S2 S1 S0
FULL ADDER	FULL ADDER	FULL ADDER	HALF ADDER

The 4-bit binary adder, 7483, contains four full adders cascaded together to perform hex nibble addition. This adder has a carry input, C_{IN}, to the least significant adder, and a C_{OUT} from the most significant adder allowing one to cascade several 7483 chips to perform multi-nibble addition.

The symbols for the adders used in this lab are shown in Figure 1.

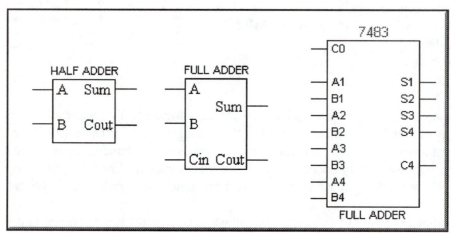

Figure 1

Part 1   Procedure

1. Complete the function table for the half adder.

2. Extract the Boolean equation from the function table that represents the Carry output with respect to inputs A and B.

    Carry = _____

3. Write the Boolean equation that represents the Sum output with respect to inputs A and B.

    Sum = _____

B	A	Carry	Sum
0	0		
0	1		
1	0		
1	1		

Half adder function table

4. Draw the Sum and Carry circuits based on your equations from Step 2 and Step 3.

5.   Open the Max+plus II software. Assign the project name **adder1** and MAX7000S as the device family.

6.   Open a new Graphic Editor file and construct the circuit from Step 4.

7.   Open a new Waveform Editor file, set the Grid Size to 100 ns, then construct the waveforms shown in Figure 2.

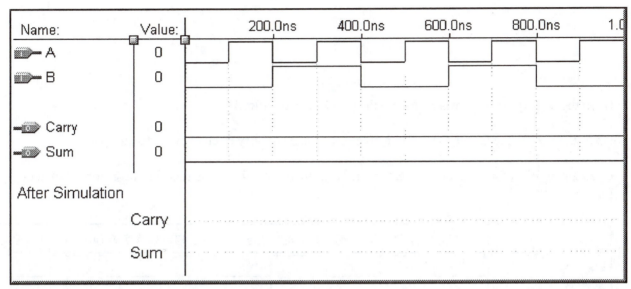

Figure 2

8.   Verify the waveforms, after simulation, match the function table. The Carry output should go to a logic-HIGH only when two or three of the inputs, A, B, and C_{IN} are at a Logic-HIGH.

9.   Draw the simulated waveforms at the bottom of Figure 2.

10.   Save the editor files to Drive A as **adder1**, then exit the Graphic and Waveform Editors.

Part 2   Procedure

1.   Complete the function table for the full adder.

2.   Extract the Boolean equation from the function table that represents the Carry output with respect to inputs A and B.

Carry = _____

3.   Extract the Boolean equation from the function table that represents the Sum output with respect to inputs A and B.

Sum = _____

4.   Draw the Sum and Carry circuits based on your equations from Step 2 and Step 3.

C_{IN}	B	A	Carry	Sum
0	0	0		
0	0	1		
0	1	0		
0	1	1		
1	0	0		
1	0	1		
1	1	0		
1	1	1		

Full adder function table

5. Open the Max+plus II software. Assign the project name **adder2**.

6. Open a new Graphic Editor file and construct the Sum and Carry circuits of Part 2, Step 4.

7. Open a new Waveform Editor file, set the Grid Size to 100 ns, then construct the waveforms shown in Figure 3.

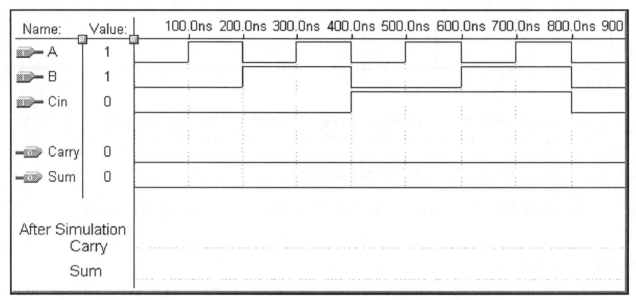

Figure 3

8. Verify that the waveforms match the function table. The Carry output should go to a logic-HIGH only when two or three of the inputs, A , B, and C_{IN} are at a logic-HIGH.

9. Draw the simulated waveforms at the bottom of Figure 3.

10. Save the editor files to Drive A as **adder2**, then exit the Graphic and Waveform Editors.

Part 3   Procedure

1. Open the Max+plus II software. Assign the project name **adder3**.

2. Open a new Graphic Editor file and construct the circuit shown in Figure 4, referring to the following instructions to create BUS lines and to label wires.

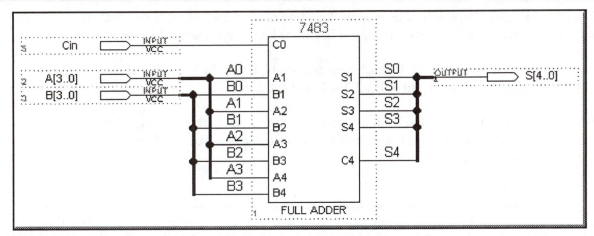

Figure 4

3. After placing the input symbol to the left of the 7483 symbol (Figure 5), place the mouse pointer on the right end of the input symbol, click and drag the mouse right ½ inch, then down 1 inch. Leave the line highlighted. Select **Options - Line Style** and click on the thick line (Figure 6) to select the **BUS** option.

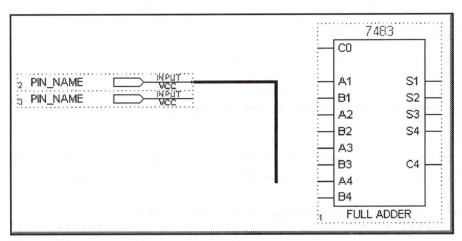

Figure 5

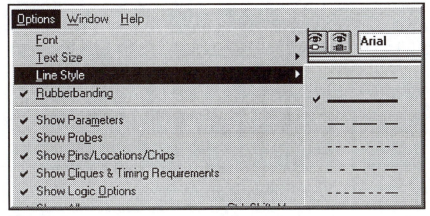

Figure 6

4. To label a line, place the mouse pointer on the line, then click on the left mouse button. The line should be highlighted with a flashing insertion point just below the line. Type the label.

5. The input buses, A[3..0] and B[3..0], each represent 4 bits: Bit 3, Bit 2, Bit 1, and Bit 0. The output bus, S[4..0] represents 5 bits: Bit 4, Bit 3, Bit 2, Bit 1, and Bit 0.

6. Open a new Waveform Editor file, set the Grid Size to 200 ns, and create the waveforms shown in Figure 8. When the bus line is highlighted, select the count over-ride button (Figure 7) in the Draw tool bar.

Figure 7

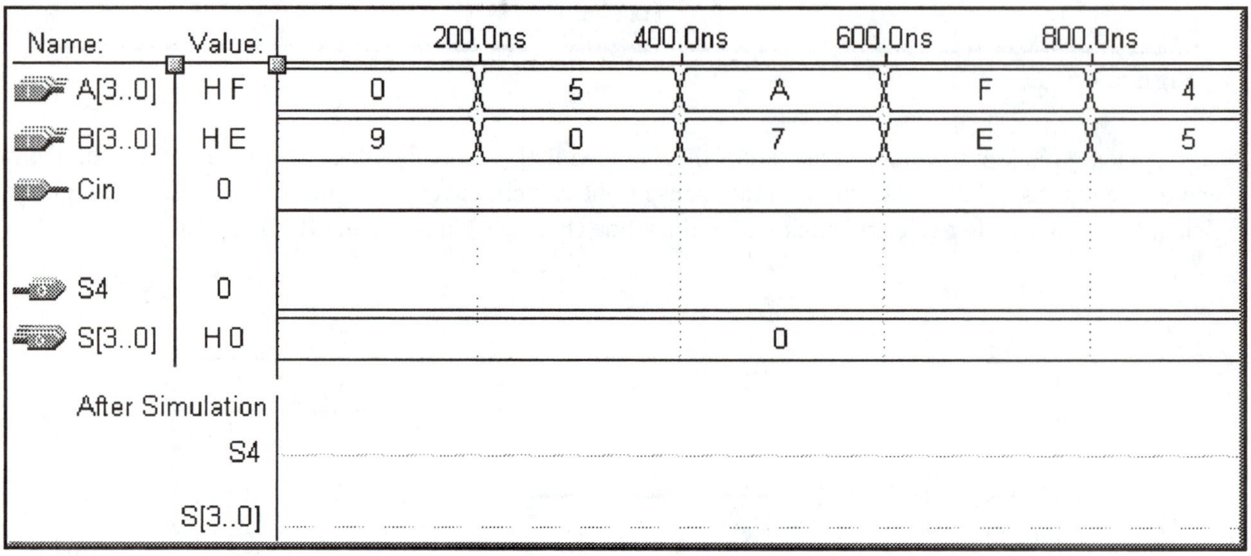

Name:	Value:	200.0ns	400.0ns	600.0ns	800.0ns
A[3..0]	H F	0	5	A	F	4
B[3..0]	H E	9	0	7	E	5
Cin	0				
S4	0				
S[3..0]	H 0			0	
After Simulation					
S4					
S[3..0]					

Figure 8

7. When the Overwrite Count Value box appears when defining Waveform A, set **Increment By:** to 5 before pressing the **OK** button. For Waveform B, set **Starting Value:** to 9 and **Increment By:** to 7.

8. Draw the resulting waveforms after simulation in the space provided in Figure 8.

9. Complete each addition problem in binary. **(Show all work in binary)**

@100 ns	@300 ns	@500 ns	@700 ns	@900 ns
0 0 0 0	0 1 0 1	1 0 1 0	1 1 1 1	0 1 0 0
+ 1 0 0 1	+ 0 0 0 0	+ 0 1 1 1	+ 1 1 1 0	+ 0 1 0 1

10. Compare your answers for each problem to the waveforms. Do your math results match the output waveforms for each time segment?   (Yes/No)

11. Save the editor files to Drive A as **adder3**, then exit the Graphics and Waveform Editors.

Part 4   Procedure

1.   Open the Max+plus II software. Assign the project name **adder4**.

2.   Open a new Graphic Editor file.

3.   Cascade two 7483 chips together to perform the following math process.

$$A_7\ A_6\ A_5\ A_4\ \ A_3\ A_2\ A_1\ A_0$$
$$+\ \underline{B_7\ B_6\ B_5\ B_4\ \ B_3\ B_2\ B_1\ B_0}$$
$$S_8\ S_7\ S_6\ S_5\ \ S_4\ \ S_3\ S_2\ S_1\ S_0$$

4.   Open a new Waveform Editor file and create a set of waveforms, A[7..0], B[7..0], C_{IN}, S_8 and S[7..0] to demonstrate your circuit is operating properly.

5.   Obtain a hard copy of the Graphics and Waveform Editors after simulation. Label these pages **Part 4, Step 4A** and **Part 4, Step 4B**.

6.   Demonstrate the 8-bit adder to your instructor. Obtain the signature of approval on the answer page.

7.   Save the editor files to Drive A as **adder4**, then exit the Graphic and Waveform Editors.

Part 5   Procedure

1.   Connect the circuit card containing the EPM7128SLC84 chip to the computer's printer port. If the computer has a software key attached to LPT1, connect the card to the parallel port on LPT2. See your instructor to determine the correct connection port.

2.   Open the Max+plus II software. Assign the project name **adder4**.

3.   Open the **adder4.gdf** file created in Part 4 of this lab.

4.   Open the **adder4.scf** file created in Part 4 of this lab.

5.   Run the compiler and simulator. Correct all errors before continuing.

6.   During compilation, a report file containing technical information including pin assignments for the EPM7128SLC84 was created and stored on your disk. Use a word processor to open this **adder4.rpt** file. Set the font for the word processor to Courier 10 point so that the symbol with the pin assignments will be easier to read.

7.   Identify and record the input and output pin numbers in Table 1 for the adder4 circuit using the **adder4.rpt** file.

"A" Inputs	"B" Inputs	"S" Inputs	C_{IN}
A_7: Pin ____	B_7: Pin ____	S_8: Pin ____	C_{IN}: Pin ____
A_6: Pin ____	B_6: Pin ____	S_7: Pin ____	
A_5: Pin ____	B_5: Pin ____	S_6: Pin ____	
A_4: Pin ____	B_4: Pin ____	S_5: Pin ____	
A_3: Pin ____	B_3: Pin ____	S_4: Pin ____	
A_2: Pin ____	B_2: Pin ____	S_3: Pin ____	
A_1: Pin ____	B_1: Pin ____	S_2: Pin ____	
A_0: Pin ____	B_0: Pin ____	S_1: Pin ____	
		S_0: Pin ____	

Table 1

8. Select **Programmer** in the Max+plus II main menu item (left of the File option).

9. Proceed to program the EPM7128SLC84 chip following the instructions in Appendix C or refer to the circuit board manufacturer's programming instructions.

10. Assume the EPM7128SLC84 chip was successfully programmed, construct the circuit shown in Figure 9. Position the LEDs and switches in numeric sequence, with the most significant on the left side.

11. Demonstrate the 8-bit adder to the instructor. Obtain the signature of approval directly on the answer page.

12. Create a cover page and write a summary pertaining to the results obtained from this lab.

13. Place all papers for this lab in the following sequence, then submit the lab to your instructor for grading.

- Cover page
- Typed summary
- The completed answer page for this lab
- Hard copy of the Graphics Editor, **Part 4, Step 4A**
- Hard copy of the Waveform Editor, **Part 4, Step 4B**

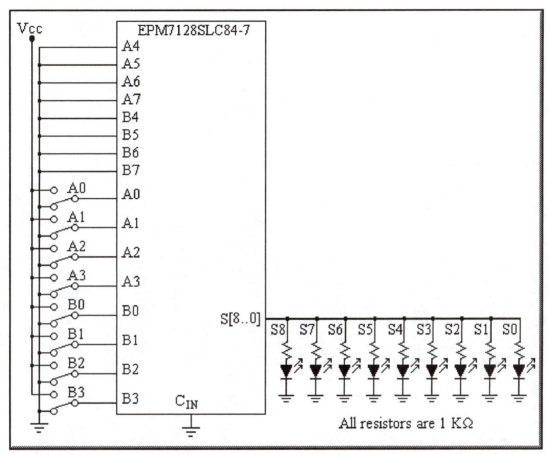

Figure 9

Lab 5: Adders Answer Page

Name: _____

Part 1

2.   Carry = _____

3.   Sum = _____

4.

B	A	Carry	Sum
0	0		
0	1		
1	0		
1	1		

Half adder function table

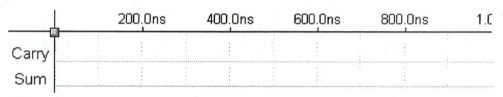

Figure 2

Part 2

2.   Carry = _____

3.   Sum = _____

4.

C_{IN}	B	A	Carry	Sum
0	0	0		
0	0	1		
0	1	0		
0	1	1		
1	0	0		
1	0	1		
1	1	0		
1	1	1		

Full adder function table

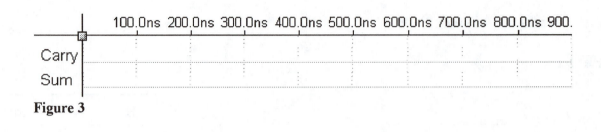

Figure 3

Part 3

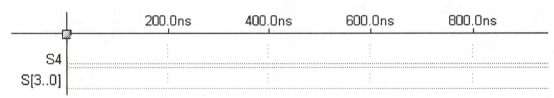

Figure 8

@100 ns	@300 ns	@500 ns	@700 ns	@900 ns
0 0 0 0	0 1 0 1	1 0 1 0	1 1 1 1	0 1 0 0
+ 1 0 0 1	+ 0 0 0 0	+ 0 1 1 1	+ 1 1 1 0	+ 0 1 0 1

10. Yes/No

Part 4

6. Demonstrated to: _____ Date: _____

Part 5

11. Demonstrated to: _____ Date: _____

Grade: _____

Lab 6: Adder Applications

Objectives:

1. Construct and demonstrate an adder/subtractor network
2. Construct and demonstrate a BCD adder
3. Construct and demonstrate a BCD to binary convertor

Materials List:

♦ Max+plus II software by Altera Corporation
♦ University Board by Altera Corporation (optional)
♦ Computer requirements:
  Minimum 486/66 with 8 MB RAM
♦ Floppy disk

Discussion:

The first circuit constructed in Figure 1 of Part 1 contains a "Programmable Inverter." The four Exclusive ORs share a common control line, C_{IN}. C_{IN} is Exclusive ORed with B[3..0].

Cin	B	XOR
0	0	0
0	1	1
1	0	1
1	1	0

XOR gate function table

Examine the function table for the XOR gate. Note that the output is identical to input B when the control input, C_{IN}, is a logic-LOW. The top half of the function table yields a buffered output of input B. The bottom half of the function table shows the output to be the inverse of input B when the control input, C_{IN}, is a logic-HIGH.

The 7483 four-bit adder adds #A + #B + C_{IN} when C_{IN} is a logic-LOW, to give a sum. When C_{IN} is a logic-HIGH, the 7483 adds #A + #$\overline{B}$ + 1, performing 2's complement addition, the equivalent of subtraction.

```
    Add, Cin = 0                Subtract, Cin = 1

    #A + #B                     #A - #B

              Cin                         Cin                    1
    A3 A2 A1 A0                 A3 A2 A1 A0 →   A3 A2 A1 A0
  + B3 B2 B1 B0                - B3 B2 B1 B0 → + B̄3 B̄2 B̄1 B̄0
    C3 S3 S2 S1 S0                              C3 S3 S2 S1 S0
```

If C3 for subtraction is a logic-HIGH, the answer, S[3..0], is in true form. If C3 is a logic-LOW, then the answer, S[3..0], is negative and in 2's complement form.

The second circuit, Figure 4, uses the 7483 to performing BCD addition. The 7483 only adds binary numbers and the result is binary. Any sum above 9 is invalid for BCD. If the addition was 5 + 4, the answer is 9. This is OK since this is a true statement in decimal. Since the carry output is a logic-LOW, the second 7483 chip adds zero to the answer of the first 7483. The final answer is 9, 1001_{BCD}.

If the process was 5 + 5, the answer from the first 7483 would be equivalent to A_H ($0101_2 + 0101_2 = 1010_2$, with a 0 carry). Since Bit 2 **or** Bit 1 will be a logic-HIGH **and** Bit 3 will be a logic-HIGH, the Carry output will be a logic-HIGH. This carry output will cause the "B" inputs to the second 7483 chip to equal 6. The second 7483 then adds 6 to the answer of the first 7483 to give zero for the answer. The logic-HIGH on the Carry output and the Zero from the second adder gives 10_{10} for the final answer. In this circuit, $5 + 5 = 10$ ($0101_{BCD} + 0101_{BCD} = 0001\ 0000_{BCD}$, or 10_{10}), not A_H.

Figure 4 can be used to convert binary numbers to BCD numbers by adding zero to the binary number.

Figure 5 converts BCD numbers to binary. As long as the inputs A[7..0] are valid BCD characters, the output will be the binary equivalent. To predict the output for any BCD number applied, trace the bits to the 7483 on the left, add the bits, then trace the outputs to the 7483 on the right and add those bits.

Part 1   Procedure

1.   Open the Max+plus II software. Assign the project name **addapps1** and MAX7000S as the device family.

2.   Open a new Graphic Editor file and construct the circuit shown in Figure 1.

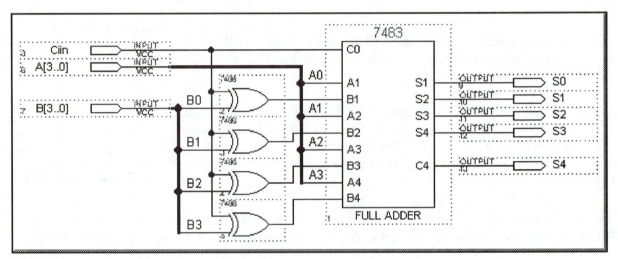

Figure 1

3.   Open a new Waveform Editor file, set the Grid Size to 200 ns, then create Waveform A as a bus containing A0, A1, A2, and A3. This bus should start at 3 and increment by 11. Create Bus B, B[3..0], starting at 9 and increment by 4.

4.   Create the SUBT/ADD input as a logic-LOW for 600 ns, then a logic_HIGH for 400 ns. Create output waveforms as labeled in Figure 1.

5.   Draw the output waveforms after simulation in Figure 2.

6.   Complete the problems listed below. **Show all work in binary**.

@ 100 ns	@ 300 ns	@ 500 ns	@ 700 ns	@ 900 ns
0011	1110	1001	0100	1111
+ 1001	+ 1101	+ 0001	− 0101	− 1001

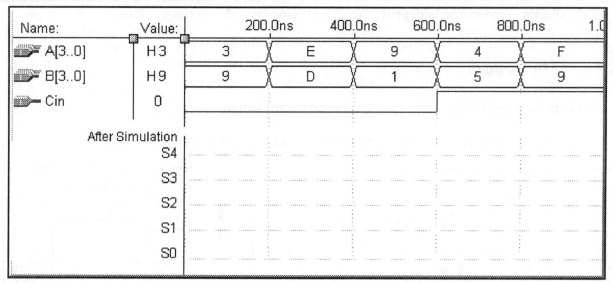

Figure 2

7. Compare your answers to the problems to the output waveforms you drew in Figure 2. Do the output waveforms at each time interval match your answers? (Yes/No)

8. Change Waveform A[3..0] to start at B_H, incrementing by 11, and Waveform B to start at 3 and increment by 7. The new set of waveforms should look like those in Figure 3.

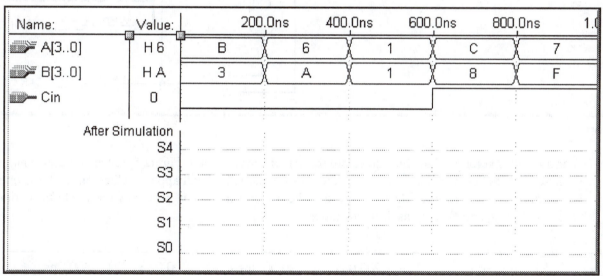

Figure 3

9. Draw the new set of output waveforms after simulation in Figure 3.

10. Complete the problems listed below. **Show all work in binary**.

@ 100 ns	@ 300 ns	@ 500 ns	@ 700 ns	@ 900 ns
1 0 1 1	0 1 1 0	0 0 0 1	1 1 0 0	0 1 1 1
+ 0 0 1 1	+ 1 0 1 0	+ 0 0 0 1	− 1 0 0 0	− 1 1 1 1

11. Compare your answers to the problems to the output waveforms you drew in Figure 3. Do the output waveforms at each time interval match your answers? (Yes/No)

12.   Save all files to Drive A as **addapps1**, then exit the Graphic and Waveform Editors.

Part 2   Procedure

1.   Open the Max+plus II software. Assign the project name **addapps2**.

2.   Open a new Graphic Editor file and construct the circuit shown in Figure 4.

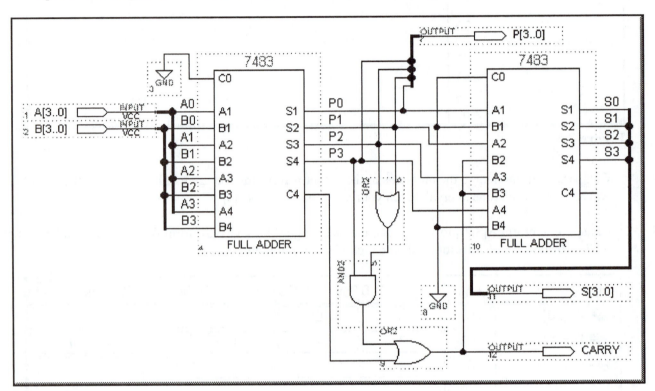

Figure 4

3.   Open a new Waveform Editor file and create the waveforms shown in Figure 5. Once you create an input bus line, double click on the bus line. An Enter Group dialog box will appear. Click on the DEC option in the Radix box. The numeric values displayed in the waveform are now decimal values. Define both input bus lines, A[3..0] and B[3..0], as decimal values.

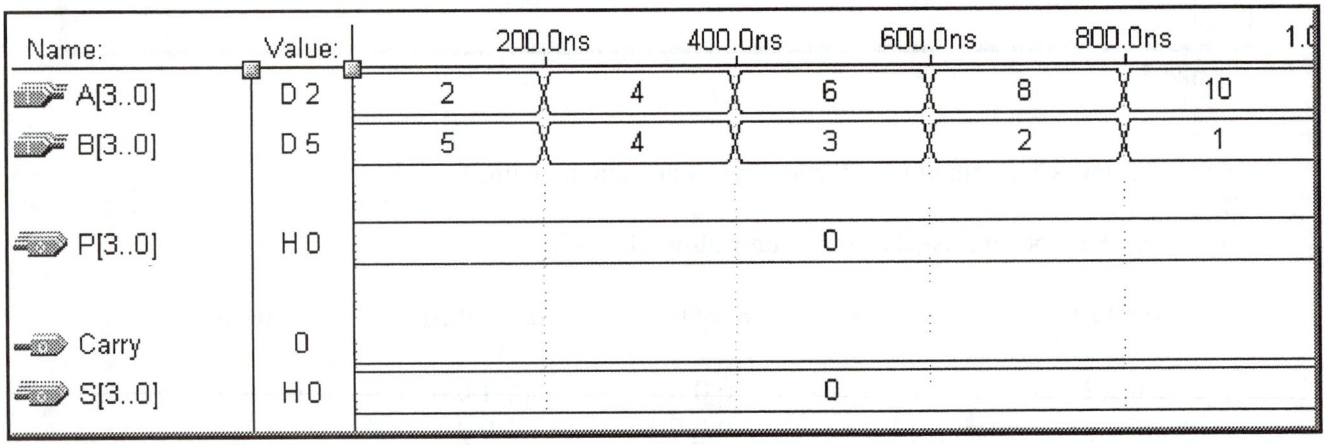

Name:	Value:	200.0ns	400.0ns	600.0ns	800.0ns	1.0
A[3..0]	D 2	2	4	6	8	10
B[3..0]	D 5	5	4	3	2	1
P[3..0]	H 0			0		
Carry	0					
S[3..0]	H 0			0		

Figure 5

4.   After simulation, draw the output waveforms in the space provided at the bottom of Figure 5.

5.   Perform the following math in binary, as illustrated in Figure 5. Enter the Carry bit from the left 7483 as Bit 2 and Bit 1 for the second addition process. The output logic level based on S2 or S3 and S4 or C4 of the left 7483 is to be recorded as the Carry bit.

@ 100 ns	@ 300 ns	@ 500 ns	@ 700 ns	@ 900 ns
0 0 1 0	0 1 0 0	0 1 1 0	1 0 0 0	1 0 1 0
+ 0 1 0 1	+ 0 1 0 0	+ 0 0 1 1	+ 0 0 1 0	+ 0 0 0 1
+ 0 0	+ 0 0	+ 0 0	+ 0 0	+ 0 0
Carry Sum	Carry Sum	Carry Sum	Carry Sum	Carry Sum

6.   Do your answers match the outputs of the circuit?   (Yes/No)

7.   Save all files to Drive A as **addapps2**, then exit the Graphic and Waveform Editors.

Part 3   Procedure

1.   Open the Max+plus II software. Assign the project name **addapps3**.

2.   Open a new Graphic Editor file and construct the circuit and waveforms shown in Figure 6.

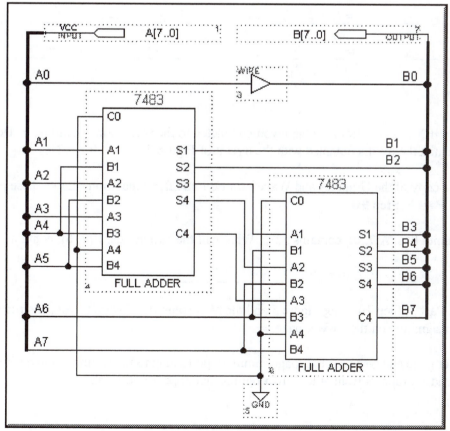

Figure 6

3. Note that the input and output connectors in Figure 6 have been rotated 180 degrees. To rotate a symbol 180 degrees, single click on the symbol to highlight the symbol, then select **Edit - Rotate - 180**.

4. Open a new Waveform Editor file and create waveform A[7..4] starting at 0, increment by 1. Set the "Value" to decimal.

5. Create waveform A[3..0] starting at 9, decrement by 1 (increment by minus 1). Set the "Value" to decimal. Create the output bus, B[7..0], with its value set for hexadecimal. Your waveforms should look like those shown in Figure 7.

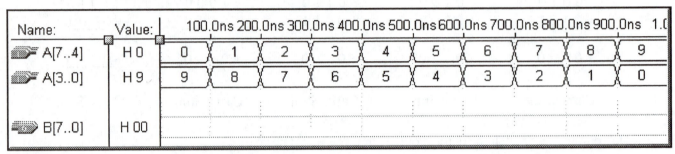

Figure 7

6. Draw the resulting wave, B[7..0], after simulation in the area provided in Figure 5.

7. Complete the number conversions for each decimal value below.

$09_{10} =$ _____ BCD $27_{10} =$ _____ BCD $45_{10} =$ _____ BCD $63_{10} =$ _____ BCD

$=$ _____ 2 $=$ _____ 2 $=$ _____ 2 $=$ _____ 2

$=$ _____ H $=$ _____ H $=$ _____ H $=$ _____ H

8. Compare the HEX answers from the table you completed to the waveforms in Figure 7. Do your predictions match the results obtained with the circuit of Figure 7?   (Yes/No)

9. Obtain a hard copy of the Graphics and Waveform Editors after simulation. Label these pages **Part 3, Step 9A** and **Part 3, Step 9B**.

10. Assume the input bus, A[7..0], contains 52_{10}. What will the output bus, B[7..0], contain?

                   B[7..0] = _____

11. Demonstrate Part 3, Step 10 using Figure 5 and the Max+plus II software to your instructor. Obtain the authorization signature on the answer page.

12. Create a cover page and write a 1 to 2 page summary pertaining to the results obtained from this lab. Include embedded graphics from at least two figures that appear in this lab.

13.   Place all papers for this lab in the following sequence, then submit the lab to your instructor for grading.

- Cover page
- Typed summary
- The completed answer pages for this lab
- Hard copy of the Graphic Editor, **Part 3, Step 9A**
- Hard copy of the Waveform Editor, **Part 3, Step 9B**

Part 1

6.

@ 100 ns	@ 300 ns	@ 500 ns	@ 700 ns	@ 900 ns
0 0 1 1	1 1 1 0	1 0 0 1	0 1 0 0	1 1 1 1
+ 1 0 0 1	+ 1 1 0 1	+ 0 0 0 1	- 0 1 0 1	- 1 0 0 1

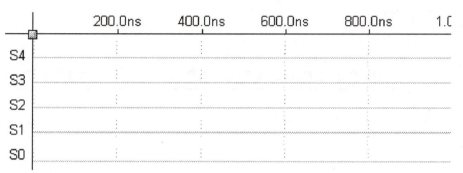

Figure 2

7.   Yes   No

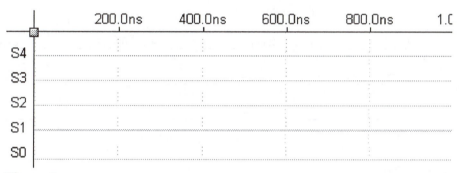

Figure 3

@ 100 ns	@ 300 ns	@ 500 ns	@ 700 ns	@ 900 ns
1 0 1 1	0 1 1 0	0 0 0 1	1 1 0 0	0 1 1 1
+ 0 0 1 1	+ 1 0 1 0	+ 0 0 0 1	- 1 0 0 0	- 1 1 1 1

Part 2

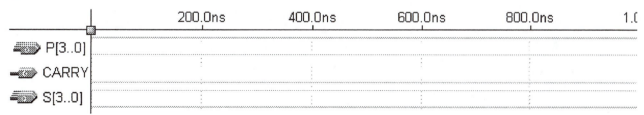

Figure 5

5.

@ 100 ns	@ 300 ns	@ 500 ns	@ 700 ns	@ 900 ns

```
   0 0 1 0       0 1 0 0       0 1 1 0       1 0 0 0       1 0 1 0
 + 0 1 0 1     + 0 1 0 0     + 0 0 1 1     + 0 0 1 0     + 0 0 0 1


 + 0     0     + 0     0     + 0     0     + 0     0     + 0     0


 Carry Sum     Carry Sum     Carry Sum     Carry Sum     Carry Sum
```

6.   Yes   No

Part 3

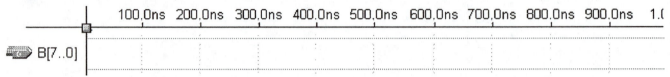

Figure 7

7.

$09_{10} = $ _____ BCD $27_{10} = $ _____ BCD $45_{10} = $ _____ BCD $63_{10} = $ _____ BCD

$= $ _____ $_2$ $= $ _____ $_2$ $= $ _____ $_2$ $= $ _____ $_2$

$= $ _____ $_H$ $= $ _____ $_H$ $= $ _____ $_H$ $= $ _____ $_H$

8.   Yes   No

10.   _____

11.   Demonstrated to: _____ Date: _____

Grade: _____

Lab 7: Parity

Objectives:

1. Implement a basic parity circuit using XOR gates
2. Use the 74180 as a parity generator
3. Use the 74180 as a parity checker
4. Analyze a parity generator/checker circuit and modify the circuit to eliminate undesirable glitches in the output signal

Materials List:

♦ Max+plus II software by Altera Corporation
♦ University Board by Altera Corporation (optional)
♦ Computer requirements:
  Minimum 486/66 with 8 MB RAM
♦ Floppy disk

Discussion:

Transmitted data in a digital system may be altered due to external electrical interference or an internal defective part. If the system generates and transmits a parity bit with the data, the parity checker at the receiver end will generate an error signal. A parity bit is generated during the memory write cycle time and is checked during the memory read cycle time. If an error is detected, a memory error message is displayed on the monitor and the system is halted. An error detected in data received by a modem may send an interrupt signal to the transmitter requesting that the data be retransmitted. The operator may not know that transmission errors occurred.

This lab shows how to use the XOR gate to create a parity generator, then illustrates how to wire a 74280 integrated circuit as a parity generator or checker. The parity generator, parity checker, and control signals will be combined to create a parity error detection circuit typical in a computer or modem system.

Part 1   Procedure

1. Open the Max+plus II software and assign the project name **parity1** and MAX7000S as the device family.

2. Open a new Graphic Editor file, then construct the circuit shown in Figure 1.

3. Open a new Waveform Editor file, set the Grid Size to 100 ns, and construct the waveforms shown in Figure 2.

4. Draw the output waveform in the space provided in Figure 2 after simulating the circuit.

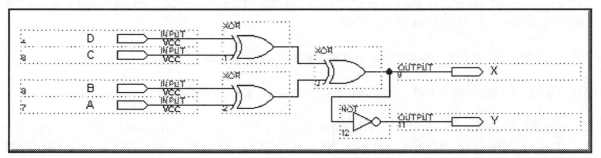

Figure 1

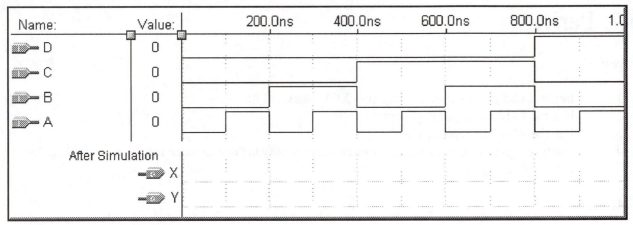

Figure 2

Time Segment	X D C B A (in binary)	Number of 1s in X D C B A	Y D C B A (in binary)	Number of 1s in Y D C B A
0 ns- 100 ns				
100 ns- 200 ns				
200 ns- 300 ns				
300 ns- 400 ns				
400 ns- 500 ns				
500 ns- 600 ns				
600 ns- 700 ns				
700 ns- 800 ns				
800 ns- 900 ns				
900 ns- 1 μs				

Table 1

5.   Complete Table 1.

6.   Based on the results obtained in Figure 1, the "X" output is an (ODD/EVEN) parity generator and the "Y" output is an (ODD/EVEN) parity generator.

7.   Save both editor files to Drive A as **parity1**, then exit the Graphic and Waveform Editors.

Part 2   Procedure

Rarely will you find a parity circuit constructed out of XORs. Designers will use integrated circuits. The 9-Bit Odd/Even Parity Generator/Checker used in this lab is the 74280. This IC can be used for either Even or Odd parity systems and has a cascadable input for *n*-bits.

1.   Open the Max+plus II software and assign the project name **parity2**.

2.   Open a new Graphic Editor file, then construct the circuit shown in Figure 3.

3.   Open a new Waveform Editor file, set the Grid Size to 100 ns, and construct the waveforms shown in Figure 4. Set the Starting Value: to 17 and Increment By: to 23 in the Overwrite Count Value dialog box.

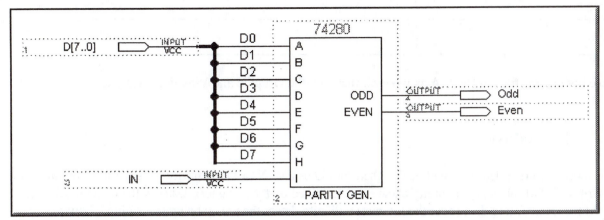

Figure 3

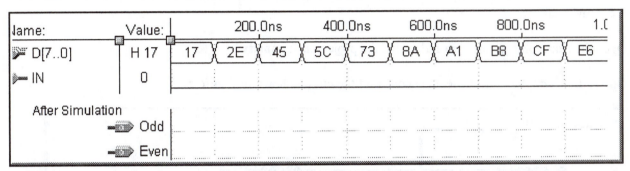

Figure 4

4. Draw the output waveform in the space provided in Figure 4 after simulating the circuit.

5. Complete Table 2 showing the odd and even output bits for each data applied to the 74280 in Figure 3.

D[7..0]	D[7..0] (in binary)	Odd Output Bit	Even Output Bit
17	_____ ₂	_____	_____
2E	_____ ₂	_____	_____
45	_____ ₂	_____	_____
5C	_____ ₂	_____	_____
73	_____ ₂	_____	_____
8A	_____ ₂	_____	_____
A1	_____ ₂	_____	_____
B8	_____ ₂	_____	_____
CF	_____ ₂	_____	_____
E6	_____ ₂	_____	_____

Table2

6. Write a paragraph explaining the results obtained in Figure 4 with respect to the circuit in Figure 3.

_____

_____

7. Save both editor files to Drive A as **parity2**, then exit the Graphic and Waveform Editors.

Part 3   Procedure

A system using parity error detection will be designed for either EVEN or ODD parity. If used in a computer for reading or writing RAM memory, the parity choice is determined by the designer. Usually the communications software used for transmitting data (over the Internet) will auto detect the parity being transmitted, however for some software, the operator must set his or her parity to match the parity of the system to which it is connected. The rest of this lab is based on a parity generator/checker system that may be used inside a computer for reading and writing RAM memory.

1. Open the Max+plus II software and assign the project name **parity3**.

2. Open a new Graphic Editor file, then construct the circuit shown in Figure 5.

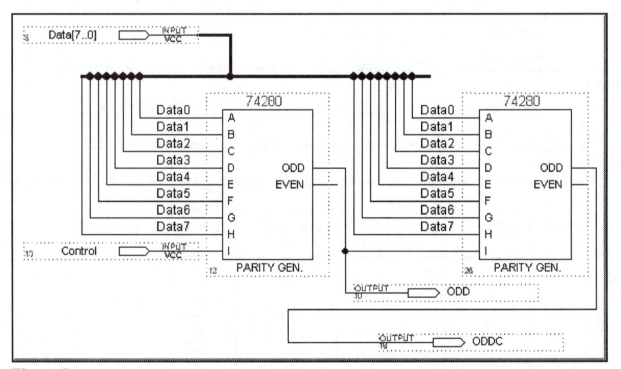

Figure 5

3. Open a new Waveform Editor file, set the Grid Size to 100 ns, and construct the waveforms shown in Figure 6. For the Data[7..0] waveform, set the Starting Value: to 75 and Increment By: to 183 in the Overwrite Count Value dialog box.

4. Complete Table 3 for the time segment 0 ns to 500 ns.

5. The ODD output represents (EVEN/ODD) parity for the time segment 0 ns to 500 ns when the input control line is a logic-LOW.

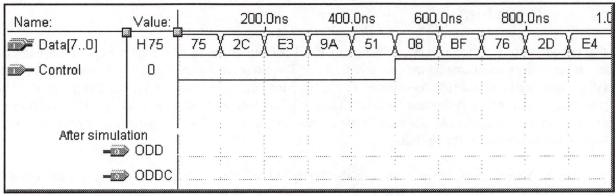

Figure 6

Control	Data[7..0]	Data[7..0] (in binary)	ODD (1 or 0)	ODDC (1 or 0)
0	75	_____2	____	____
0	2C	_____2	____	____
0	E3	_____2	____	____
0	9A	_____2	____	____
0	51	_____2	____	____

Table 3

6. The **ODDC** output from 0 ns to 500 ns represents active-(LOW/HIGH) levels when an error is detected.

7. Complete Table 4 for the time segment 500 ns to 1 μs.

Control	Data[7..0]	Data[7..0] (in binary)	ODD (1 or 0)	ODDC (1 or 0)
1	08	_____2	____	____
1	BF	_____2	____	____
1	76	_____2	____	____
1	2D	_____2	____	____
1	E4	_____2	____	____

Table 4

8. The **ODD** output represents (EVEN/ODD) parity for the time segment 500 ns to 1 μs when the input control line is a logic-HIGH.

9. The **ODDC** output from 500 ns to 1 μs represents active- (LOW/HIGH) levels when an error is detected.

10. Based on your observation, which 74280 IC in Figure 5 is the Parity Generator? (Left/Right)

11. What you should notice is that **ODDC** is identical to the control input. If the circuit does not detect an error (either from 0 to 500 ns when Control = 0 or from 500 ns to 1 μs when Control = 1), **ODDC** will be a constant value. If an error occurs, **ODDC** will become "active" to represent the error.

12. Save both editor files to drive A as **parity3**, then exit the Graphic and Waveform Editors.

Part 4   Procedure

Note that the output of waveform OUTC of the parity checker (chip on the right in Figure 5) produces undesirable glitches that are errors when data on the data bus changes. The circuit of Figure 5 needs to be modified so that these errors don't show up in the output. As you may recall, the parity bit is generated and saved along with the data during memory write. Parity is checked when the data and parity bits are read from memory. The output of the parity checker may be controlled by the Read/Write control line, which enables the parity bit from the checker to pass to the output only during the read time.

1.   Open the Max+plus II software and open the **parity3** Graphic and Waveform files located on your disk.

2.   Change (assign) the project to **parity4**. Save both editor files to Drive A as **parity4**.

3.   Modify the parity generator/checker circuit as shown in Figure 7.

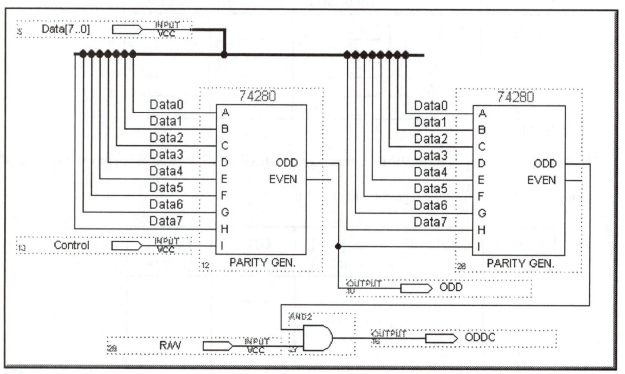

Figure 7

4.   Set the Grid Size to 20 ns and be sure the Snap to Grid option is turned on. Add a constant logic-HIGH R/W control input to your Waveform Editor file. Highlight the following sections of the R/W waveform, making each section a logic-LOW: 100 to 120 ns, 200 to 220 ns, 300 to 320 ns, 400 to 420 ns, 500 to 520 ns, 600 to 620 ns, 700 to 720 ns, 800 to 820 ns, and 900 to 920 ns.

5.   Change the Control waveform to a constant logic-LOW.

6.   Compile, then simulate the circuit. Examine the output waveform, ODDC, from the parity checker. Are the undesirable glitches still present in this output waveform?   (Yes/No)

7.   Does the parity checker detect any parity errors from 0 ns to 1 μs?   (Yes/No)

8.   Save all files to drive A as **parity4**, but DO NOT EXIT the editors.

Part 5   Procedure

1.   Open the Max+plus II software and open the **parity4** Graphic and Waveform files located on your disk.

2.   Change (assign) the project to **parity5**. Save both editor files as **parity5**.

3.   Since the circuit is designed for ODDC to be a logic-HIGH only when the parity checker detects an error, you will not see an error signal for there are no errors coming from Data[7..0] in the Waveform Editor. To simulate an error while reading data stored in memory, add an AND gate in the Data0 line as shown in Figure 8.

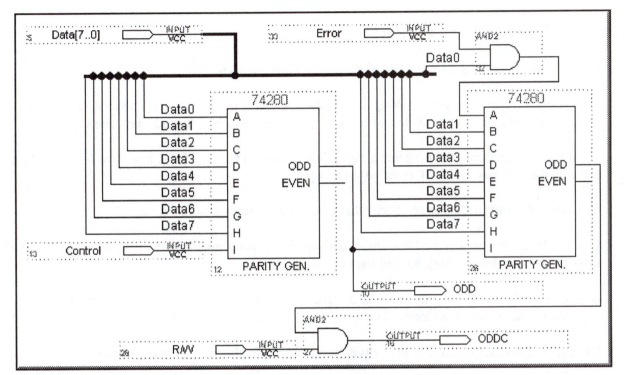

Figure 8

4.   Add a constant logic-HIGH Error signal to the Waveform Editor.

5.   Press the Compile and Simulate buttons, correcting all errors before continuing.

6.   Analyze the output waveform after simulation. Does ODDC show any errors? (any time the output goes to a logic-HIGH)   (Yes/No)

7.   Highlight and change the error waveform from 300 ns to 500 ns to a constant logic-LOW.

8.   Press the Simulator button.

9.   Analyze the output waveform after simulation. Does ODDC show any errors? (any time the output goes to a logic-HIGH)   (Yes/No)

10.   Explain why **ODDC** shows errors when the error input is a logic-LOW but not when error input is a logic-HIGH.

_____

_____

_____

11.   Obtain a hard copy of your modified circuit and simulated waveforms with the R/W control input. Label these hard copies **Part 5, Step 9A** and **Part 5, Step 9B**.

12.   Save both editor files to Drive A as **parity5**, then exit the Graphic and Waveform Editors.

Part 6   Procedure   (Optional)

1.   Open the Max+plus II software. Assign the project name **parity6**.

2.   Open a new Graphic Editor file. Using two 74280 ICs, create a circuit to generate an even parity bit based on D[15..0] during a memory write and check for possible errors in data read from memory.

3.   Open a new Waveform Editor file and assign d7b9 to the data bus, D[15..0], from 0 to 500 ns and assign FdCF to the data bus, D[15..0], from 500 ns to 1 µs.

4.   Compile and simulate the circuit. Verify that the circuit operates as stated in Step 2.

5.   Obtain a hard copy of your modified circuit and simulated waveforms with the R/W control input. Label these hard copies **Part 6, Step 5A** and **Part 6, Step 5B**.

6.   Demonstrate the results obtained from the designed circuit to your instructor. Obtain the signature of approval on the answer page for this lab.

7.   Save both editor files to Drive A as **parity6**, then exit the Graphic and Waveform Editors.

8.   Write a 1 to 2 page summary pertaining to the results obtained from this lab. Compare and contrast Figures 5 and 7, highlighting the advantages of Figure 7. Include embedded figures and waveforms in your summary.

9.   Place all papers for this lab in the following sequence, then submit the lab to your instructor for grading.

- Cover page
- Typed summary
- The completed answer page for this lab
- Hard copy of the Graphics Editor, **Part 5, Step 9A**
- Hard copy of the Waveform Editor, **Part 5, Step 9B**
- Hard copy of the Graphics Editor, **Part 6, Step 5A**
- Hard copy of the Waveform Editor, **Part 6, Step 5B**

Lab 7: Parity Answer Page

Part 1

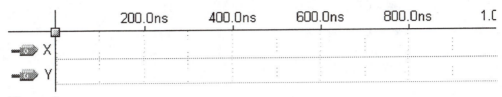

Figure 2

Time Segment	X D C B A (in binary)	Number of 1s in X D C B A	Y D C B A (in binary)	Number of 1s in Y D C B A
0 ns - 100 ns	_____	_____	_____	_____
100 ns - 200 ns	_____	_____	_____	_____
200 ns - 300 ns	_____	_____	_____	_____
300 ns - 400 ns	_____	_____	_____	_____
400 ns - 500 ns	_____	_____	_____	_____
500 ns - 600 ns	_____	_____	_____	_____
600 ns - 700 ns	_____	_____	_____	_____
700 ns - 800 ns	_____	_____	_____	_____
800 ns - 900 ns	_____	_____	_____	_____
900 ns -1 μs	_____	_____	_____	_____

Table 1

6.   ODD   EVEN

Part 2

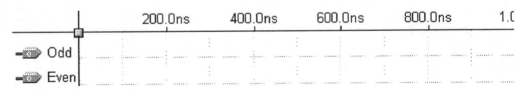

Figure 4

6. _____

_____

_____

_____

_____

_____

_____

D[7..0]	D[7..0] (in binary)	Odd Output Bit	Even Output Bit
17	_____ 2	_____	_____
2E	_____ 2	_____	_____
45	_____ 2	_____	_____
5C	_____ 2	_____	_____
73	_____ 2	_____	_____
8A	_____ 2	_____	_____
A1	_____ 2	_____	_____
B8	_____ 2	_____	_____
CF	_____ 2	_____	_____
E6	_____ 2	_____	_____

Table2

Part 3

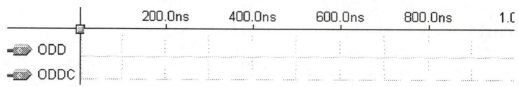

Figure 6

5. EVEN ODD

6. LOW HIGH

Control	Data[7..0]	Data[7..0] (in binary)	ODD (1 or 0)	ODDC (1 or 0)
0	75	_____2	_____	_____
0	2C	_____2	_____	_____
0	E3	_____2	_____	_____
0	9A	_____2	_____	_____
0	51	_____2	_____	_____

Table 3

7. EVEN ODD

8. LOW HIGH

9. Left Right

Control	Data[7..0]	Data[7..0] (in binary)	ODD (1 or 0)	ODDC (1 or 0)
1	08	_____2	_____	_____
1	BF	_____2	_____	_____
1	76	_____2	_____	_____
1	2D	_____2	_____	_____
1	E4	_____2	_____	_____

Table 4

Part 4

6. YES NO

7. YES NO

Part 5

6. YES NO

9. YES NO

10. _____

_____

Part 6

6. Demonstrated to: _____ Date: _____

Grade: _____

Lab 8: Comparators

Objectives:

1. Use the Exclusive-OR gate as a comparator
2. Build a 4-bit magnitude comparator using basic logic gates
3. Use the 7485 4-bit magnitude comparator for 4-bit and 8-bit binary comparisons

Materials List:

- Max+plus II software by Altera Corporation
- University Board by Altera Corporation (optional)
- Computer requirements:
    Minimum 486/66 with 8 MB RAM
- Floppy disk

Discussion:

A comparator is a circuit that determines the relationship of two numbers. Typical outputs of the comparator are greater than (A > B), less than (A < B), and equal to (A = B). Either the exclusive-OR or the Exclusive-NOR gates are used for basic comparisons.

Examine the circuit and waveforms shown in Figure 1. When inputs A and B are both logic-HIGH or logic-LOW, output AequalB is a logic-HIGH. If the inputs are of different logic levels, output AequalB is a logic-LOW. This circuit may be used to compare for equality. This circuit produces an "active-HIGH" output based on equality.

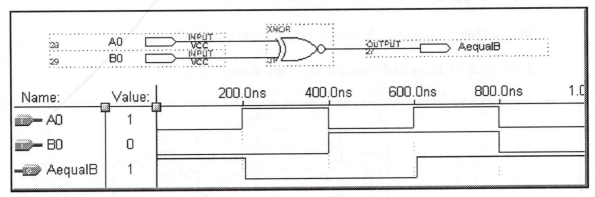

Figure 1

To determine inequality, one input is ANDed with the inverse of the other input. If A AND not B equal a logic-HIGH, then A > B. If not A AND B equal a logic-HIGH, then A < B. The circuit shown in Figure 2 will produce an active high output on either A > B, A < B, or A = B.

Of course, larger bit comparisons will require larger circuits. The 7485 4-bit magnitude comparator will be used to compare 4- and 8-bit numbers instead of using a complex network of logic gates.

Part 1   Procedure

1. Open the Max+plus II software. Assign the project name **compare2** and MAX7000S as the device family.

2. Open a new Graphic Editor and construct the circuit of Figure 2.

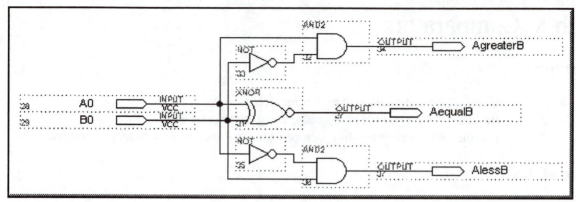

Figure 2

3. Open a new Waveform Editor, set the Grid Size to 200 ns, then create waveforms A0 and B0 as shown in Figure 1. Create the three output waveforms identified in Figure 2.

4. Run the compiler and simulator. Correct all errors before continuing.

5. Analyze the output waveforms with respect to the inputs, then complete Table 1.

6. Save all files to Drive A as **compare2**, then exit the Graphic and Waveform Editors.

Inputs		Outputs		
B0	A0	A>B	A<B	A=B
0	0			
0	1			
1	0			
1	1			

Table 1

Part 2   Procedure

1. Open the Max+plus II software. Assign the project name **compare3**.

2. Open a new Graphic Editor and construct the circuit shown in Figure 3.

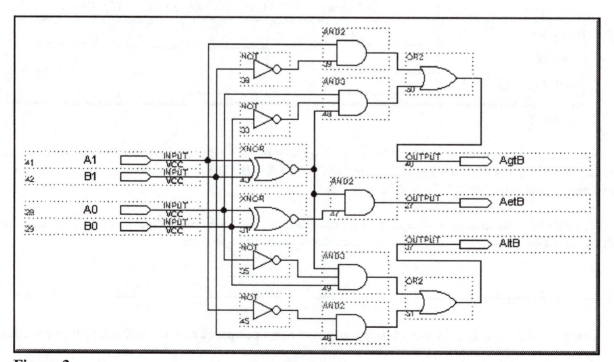

Figure 3

Lab 8: Comparators

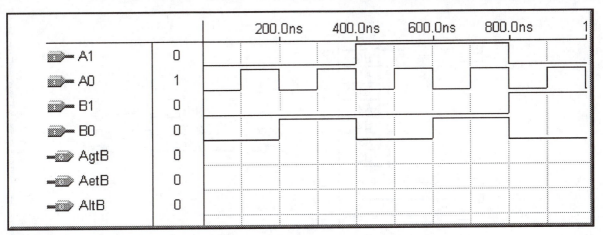

Figure 4

3.   Open a new Waveform Editor, set the Grid Size to 100 ns, and create the waveforms shown in Figure 4.

4.   Run the compiler and simulator. Correct all errors before continuing.

5.   Neatly and accurately draw the output waveforms in the space provided in Figure 4.

6.   Analyze the output waveforms with respect to inputs, then complete Table 2.

Time	Inputs		Outputs		
	B_1B_0	A_1A_0	A>B	A<B	A=B
50 ns	0 0	0 0			
150 ns	0 0	0 1			
250 ns	0 1	0 0			
350 ns	0 1	0 1			
450 ns	0 0	1 0			

Time	Inputs		Outputs		
	B_1B_0	A_1A_0	A>B	A<B	A=B
550 ns	0 0	1 0			
650 ns	0 1	1 1			
750 ns	0 1	1 0			
850 ns	1 0	0 1			
950 ns	1 0	0 0			

Table 2

7.   Is input A1 dominant over input A0?   (Yes/No)

8.   Name the output(s) that take on an active-HIGH characteristic. _____

9.   Save all files to Drive A as **compare3**, then exit the Graphic and Waveform Editors.

Part 3   Procedure

1.   Open the Max+plus II software. Assign the project name **compare4**.

2.   Open a new Graphic Editor and construct the circuit shown in Figure 6.

3.   Open a new Waveform Editor, set the Grid Size to 100 ns, and construct the waveforms shown in Figure 7.

4.   Highlight waveform A[3..0] and press the Over Write Group button in the Draw tool bar (see Figure 5). Enter "C" for the Group Value. Assign the Group Value "7" to waveform B[3..0].

Figure 5

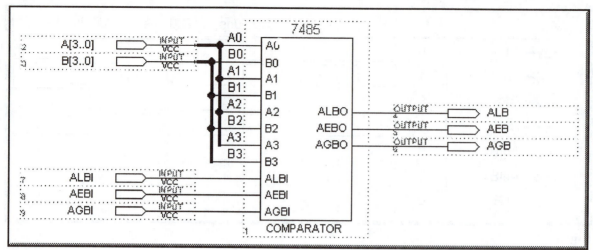

Figure 6

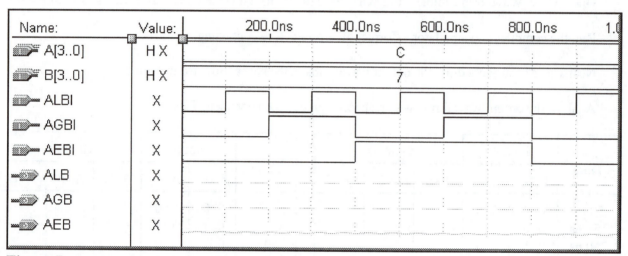

Figure 7

5. Compile and simulate the circuit. Draw the output waveforms in the space provided in Figure 7.

6. Did the logic level of the cascade inputs affect the outputs of the 7485 when A[3..0] = "C" and B[3..0] = "7"?   (Yes/No)   Explain why or why not.

    _____

    _____

7. Change B[3..0] to a value of "D" from 0 ns to 1 µs.

8. Explain how the circuit operation (after simulation) was altered when B[3..0] is "D."

    _____

9. Change B[3..0] to a value of "C" from 0 ns to 1 µs.

10. Complete Table 3 based on the results when A[3..0] and B[3..0] contain "C_H."

Time Segment when	Cascade Inputs A>B A<B A=B	Outputs A>B A<B A=B
0 ns to 100 ns	___ ___ ___	___ ___ ___
100 to 200 ns	___ ___ ___	___ ___ ___
200 to 300 ns	___ ___ ___	___ ___ ___
300 to 400 ns	___ ___ ___	___ ___ ___
400 to 500 ns	___ ___ ___	___ ___ ___
500 to 600 ns	___ ___ ___	___ ___ ___
600 to 700 ns	___ ___ ___	___ ___ ___
700 to 800 ns	___ ___ ___	___ ___ ___
800 to 900 ns	___ ___ ___	___ ___ ___
900 ns to 1 µs	___ ___ ___	___ ___ ___

Table 3

11.   Based on the results recorded for Table 3, which cascade input is dominant?   _____

12.   Save all files to Drive A as **compare4**, then exit the Graphic and Waveform Editors.

Part 4   Procedure

1.   Open the Max+plus II software and assign the project name **compare5**.

2.   Create an 8-bit magnitude comparator using two 7485s with data inputs A[7..0] and B[7..0]. The cascade inputs must be hard wired to either Vcc or ground as required by the IC specifications.

3.   Demonstrate that the 8-bit magnitude comparator produces the desired output comparisons, A[7..0] > B[7..0], A[7..0] = B[7..0], and A[7..0] < B[7..0] for various values of numbers A and B.

4.   Demonstrate your 8-bit magnitude comparator to your instructor. Obtain the signature on the answer page for this lab.

5.   Obtain hard copies of the Graphic and Waveform editors showing the 8-bit magnitude comparator. Label these hard copies **Part 4, Step 5A** and **Part 4, Step 5B**.

6.   Exit the Max+plus II software, saving all files to Drive A as **compare5** upon exit.

7.   Write a summary pertaining to the results obtained from this lab. Include tables and figures to supplement your discussion.

8.   Place all papers for this lab in the following sequence, then submit the materials to your instructor for grading.

- Cover page
- Typed summary
- The completed answer page
- Hard copy of the Graphic Editor, **Part 4, Step 5**
- Hard copy of the Waveform Editor, **Part 4, Step 5**

Part 1

Inputs		Outputs		
B0	A0	A>B	A<B	A=B
0	0			
0	1			
1	0			
1	1			

Table 1

Part 2

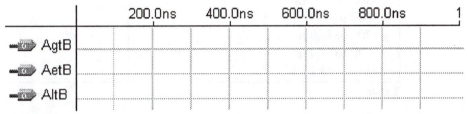

Figure 3

Time	Inputs		Outputs		
	B_1B_0	A_1A_0	A>B	A<B	A=B
50 ns	0 0	0 0			
150 ns	0 0	0 1			
250 ns	0 1	0 0			
350 ns	0 1	0 1			
450 ns	0 0	1 0			

Time	Inputs		Outputs		
	B_1B_0	A_1A_0	A>B	A<B	A=B
550 ns	0 0	1 0			
650 ns	0 1	1 1			
750 ns	0 1	1 0			
850 ns	1 0	0 1			
950 ns	1 0	0 0			

Table 2

7.   (Yes/No)

8.   _____

Part 3

Figure 5

6.   (Yes/No)   Explain why or why not.

_____

_____

8.   _____

Time Segment when	Cascade Inputs A>B A<B A=B			Outputs A>B A<B A=B		
0 ns to 100 ns	__	__	__	__	__	__
100 to 200 ns	__	__	__	__	__	__
200 to 300 ns	__	__	__	__	__	__
300 to 400 ns	__	__	__	__	__	__
400 to 500 ns	__	__	__	__	__	__
500 to 600 ns	__	__	__	__	__	__
600 to 700 ns	__	__	__	__	__	__
700 to 800 ns	__	__	__	__	__	__
800 to 900 ns	__	__	__	__	__	__
900 ns to 1 μs	__	__	__	__	__	__

Table 3

11.   _____

Part 4

4.   Demonstrated to: _____ Date: _____

Grade: _____

Lab 9: Encoders

Objectives:

    1.   Construct a basic encoder using logic gates
    2.   Verify that the 74147 and 74148 ICs operate according to their respective function tables in the data specification sheets
    3.   Cascade multiple 74148s to create a 16-line to 4-line encoder

Materials List:

- II software by Altera Corporation
- University Board by Altera Corporation (optional)
- Computer requirements:
  - Minimum 486/66 with 8 MB RAM
- Floppy disk

Discussion:

The encoder is a circuit that converts intelligent information like the keys on a keyboard to a binary-based code of 1s and 0s. Two encoders in chip form are the 74147, 10-line to 4-line BCD encoder, and the 74148 8-line to 3-line octal encoder. Both are priority encoders in that the highest numbered active input dictates the output logic levels. The logic symbols (Figure 1) show all inputs and outputs with bubbles, identifying these pins as active-LOW. The bit pattern on the outputs will represent the 1's complement of the input selected.

Even though the 74147 is a 10-line to 4-line encoder, there are only 9 physical inputs. By not selecting any input on the 74147, none of the outputs will be active, thus representing zero.

The 74148 enable input, E_{IN}, and enable output, E_{ON}, allow multiple 74148s to be cascaded for bigger encoder systems.

Table 1 represents the DCBA output logic levels for ten inputs of a 10-line to 4-line encoder. The table shows active-HIGH inputs and active-HIGH outputs. A designer would write output sum of product expressions for outputs A, B, C, and D, then simplify these complex expressions using Boolean identities and rules or Karnaugh maps. By observation, you may notice that output A is a logic-HIGH when input 1 or input 3 or input 5 or input 7 or input 9 are active. This may be expressed by a 5-input OR gate. Output B is a logic-HIGH when inputs 2, 3, 6, or 7 are a logic-HIGH. This is a 4-input OR gate. By similar observation, outputs C and D may be determined, hence resulting in a circuit that looks like Figure 2.

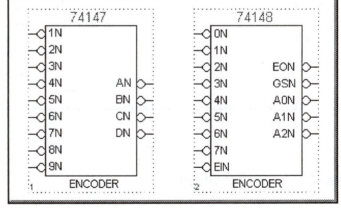

Figure 1

Will this circuit work as an encoder? Yes, as long as only one input is "active" at a time. However, the 74147 and 74148 ICs are priority encoders, in that only the highest numeric active input will be encoded. The 74148 also has an active-LOW enable input, which allows the IC to be turned on or off.

No.	Inputs										Outputs			
	0	1	2	3	4	5	6	7	8	9	D	C	B	A
0	0	0	0	0	0	0	0	0	0	0	0	0	0	0
1	0	1	0	0	0	0	0	0	0	0	0	0	0	1
2	0	0	1	0	0	0	0	0	0	0	0	0	1	0
3	0	0	0	1	0	0	0	0	0	0	0	0	1	1
4	0	0	0	0	1	0	0	0	0	0	0	1	0	0
5	0	0	0	0	0	1	0	0	0	0	0	1	0	1
6	0	0	0	0	0	0	1	0	0	0	0	1	1	0
7	0	0	0	0	0	0	0	1	0	0	0	1	1	1
8	0	0	0	0	0	0	0	0	1	0	1	0	0	0
9	0	0	0	0	0	0	0	0	0	1	1	0	0	1

Table 1

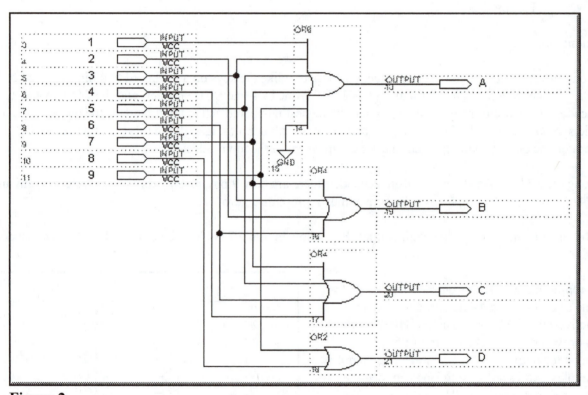

Figure 2

Part 1   Procedure

1.   Open the II software. Assign the project name **encode1** and MAX7000S as the device family.

2.   Open a new Graphic Editor and construct the circuit shown in Figure 2.

3.   Open a new Waveform Editor, set the Grid Size to 100 ns, and create the waveforms shown in Figure 3.

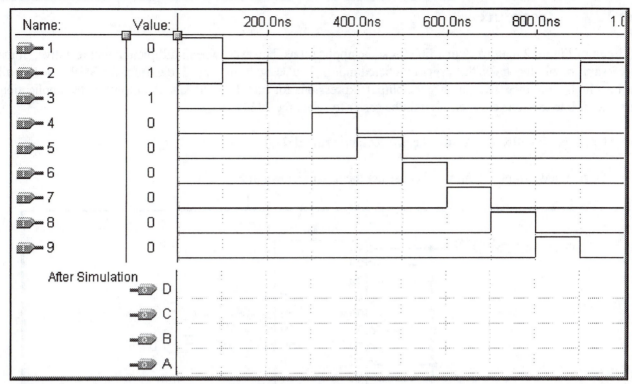

Figure 3

4.   Complete Table 2 identifying which input and output are active during each time segment listed.

Time Segment	Active Input	DCBA Output	Time Segment	Active Input	DCBA Output
0-100 ns			500-600 ns		
100-200 ns			600-700 ns		
200-300 ns			700-800 ns		
300-400 ns			800-900 ns		
400-500 ns			900 ns-1µs		

Table 2

5.   During the time segments 0-900 ns when only one input is active at a time, did the output BCD code represent that active input?   (Yes/No)

6.   Explain what happened during the 900 ns to 1 µs interval when multiple inputs are active simultaneously.

_____

7.   Would the circuit of Figure 2 be used in an application to convert numbers typed on a keypad to their BCD equivalents? (Yes/No)   Explain why or why not.

_____

8.   Save all files to Drive A as **encode1**, then exit the Graphic and Waveform Editors.

Part 2   Procedure

The circuit of Figure 2 may work just fine for some applications, however, when multiple inputs are active, it may be necessary to only recognize the larger numbered input. The designer may need to extract the SOP based on all input bits, highs and lows, and simplify the output expressions for each D, C, B, and A output. If the application requires a 10-line to 4-line encoder, it might be easier to select the 74147 IC.

1.   Open the II software. Assign the project name **encode2**.

2.   Open a new Graphic Editor and construct the circuit shown in Figure 4.

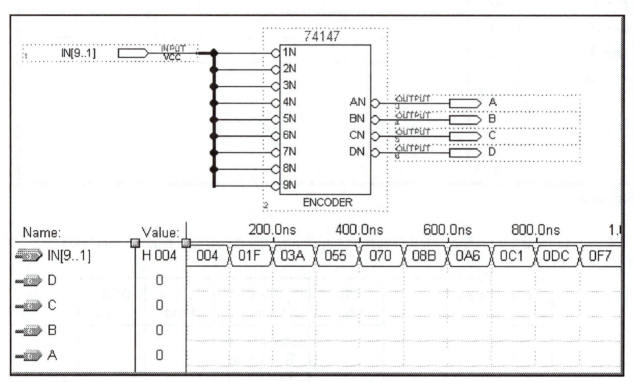

Figure 4

3.   Open a new Waveform Editor and create the waveforms shown in Figure 4. Enter these values, incrementing by 27, using the Count Overwrite Value dialog box.

4.   The compiler shows 9 or more errors in your circuit. What were the errors in the circuit and what was necessary to correct these errors?

_____

_____

5.   Run the simulator. Are there errors that prevent the software from simulating the circuit? (Yes/No) If yes, correct the errors and record what the problem was and what was done before the circuit was successfully simulated.

_____

_____

6.   Which input is reflected by the logic levels on the DCBA outputs? _____

7. Why are the DCBA outputs constant even though the inputs are varying?

    _____

8. Highlight the IN[9..1] waveform and overwrite this waveform with **3FD** by entering this number into the Overwrite Group Value dialog box.

9. Simulate the circuit. Record the DCBA bit pattern on the outputs:
    D = __ C = __ B = __ A = __

10. Convert 3FD to its 12-bit binary equivalent.

    $B_{11}B_{10}B_9B_8$ $B_7B_6B_5B_4$ $B_3B_2B_1B_0$

    $3FD_H$ = _____

11. Bits B_{11}, B_{10}, and B_0 are *not* used in Figure 4 so the DCBA outputs are determined by B_9 thru B_1.

12. Convert the hex numbers in Table 3 to binary, then predict the DCBA output of the 74147 with these hex numbers applied.

13. Apply the bit pattern of Table 3 as IN[9..0] to the circuit of Figure 4, re-simulate the circuit, and verify your DCBA predictions in Table 3.

14. Save all files to Drive A as **encode2**, then exit the Graphic and Waveform Editors.

Hex	$B_{11}B_{10}B_9B_8$ $B_7B_6B_5B_4$ $B_3B_2B_1B_0$	D C B A
3FD	_____	_____
3FB	_____	_____
3F7	_____	_____
3EF	_____	_____
3DF	_____	_____
3BF	_____	_____
37F	_____	_____
3FF	_____	_____

Table 3

Part 3   Procedure

The 74148 has active-LOW inputs and active-LOW outputs similar to the 74147, except the 74148 has an enable input, E_{IN}, and enable output, E_{ON}, used for cascading multiple chips. The G_{SN} output may be used as a flag (or interrupt) signal identifying when a conversion takes place.

1. Open the II software. Assign the project name **encode3**.

2. Open a new Graphic Editor and construct the circuit and waveforms shown in Figure 5.

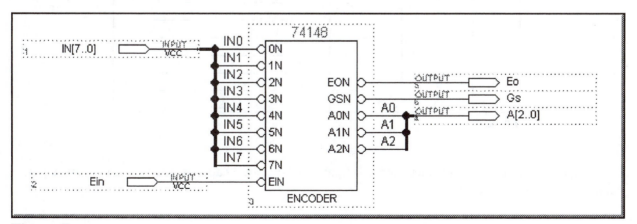

Figure 5

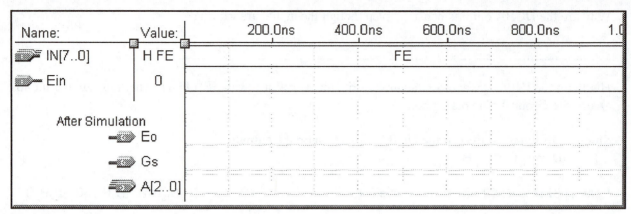

Figure 6

3. Open a new Waveform Editor and create the waveforms shown in Figure 6.

4. Draw the output waveforms after simulation in the area provided in Figure 6.

5. The inputs to the 74148 are active-(HIGH/LOW).

6. Which input(s) in Figure 5 are "active"? _____ and _____

7. What logic levels (1 or 0) are the outputs of the 74148 in Figure 5?

    Eo = ___   Gs = ___   A2 = ___   A1 = ___   A0 = ___

8. The logic levels on A2, A1, and A0 represent which active input?   1 2 3 4 5 6 7

9. Complete Table 4 by identifying what hexadecimal code is necessary for IN[7..0] that will cause only the corresponding input to become active. Record the logic levels on the outputs for each row.

E_{IN}	Active Input	IN[7..0]	Outputs Eo Gs A2 A1 A0				
0	0	FE	__	__	__	__	__
0	1	___	__	__	__	__	__
0	2	___	__	__	__	__	__
0	3	___	__	__	__	__	__
0	4	___	__	__	__	__	__
0	5	___	__	__	__	__	__
0	6	___	__	__	__	__	__
0	7	___	__	__	__	__	__
1	X	X	__	__	__	__	__

Table 4

10. With E_{IN} = 0, apply different values for IN[7..0] and identify what happens when more than one input, IN[7..0], is active at a time.

_____

11. Save all files to Drive A as **encode3**, then exit the Graphic and Waveform Editors.

Part 4   Procedure

1.   Open II software. Assign the project name **encode4**.

2.   Open a new Graphic Editor. Cascade two 74148 ICs to make a 16-line, IN[15..0], to 4-line, DCBA, encoder network. Include an output flag that will become active only when one or more IN[15..0] inputs, and E_{IN} are active.

3.   Open a new Waveform Editor and create a set of waveforms for IN[15..0] and E_{IN} that will produce the desired outputs to demonstrate that the circuit operates properly.

4.   Demonstrate your 16-line to 4-line encoder to your instructor. Obtain the signature on the answer page for this lab.

5.   Obtain hard copies of your 16-line to 4-line encoder. Label these hard copies **Part 4, Step 5A** and **Part 4, Step 5B**.

6.   Save all files to Drive A as **encode5**, then exit the Graphics and Waveform Editors.

7.   Write a 1 to 2 page summary containing charts and/or graphics pertaining to the results obtained from this lab.

8.   Place all papers for this lab in the following sequence, then submit the materials to your instructor for grading.

- Cover page
- Typed summary
- The completed answer page
- Printout of the Graphics Editor, **Part 4, Step 5A**
- Printout of the Waveform Editor, **Part 4, Step 5B**

Lab 9: Encoders Answer Page

Name: _____

Part 1

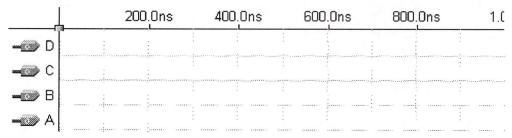

Figure 3

Time Segment	Active Input	DCBA Output	Time Segment	Active Input	DCBA Output
0–100 ns 100–200 ns 200–300 ns 300–400 ns 400–500 ns			500–600 ns 600–700 ns 700–800 ns 800–900 ns 900 ns–μS		

Table 2

5. (Yes/No)

6. _____

7. (Yes/No)   Explain why or why not.

_____

Part 2

3. _____

_____

4. (Yes/No)

_____

_____

5. _____

6. _____

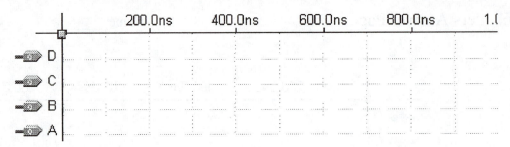

Figure 4

8.   D = __ C = __ B = __ A = __

9.

$$3FD_H = \frac{\qquad\qquad\qquad\qquad}{B_{11}B_{10}B_9B_8 \quad B_7B_6B_5B_4 \quad B_3B_2B_1B_0}$$

Hex	$B_{11}B_{10}B_9B_8 \; B_7B_6B_5B_4 \; B_3B_2B_1B_0$	D C B A
3FD	_____	_____
3FB	_____	_____
3F7	_____	_____
3EF	_____	_____
3DF	_____	_____
3BF	_____	_____
37F	_____	_____
3FF	_____	_____

Table 3

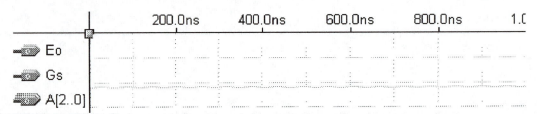

Figure 5

Part 3

5.   (HIGH/LOW)

6.   _____ and _____

7.   Eo = ___ Gs = ___ A2 = ___ A1 = ___ A0 = ___

8.   0 1 2 3 4 5 6 7

Ein	Active Input	IN[7..0]	Outputs Eo Gs A2 A1 A0
0	0	FE	__ __ __ __ __
0	1	___	__ __ __ __ __
0	2	___	__ __ __ __ __
0	3	___	__ __ __ __ __
0	4	___	__ __ __ __ __
0	5	___	__ __ __ __ __
0	6	___	__ __ __ __ __
0	7	___	__ __ __ __ __
1	X	X	__ __ __ __ __

Table 4

10. _____

Part 4

4.   Demonstrated to: _____ Date: _____

Grade: _____

Lab 10: Decoders

Objectives:

1. Use the multiple input AND or NAND gate as a decoder
2. Analyze the 7442 4-line to 10-line decoder
3. Examine the effects of the enable inputs of the 74138 3-line to 8-line decoder
4. Cascade multiple 74138 ICs to create an N-line to 2^N-line decoder

Materials list:

♦ Max+plus II software by Altera Corporation
♦ University Board by Altera Corporation (optional)
♦ Computer requirements:
   Minimum 486/66 with 8 MB RAM
♦ Floppy disk

Discussion:

The decoder is a circuit that converts binary information into intelligent information. The binary code may be data outputted by a computer, the result of an Arithmetic Logic Unit (ALU), or the calculator. The intelligence may be lit light emitting diodes (LEDs), a numeric display, or monitor.

Basic decoders are the AND or NAND gates that provide active-HIGH or active-LOW outputs when a certain input conditions exists. Consider the examples in Figure 1. Gate 1 produces a logic-HIGH output when inputs D **and** A are a logic-HIGH, while inputs C **and** B are a logic-LOW. Gate 2 produces a logic-LOW output when inputs D **and** C **and** B **and** A are a logic-HIGH. Normally, several decoder gates will be included in an integrated circuit, such as the 7442, a 4-line BCD to 10-line decimal decoder.

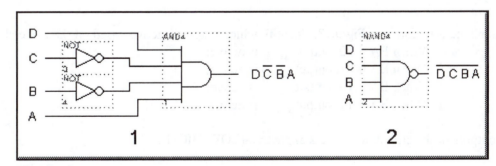

Figure 1

The 74138, 3-line to 8-line decoder, and the 74154, 4-line to 16-line decoder, include separate gate enable inputs for cascading. Quite often the 74138 or 74154 are used for memory or input/output address decoding in a microprocessor-based system.

Part 1   Procedure

1. Open the Max+plus II software. Assign the project name **decode1** and MAX7000S.

2. Open a new Graphic Editor and create the circuit shown in Figure 2.

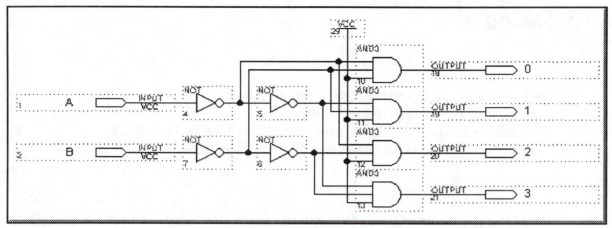

Figure 2

3. Open a new Waveform Editor. Create input A as a 5 MHz square wave and input B as a 2.5 MHz square wave. Compile and simulate your circuit and draw the input and output, I/O, waveforms in Figure 3.

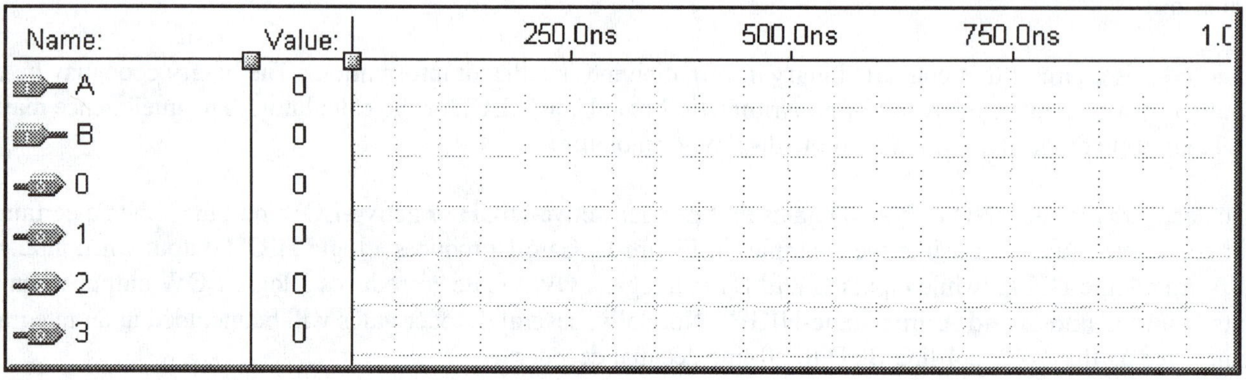

Name:	Value:	250.0ns	500.0ns	750.0ns	1.0
A	0				
B	0				
0	0				
1	0				
2	0				
3	0				

Figure 3

4. Examine the waveforms in Figure 3. Identify which output is active based on the BA code applied.
    When BA = 00, output ____ is active;
    When BA = 01, output ____ is active;
    When BA = 10, output ____ is active;
    When BA = 11, output ____ is active.

5. The outputs of the circuit in Figure 2 are active-(LOW/HIGH).

6. The circuit demonstrated in Figure 2 is a _____-line to _____-line decoder.

7. What modifications to the circuit are necessary to make the outputs active-LOW?

    _____

8. The third input to each AND gate was connected to Vcc. How would the circuit respond if these inputs were grounded instead?

    _____

9. Save all files to Drive A as **decode1**, then exit the Graphic and Waveform Editors.

Part 2   Procedure

1.   Open the Max+plus II software. Assign the project name **decode2**.

2.   Open a new Graphic Editor and construct the circuit shown in Figure 4.

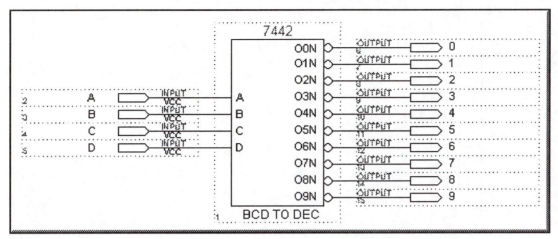

Figure 4

3.   The bubble on the outputs of the 7442 symbol imply the outputs are active-(LOW/HIGH).

4.   The inputs of the 7442 do *not* show a bubble. This implies the inputs are active-(LOW/HIGH).

5.   Open a new Waveform Editor. Create a set of waveforms for the inputs of Figure 4 so that input A = 5 MHz, input B = 2.5 MHz, input C = 1.25 MHz, and input D is .625 MHz.   DCBA should be 0000_2 at 0 ns.

6.   Compile and simulate the circuit. Draw the input and output, I/O, waveforms in Figure 5.

7.   Examine the waveforms in Figure 5. Identify which output is active, based on the DCBA code applied.
            When DCBA = 0000, output _____ is active;
            When DCBA = 0001, output _____ is active;
            When DCBA = 0010, output _____ is active;
            When DCBA = 0011, output _____ is active;
            When DCBA = 0100, output _____ is active;
            When DCBA = 0101, output _____ is active;
            When DCBA = 0110, output _____ is active;
            When DCBA = 0111, output _____ is active;
            When DCBA = 1000, output _____ is active;
            When DCBA = 1001, output _____ is active.

8.   Invert Waveform D in the Waveform Editor.

9.   Identify which output is active, based on the DCBA code applied.
            When DCBA = 1111, which outputs are active? _____
            When DCBA = 1010, which outputs are active? _____
            When DCBA = 1101, which outputs are active? _____

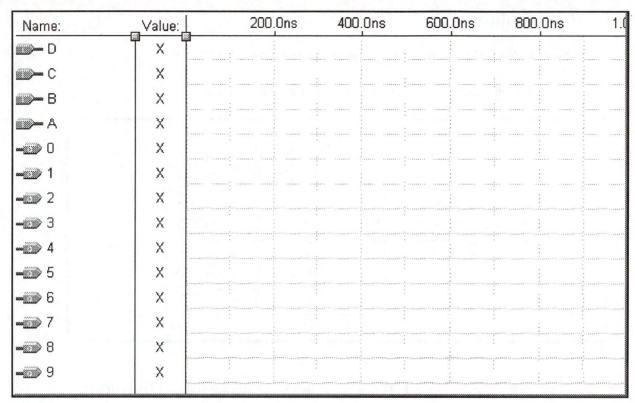

Figure 5

10. Tne 7442 is a 4-line to 10-line decimal decoder. What are valid DCBA inputs to the 7442 IC?

_____

11. What are the invalid DCBA inputs to the 7442 IC?

_____

12. Does the 7442 IC have an enable input? (Yes/No)

13. Save all files to Drive A as **decode2**, then exit the Graphic and Waveform Editors.

Part 3   Procedure

1. Open the Max+plus II software. Assign the project name **decode3**.

2. Open the **decode1.scf** file that was created in Part 1 of this lab. Save this file as **decode3.scf**.

3. Open the **decode1.gdf** file that was created in Part 1 of this lab. Save this file as **decode3.gdf**.

4. Delete the Vcc symbol in the **decode.gdf** file, replacing it with an input symbol labeled Enable.

5. What must be the logic level of the Enable input to cause the decoder to decode inputs A and B? (Logic-LOW/Logic-HIGH)

6. Delete the Enable input symbol, replacing it with the input circuit shown in Figure 6.

126   Lab 10: Decoders

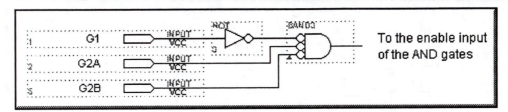

To the enable input
of the AND gates

Figure 6

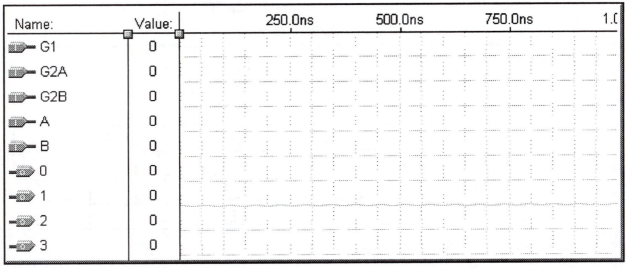

Figure 7

7.   Add input waveforms G1, G2A, and G2B to your Waveform Editor file as shown in Figure 7.

8.   Select proper logic levels for G1, G2A, and G2B so the encoder is enabled, allowing the outputs to respond to the BA inputs.

9.   Be sure that the BA inputs are as described in Part 1, Step 3 of this lab before continuing.

10.   Run the compiler and simulator. Draw all I/O waveforms in the area provided in Figure 7.

11.   To enable the 2-line to 4-line decoder, G1 must be a logic-(LOW/HIGH), G2A must be a logic-(LOW/HIGH), and G2B must be a logic-(LOW/HIGH).

12.   Save all files to Drive A as **decode3**, then exit the Graphic and Waveform Editors.

Part 4   Procedure

1.   Open the Max+plus II software. Assign the project name **decode4**.

2.   Open a new Graphic Editor and construct the circuit of Figure 8.

3.   Open a new Waveform Editor and create the waveforms shown in Figure 9.

4.   Run the compiler and simulator. Draw the resulting output waveforms in the area provided in Figure 9.

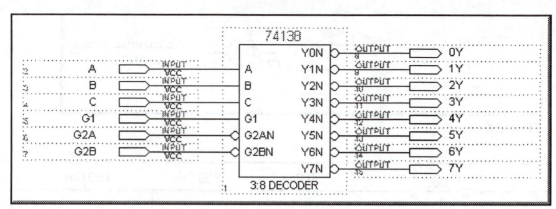

Figure 8

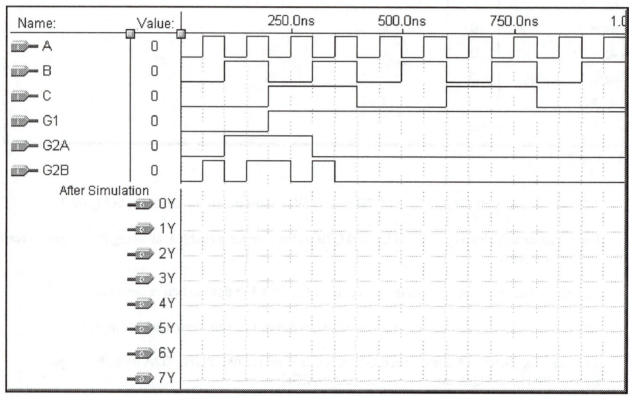

Figure 9

5. Complete Table 1 by recording the logic levels of the inputs and outputs for each time segment listed based on the results recorded in Figure 9.

Time	Inputs G1 G2A G2B C B A	Outputs 0Y 1Y 2Y 3Y 4Y 5Y 6Y 7Y
0 to 200 ns	__ X X X X X	__ __ __ __ __ __ __ __
200 to 300 ns	X __ X X X X	__ __ __ __ __ __ __ __
300 to 350 ns	X X __ X X X	__ __ __ __ __ __ __ __
350 to 400 ns	__ __ __ __ __ __	__ __ __ __ __ __ __ __

Table 1   X = irrelevant

Time	Inputs G1 G2A G2B C B A	Outputs 0Y 1Y 2Y 3Y 4Y 5Y 6Y 7Y
400 to 450 ns	— — — — — —	— — — — — — — —
450 to 500 ns	— — — — — —	— — — — — — — —
500 to 550 ns	— — — — — —	— — — — — — — —
550 to 600 ns	— — — — — —	— — — — — — — —
600 to 650 ns	— — — — — —	— — — — — — — —
650 to 700 ns	— — — — — —	— — — — — — — —
700 to 750 ns	— — — — — —	— — — — — — — —
750 to 800 ns	— — — — — —	— — — — — — — —
800 to 850 ns	— — — — — —	— — — — — — — —
850 to 900 ns	— — — — — —	— — — — — — — —
900 to 950 ns	— — — — — —	— — — — — — — —
950 ns to 1 μs	— — — — — —	— — — — — — — —

Table 2

6.   Complete Table 2 by recording the logic levels of the inputs and outputs for each time segment listed based on the results recorded in Figure 9.

7.   Based on the results recorded for G1 in Table 1 and Table 2, G1 is active-(LOW/HIGH).

8.   Based on the results recorded for G2A in Table 1 and Table 2, G2A is active-(LOW/HIGH).

9.   Based on the results recorded for G2B in Table 1 and Table 2, G2B is active-(LOW/HIGH).

10.   Based on the results recorded for the outputs in Table 1 and Table 2, the outputs active-(LOW/HIGH).

11.   Based on the results recorded for Table 1 and Table 2, which inputs are dominant?
             G1   G2A   G2B   C   B   A

12.   Assuming the 74138 is turned on, what is the relationship of the output that is active and the CBA code applied?

_____

13.   Save all files to Drive A as **decode4**, then exit the Graphic and Waveform Editors.

Part 5   Procedure

1.   Open the Graphic and Waveform Editors. Assign the project name **decode5**.

2.   Examine Table 3.

3.   Table 3 represents 32 rows, listing all possible combinations of EDCBA. Well not really, notice that the CBA code for Y0 to Y7 is identical to the CBA code for Y8 to Y15, Y16 to Y32, and Y24 to Y31. For the first 8 rows of the function table, Y0 to Y7, ED is 00. From Y8 to Y15, ED is 01, from Y16 to Y23, ED = 10, and from Y24 to Y31, ED = 11.

Inputs E D C B A	Active Output
0 0 0 0 0	Y0
. . .	. . .
0 0 1 1 1	Y7
0 1 0 0 0	Y8
. . .	. . .
0 1 1 1 1	Y15
1 0 0 0 0	Y16
. . .	. . .
1 0 1 1 1	Y23
1 1 0 0 0	Y24
. . .	. . .
1 1 1 1 1	Y31

Table 3

4. Cascade four 74138 ICs with five inputs, E, D, C, B, and A, to create a 5-line to 32-line decoder network.

5. Set the Grid Size to 30 ns and create Waveforms A, B, C, D, and E using the following multipliers in the Overwrite Count Value dialog box.

        Waveform A: Multiplied by: 1
        Waveform B: Multiplied by: 2
        Waveform C: Multiplied by: 4
        Waveform D: Multiplied by: 8
        Waveform E: Multiplied by: 16

6. Run the compiler and simulator. Correct all errors before continuing.

7. Obtain a hard copy of the Graphic and Waveform Editor files. Label these hard copies **Part 5, Step 7A** and **Part 5, Step 7B**.

8. Demonstrate the 5-line to 32-line decoder to your instructor. Obtain the signature on the answer page for this lab.

9. Write a 1 to 2 page summary pertaining to the results obtained from this lab. The summary must contain and make reference to an embedded figure and a table, both related to this lab contents.

10. Place all papers for this lab in the following sequence, then submit the lab to your instructor for grading.

    ■   Cover page
    ■   Typed summary
    ■   The completed answer pages for this lab
    ■   Hard copy of the Graphic Editor, **Part 5, Step 7A**
    ■   Hard copy of the Waveform Editor, **Part 5, Step 7B**

Part 1

Name:	Value:	250.0ns	500.0ns	750.0ns	1.0
A	0				
B	0				
0	0				
1	0				
2	0				
3	0				

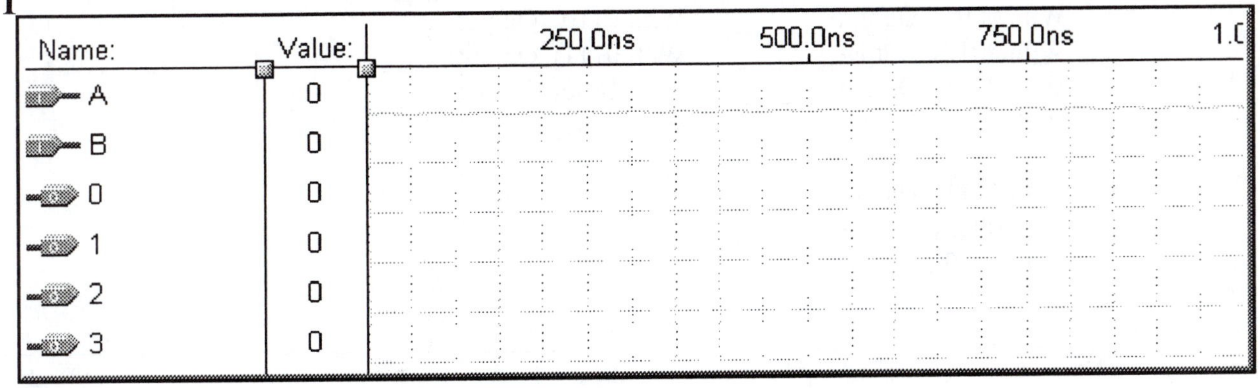

Figure 3

4.   (LOW/HIGH)

5.   00: Output _____   01: Output _____   10: Output _____   11: Output _____

6.   _____ line to _____

7.   _____

8.   _____

Part 2

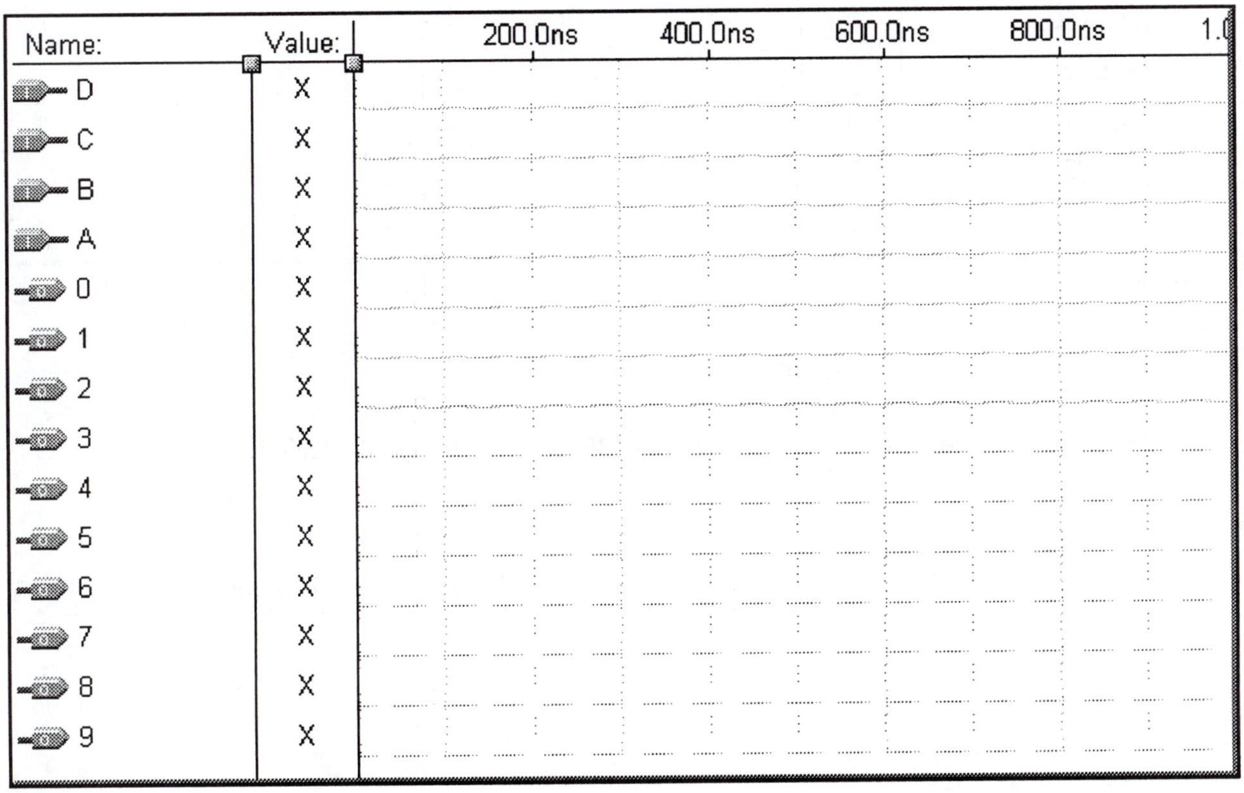

Name:	Value:	200.0ns	400.0ns	600.0ns	800.0ns	1.0
D	X					
C	X					
B	X					
A	X					
0	X					
1	X					
2	X					
3	X					
4	X					
5	X					
6	X					
7	X					
8	X					
9	X					

Figure 5

3.　　(LOW/HIGH)　　　　4.　　　　(LOW/HIGH)

7.　With 0000_2, Output: _____　　With 0101_2, Output: _____
　　With 0001_2, Output: _____　　With 0110_2, Output: _____
　　With 0010_2, Output: _____　　With 0111_2, Output: _____
　　With 0011_2, Output: _____　　With 1000_2, Output: _____
　　With 0100_2, Output: _____　　With 1001_2, Output: _____

9.　With 1111_2, Output: _____
　　With 0000_2, Output: _____
　　With 0000_2, Output: _____

10.　_____

11.　_____

12.　(Yes/No)

Part 3

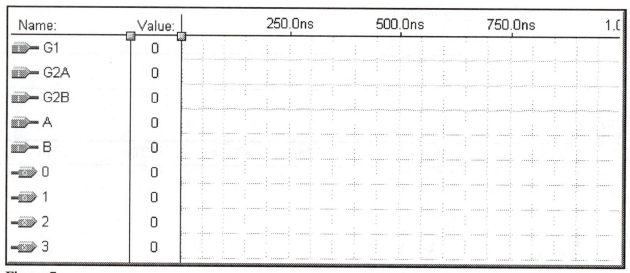

Figure 7

5.　　(Logic-LOW/Logic-HIGH)

11.　G1: (LOW/HIGH)　　　G2A: (LOW/HIGH)　　　G2B: (LOW/HIGH)

Part 4

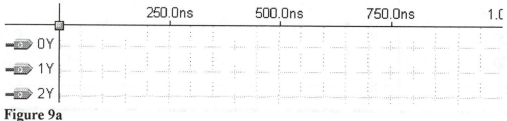

Figure 9a

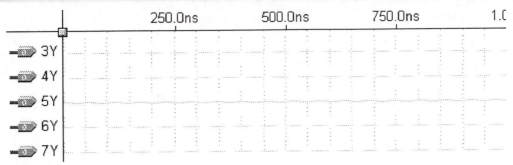

Figure 9b

Time	Inputs G1 G2A G2B C B A	Outputs 0Y 1Y 2Y 3Y 4Y 5Y 6Y 7Y
0 to 200 ns	___ X X X X X	_ _ _ _ _ _ _ _
200 to 300 ns	X ___ X X X X	_ _ _ _ _ _ _ _
300 to 350 ns	X X ___ X X X	_ _ _ _ _ _ _ _
350 to 400 ns	_ _ _ _ _ _	_ _ _ _ _ _ _ _

Table 1   X = irrelevant

Time	Inputs G1 G2A G2B C B A	Outputs 0Y 1Y 2Y 3Y 4Y 5Y 6Y 7Y
400 to 450 ns	_ _ _ _ _ _	_ _ _ _ _ _ _ _
450 to 500 ns	_ _ _ _ _ _	_ _ _ _ _ _ _ _
500 to 550 ns	_ _ _ _ _ _	_ _ _ _ _ _ _ _
550 to 600 ns	_ _ _ _ _ _	_ _ _ _ _ _ _ _
600 to 650 ns	_ _ _ _ _ _	_ _ _ _ _ _ _ _
650 to 700 ns	_ _ _ _ _ _	_ _ _ _ _ _ _ _
700 to 750 ns	_ _ _ _ _ _	_ _ _ _ _ _ _ _
750 to 800 ns	_ _ _ _ _ _	_ _ _ _ _ _ _ _
800 to 850 ns	_ _ _ _ _ _	_ _ _ _ _ _ _ _
850 to 900 ns	_ _ _ _ _ _	_ _ _ _ _ _ _ _
900 to 950 ns	_ _ _ _ _ _	_ _ _ _ _ _ _ _
950 ns to 1 μs	_ _ _ _ _ _	_ _ _ _ _ _ _ _

Table 2

7.   (LOW/HIGH)   8.   (LOW/HIGH)   9.   (LOW/HIGH)

10.   (LOW/HIGH)   11.   G1   G2A   G2B   C   B   A

12.   _____

Part 5

8.   Demonstrated to: _____ Date: _____

Grade: _____

Lab 11: Multiplexers

Objectives:

1. Analyze a 2-line to 1-line multiplexer
2. Evaluate the 74157 quad 2-line to 1-line multiplexer
3. Study a 4-line to 1-line multiplexer logic circuit
4. Analyze the output of a 74153-based on the enable and select input
5. Analyze the effects of the control inputs of a 74151 8-line to 1-line multiplexer
6. Create an octal 2-lines to 1-line multiplexer using the 74157 quad 2-line to 1-line multiplexer

Materials list:

♦   Max+plus II software by Altera Corporation
♦   University Board by Altera Corporation (optional)
♦   Computer requirements:
        Minimum 486/66 with 8 MB RAM
♦   Floppy disk

Discussion:

The basic 2-line to 1-line multiplexer can be illustrated by a toggle switch with two inputs and the common lug of the switch is the output (see Figure 1). Which data input appears on the output depends on the switch setting. The multiplexer has many data inputs and one data output.

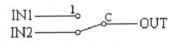

Figure 1

Figure 2 illustrates a 2-line to 1-line multiplexer using basic logic gates. The select input determines which input data appears on the output only if the Enable input is logic-HIGH. The 74157 contains four 2-line to 1-line multiplexers that share the same select and enable inputs.

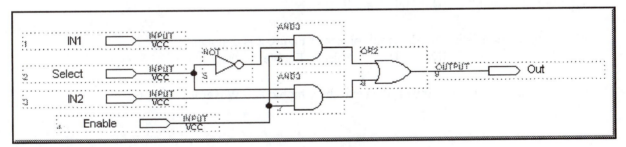

Figure 2

Multiple input multiplexers illustrated in this lab are the 74157 quad 2-line to 1-line, 74153 dual 4-line to 1-line , and 74151 8-line to 1-line multiplexers. The 74157 will be used in Parts 2 and 6 of this lab.

Part 3 of this lab focuses on the 4-line to 1-line multiplexer in gate form that is found inside a 74153. Doubling the number of inputs and adding a third select line will yield the contents of the 74151.

The 74153 is a dual 4-line to 1-line multiplexer. Each multiplexer has independent enable and data inputs but share the same BA selects. The 74153 will be used in Part 4 of this lab.

The 74151 is an 8-line to 1-line multiplexer that provides either an inverting or noninverting output. The 74151 has a single enable input and three data selects. The 74151 will be used in Part 5 of this lab.

Part 1   Procedure

1.   Open the Max+plus II software. Assign the project name **mux1** and MAX7000S as the device family.

2.   Open the Graphic Editor and construct the circuit shown in Figure 2.

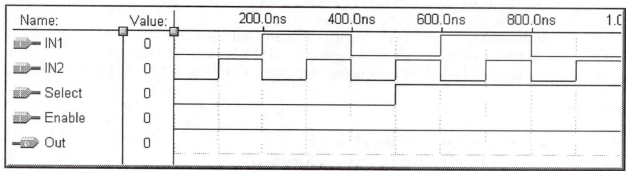

Figure 3

3.   Open a new Waveform Editor and create the waveforms shown in Figure 3.

4.   Run the Compiler and Simulator. Draw the resulting output signal in the area provided in Figure 3.

5.   Invert the enable signal then re-simulate the circuit.

6.   Based on the results obtained, the enable input to Figure 2 is active-(LOW/HIGH).

7.   When the multiplexer is enabled and the select input is a logic-LOW, which input data appeared on the output of the circuit?   (Data IN1/Data IN2)

8.   When the multiplexer is enabled and the select input is a logic-HIGH, which input data appeared on the output of the circuit?   (Data IN1/Data IN2)

9.   Which input to the 2-line to 1-line multiplexer of Figure 2 is dominant?
                        IN1   IN2   Select   Enable

10.   Save all files to Drive A as **mux1**, then exit the Graphic and Waveform Editors.

Part 2   Procedure

1.   Open the Max+plus II software. Assign the project name **mux2**.

2.   Open a new Graphic Editor and construct the circuit shown in Figure 4.

3.   Open a new Waveform Editor and create the waveforms shown in Figure 4.

4.   Draw Output Y[3..0] in the space provided in Figure 4, after simulation.

5.   Note the output did *not* change states after simulation. Why? _____

_____

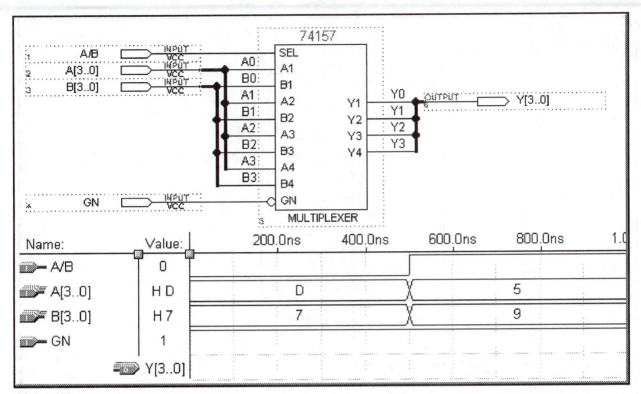

Figure 4

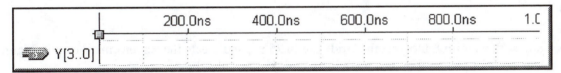

Figure 5

6. Invert the GN input and re-simulate the circuit.

7. Draw output Y[3..0] in Figure 5.

8. From your observations of the output waveform in Figure 4 and Figure 5, GN would be active- (LOW/HIGH).

9. Which data input appeared on output Y when A/B was a logic-LOW?   (A[3..0]/B[3..0])

10. Which data input appeared on output Y when A/B was a logic-HIGH?   (A[3..0]/B[3..0])

11. Save all files to Drive A as **mux2**, then exit the Graphic and Waveform Editors.

Part 3   Procedure

1. Open the Max+plus II software. Assign the project name **mux3**.

2. Open a new Graphic Editor and construct the circuit shown in Figure 6.

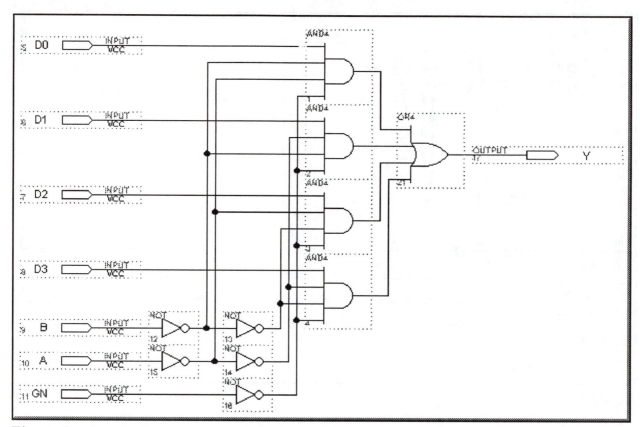

Figure 6

3. Open a new Waveform Editor, set the Grid Size to 25 ns, and create the waveforms shown in Figure 7 with the following multipliers set in the Overwrite Count Value dialog box.

Input	Multiplied By Value
D0	1
D1	2
D2	4
D3	8
A	20

Table 1

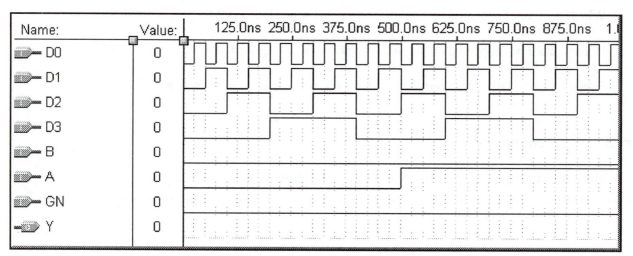

Figure 7

Lab 11: Multiplexers

4.   Press the Compiler and Simulator buttons. Correct all errors before continuing.

5.   Draw the output waveform in the area provided in Figure 7 after simulation..

6.   From 0 to 500 ns, output Y takes on the value of input (D0, D1, D2, D3).

7.   What is the BA code for the time segment from 0 to 500 ns?   (00 , 01, 10, 11)

8.   From 500 ns to 1 μs, output Y takes on the value of input (D0, D1, D2, D3).

9.   What is the BA code for the time segment from 500 ns to 1 μs?   (00 , 01, 10, 11)

10.   Invert Waveform B, then re-simulate the circuit.

11.   From 0 to 500 ns, output Y takes on the value of input (D0, D1, D2, D3).

12.   What is the BA code for the time segment from 0 to 500 ns?   (00 , 01, 10, 11)

13.   From 500 ns to 1 μs, output Y takes on the value of input (D0, D1, D2, D3).

14.   What is the BA code for the time segment from 500 ns to 1 μs?   (00 , 01, 10, 11)

15.   Invert the GN waveform then re-simulate the circuit.

16.   Record the time output Y remains at a logic-LOW state. From _____ to _____

17.   Explain why output Y remained a logic-LOW during the time segment recorded in Step 16.

      _____

18.   How many data inputs are shown in Figure 6? _____

19.   How many data outputs are shown in Figure 6? _____

20.   Figure 6 is a _____ -line to ___ -line multiplexer.

21.   Which inputs in Figure 6 determined which data appeared on output Y? _____

22.   Save all files to Drive A as **mux3**, then exit the Graphic and Waveform Editors.

Part 4   Procedure

1.   Open the Max+plus II software. Assign the project name **mux4**.

2.   Open a new Graphic Editor and construct the circuit shown in Figure 8.

3.   Open a new Waveform Editor, set the Grid Size to 500 ns, and create the waveforms shown in Figure 8.

4.   Press the Compiler and Simulator buttons. Correct all errors before continuing.

5.   Draw the output waveform in the area provided in Figure 8 after simulating the circuit.

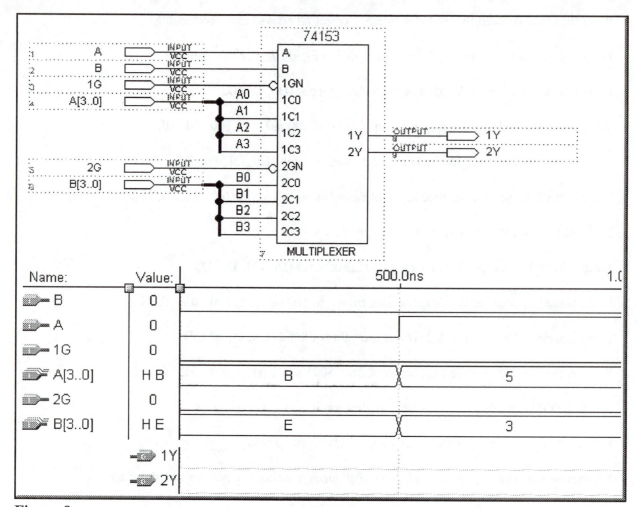

Figure 8

6. During the time segment 0 to 500 ns, the BA code is (00, 01, 10, 11).

7. From 0 to 500 ns, 1Y takes on the value of (A0, A1, A2, A3, B0, B1, B2, B3).

8. From 0 to 500 ns, 2Y takes on the value of (A0, A1, A2, A3, B0, B1, B2, B3).

9. During the time segment 500 ns to 1 μs, the BA code is (00, 01, 10, 11).

10. From 500 ns to 1 μs, 1Y takes on the value of (A0, A1, A2, A3, B0, B1, B2, B3).

11. From 500 ns to 1 μs, 2Y takes on the value of (A0, A1, A2, A3, B0, B1, B2, B3).

12. Invert Waveform B, then re-simulate the circuit.

13. During the time segment 0 to 500 ns, the BA code is (00, 01, 10, 11).

14. From 0 to 500 ns, 1Y takes on the value of (A0, A1, A2, A3, B0, B1, B2, B3).

15. From 0 to 500 ns, 2Y takes on the value of (A0, A1, A2, A3, B0, B1, B2, B3).

16. During the time segment 500 ns to 1 μs, the BA code is (00, 01, 10, 11).

17. From 500 ns to 1 μs, 1Y takes on the value of (A0, A1, A2, A3, B0, B1, B2, B3).

18. From 500 ns to 1 μs, 2Y takes on the value of (A0, A1, A2, A3, B0, B1, B2, B3).

19. Invert waveform 1G, then re-simulate the circuit.

20. Based on the results, 1G is active-(LOW/HIGH).

21. A logic-LOW on 2G (enables/inhibits) (1Y/2Y).

22. Save all files to Drive A as **mux4**, then exit the Graphic and Waveform Editors.

Part 5   Procedure

1. Open the Max+plus II software. Assign the project name **mux5**.

2. Open a new Graphic Editor. Construct the circuit shown in Figure 9.

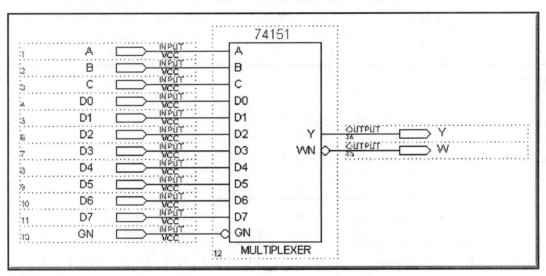

Figure 9

3. Open the Waveform Editor, set the Grid Size to 50 ns, and construct the waveforms shown in Figure 10.

4. Compile and simulate the circuit. Correct all errors before continuing.

5. Draw the output waveforms in the space provided in Figure 10.

6. Complete Table 2 based on the waveforms in Figure 10.

Time Segment	C B A	"Y" takes on the value of (select one)
0–500 ns	__ __ __	(D_7 D_6 D_5 D_4 D_3 D_2 D_1 D_0)
500 ns–1 μs	__ __ __	(D_7 D_6 D_5 D_4 D_3 D_2 D_1 D_0)

Table 2

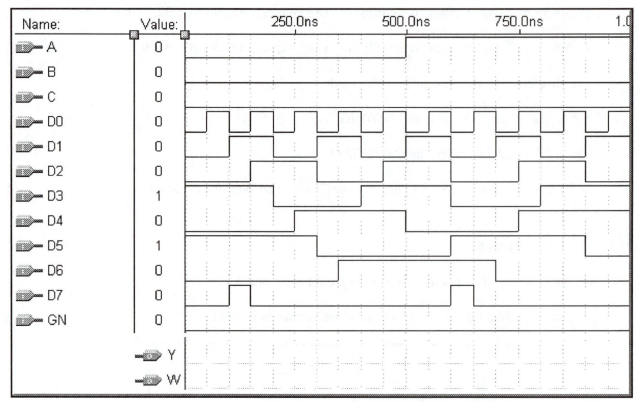

Figure 10

7.   Invert Waveform B. Re-simulate the circuit.

8.   Complete Table 3 based on the new set of waveforms after inverting Waveform B.

Time Segment	C B A	"Y" takes on the value of (select one)
0–500 ns	_ _ _	(D_7 D_6 D_5 D_4 D_3 D_2 D_1 D_0)
500 ns–1 µs	_ _ _	(D_7 D_6 D_5 D_4 D_3 D_2 D_1 D_0)

Table 3

9.   Invert Waveform C. Re-simulate the circuit.

10.   Complete Table 4 based on the new set of waveforms after inverting Waveform C.

Time Segment	C B A	"Y" takes on the value of (select one)
0–500 ns	_ _ _	(D_7 D_6 D_5 D_4 D_3 D_2 D_1 D_0)
500 ns–1 µs	_ _ _	(D_7 D_6 D_5 D_4 D_3 D_2 D_1 D_0)

Table 4

11.   When C = 1, B = 0, and A = 0, which data input will appear on output Y? _____

12.   When C = 1, B = 0, and A = 1, which data input will appear on output Y? _____

13.   Which output in Figure 10 inverts the data? _____

14.   Save all files to Drive A as **mux5**, then exit the Graphic and Waveform Editors.

Part 6   Procedure

1.   Open a new Graphic and Waveform Editors. Assign the project name **mux6**.

2.   Use a 74151 multiplexer to implement the function shown in the table to the right.

3.   Create a set of input waveforms showing the CBA pattern of Table 5 and apply the proper data bits that will produce output Y.

4.   Once you verify the circuit operation matches the data shown in Table 5, obtain a hard copy of the Graphic and Waveform Editor files. Label these hard copies **Part 6, Step 4A** and **Part 6, Step 4B**, respectively.

C	B	A	Output Y
0	0	0	1
0	0	1	0
0	1	0	0
0	1	1	1
1	0	0	0
1	0	1	0
1	1	0	1
1	1	1	1

Table 5

5.   Write the Boolean expression for output Y with respect to the data and select inputs.

        Y = _____

6.   Save all files to Drive A as **mux6**, then exit the Graphic and Waveform Editors.

Part 7   Procedure

1.   Open the Max+plus II software. Assign the project name **mux7**.

2.   Open a new Graphic Editor.

3.   Cascade 74157 ICs to multiplex A[7..0] with A[15..8] to obtain Y[7..0]. The low byte lines of A[15..0] will appear on Y[7..0] when the select line is a logic-LOW. The high byte lines of A[15..0] will appear on Y[7..0] when the select line is a logic-HIGH.

4.   Open a new Waveform Editor.

5.   Assign waveform A[15..0] to be $7b95_{16}$. Create the necessary control waveforms to pass A[7..0], then A[15..8] to Y[7..0].

6.   Compile and simulate your circuit. Correct all errors before continuing.

7.   Obtain a hard copy of the Graphic and Waveform Editor files. Label these hard copies **Part 7, Step 7A** and **Part 7, Step 7B**, respectively.

8.   Demonstrate the octal 2-line to 1-line multiplexer to the instructor. Obtain the signature of approval on the answer page for this lab.

9.	Save all files to Drive A as **mux7**, then exit the Graphic and Waveform Editors.

10.	Write a 1 to 2 page summary containing and making reference to at least one embedded figure and a table obtained from this lab.

11.	Place all papers for this lab in the following sequence, then submit the lab to your instructor for grading.

- Cover page
- Typed summary
- The completed lab
- Printout of the Graphic Editor, **Part 6, Step 4A**
- Printout of the Waveform Editor, **Part 6, Step 4B**
- Printout of the Graphic Editor, **Part 7, Step 7A**
- Printout of the Waveform Editor, **Part 7, Step 7B**

Lab 11: Multiplexers Answer Page

Name:_____

Part 1

Figure 3

6.   (LOW/HIGH)

7.   (Data IN/Data IN2)

8.   (Data IN1/Data IN2)

9.   IN1   IN2   Select   Enable

Part 2

Figure 4

5.

_____

8.   (LOW/HIGH)   9.   (IN1/IN2)   10.   (IN1/IN2)

Part 3

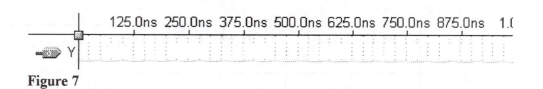

Figure 7

6.   D0 D1 D2 D3   7.   00 01 10 11

8.   D0 D1 D2 D3   9.   00 01 10 11

11.   D0 D1 D2 D3   12.   00 01 10 11

13.   D0 D1 D2 D3   14.   00 01 10 11

16.   From _____ to _____

17.   _____

18.   _____   19.   _____   20.   _____ - line to _____ - line mux.

21.   _____

Part 4

6.   (00, 01, 10, 11)   7.   (A0, A1, A2, A3, B0, B1, B0, B3)

8.   (A0, A1, A2, A3, B0, B1, B0, B3)   9.   (00, 01, 10, 11)

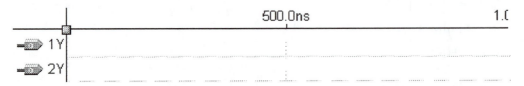

Figure 8

10.   (A0, A1, A2, A3, B0, B1, B2, B3)   11.   (A0, A1, A2, A3, B0, B1, B2, B3)

13.   (00, 01, 10, 11)   14.   (A0, A1, A2, A3, B0, B1, B2, B3)

15.   (A0, A1, A2, A3, B0, B1, B2, B3)   16.   (00, 01, 10, 11)

17.   (A0, A1, A2, A3, B0, B1, B2, B3)   18.   (A0, A1, A2, A3, B0, B1, B2, B3)

20.   LOW / HIGH   21.   (1Y / 2Y)

Part 5

Figure 10

Time Segment	C B A	"Y" takes on the value of (select one)
0–500 ns	___ ___ ___	(D_7 D_6 D_5 D_4 D_3 D_2 D_1 D_0)
500 ns–1 µs	___ ___ ___	(D_7 D_6 D_5 D_4 D_3 D_2 D_1 D_0)

Table 2

Time Segment	C B A	"Y" takes on the value of (select one)
0–500 ns	___ ___ ___	(D_7 D_6 D_5 D_4 D_3 D_2 D_1 D_0)
500 ns–1 µs	___ ___ ___	(D_7 D_6 D_5 D_4 D_3 D_2 D_1 D_0)

Table 3

11.   _____   12.   _____   13.   _____

Part 6

5. _____

Part 7

8.   Demonstrated to: _____ Date: _____

Grade: _____

Lab 12: Demultiplexers

Objectives:

1. Evaluate a basic 1-line to 2-line demultiplexer
2. Analyze a 2-line to 4-line multiplexer
3. Use the 74138 as a demultiplexer with no data inversion
4. Modify the 73138 demultiplexer to invert data
5. Create a circuit using an 8-line to 1-line multiplexer and a 1-line to 8-line demultiplexer

Materials List:

♦ Max+plus II software by Altera Corporation
♦ University Board by Altera Corporation (optional)
♦ Computer requirements:
    Minimum 486/66 with 8 MB RAM
♦ Floppy disk

Discussion:

A demultiplexer has a single data input and will send that data to one of many outputs. The number of outputs is determined by total possible combinations of the number of select inputs.

The basic 1-line to 2-line demultiplexer is shown in Figure 1. Data applied to the input will appear on one of the outputs, depending on the setting of the switch. Other names for the demultiplexer are data selector or data distributor.

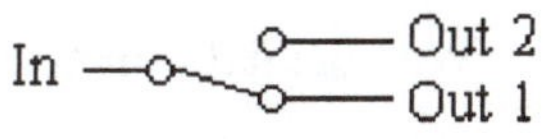

In ——o   o—— Out 2
          o—— Out 1

Figure 1

Figure 2 shows a demultiplexer using logic gates. The logic level on the select input determines on which output the data will appear.

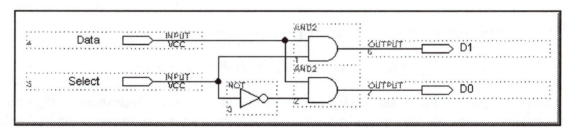

Figure 2

Any decoder that has an enable input may be used as a demultiplexer. Circuits that are designed to pass data from a single input to one of many outputs is a demultiplexer, where as a circuit whose outputs either turn on or turn off another circuit is a decoder.

This lab will illustrate the operation of several demultiplexers using logic gates and integrated circuits.

Part 1   Procedure

1. Open the Max+plus II software. Assign the project name **demux1** and MAX7000S as the device family.

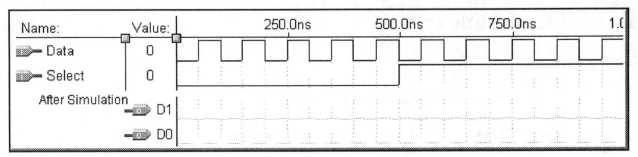

Figure 3

2.   Open a new Graphic Editor and construct the circuit shown in Figure 2.

3.   Open a new Waveform Editor, set the Grid Size to 50 ns, then create the waveforms shown in Figure 3.

4.   Draw the output waveforms in the area provided in Figure 3, after simulation.

5.   What output did the input data appear on when the select line was a logic-LOW? (D1/D0)

6.   What output did the input data appear on when the select line was a logic-HIGH? (D1/D0)

7.   The data input is active-(LOW/HIGH).

8.   The data outputs are active-(LOW/HIGH).

9.   Was the data inverted as data was passed through the circuit in Figure 2? (Yes/No)

10.   Save all files to Drive A as **demux1**, then exit the Graphic and Waveform Editors.

Part 2   Procedure

1.   Open the Max+plus II software. Assign the project name **demux2**.

2.   Open a new Graphic Editor file and construct the circuit shown in Figure 4.

3.   Open the Waveform Editor, set the Grid Size to 50 ns, and create waveforms shown in Figure 5. The casual minded observer may recognize that the circuit in Figure 5 is very similar to Figure 2 in Lab 10.

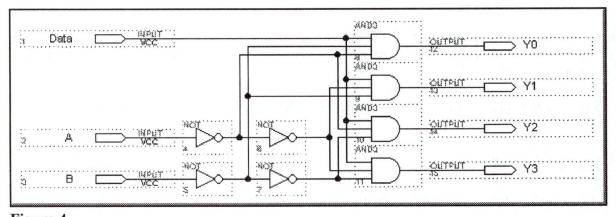

Figure 4

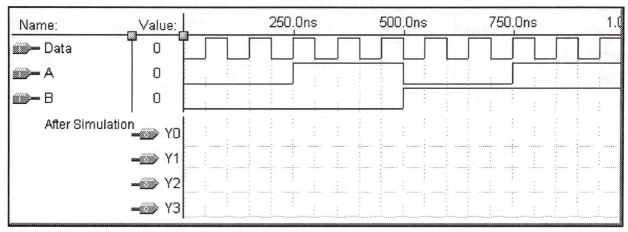

Figure 5

4.   Draw the output waveforms after simulation in the area provided in Figure 5.

5.   What output did the data appear on when the BA code was 00_2?   (Y0 , Y1 , Y2 , Y3)

6.   What output did the data appear on when the BA code was 01_2?   (Y0 , Y1 , Y2 , Y3)

7.   What output did the data appear on when the BA code was 10_2?   (Y0 , Y1 , Y2 , Y3)

8.   What output did the data appear on when the BA code was 11_2?   (Y0 , Y1 , Y2 , Y3)

9.   Was the data inverted as data was passed through the circuit in Figure 4? (Yes/No)

10.   Save all files to Drive A as **demux2**, then exit the Graphic and Waveform Editors.

Part 3   Procedure

1.   Open the Max+plus II software. Assign the project name **demux3**.

2.   Open a new Graphic Editor and create the circuit and waveforms shown in Figure 6.

3.   Open a new Waveform Editor, set the Grid Size to 25 ns, then create the waveforms shown in Figure 7.

4.   Draw the output waveforms after simulation in the area provided in Figure 7.

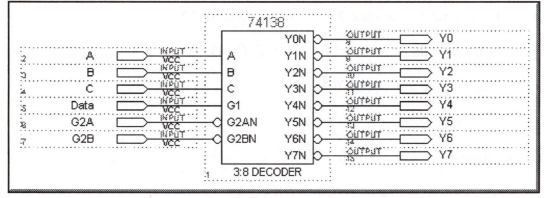

Figure 6

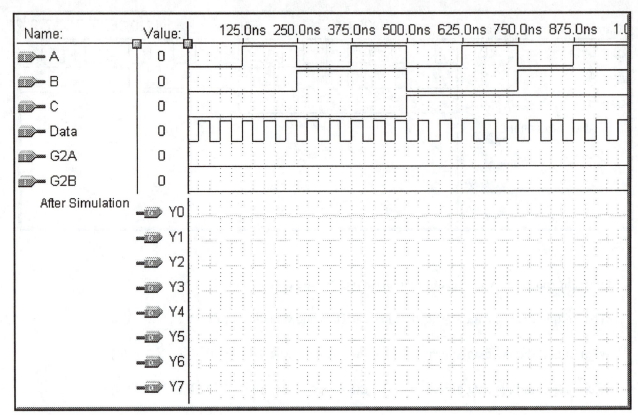

Figure 7

Time	G2B	G2A	C B A	Active Output
0–125 ns	——	——	———	——
125–250 ns	——	——	———	——
250–375 ns	——	——	———	——
375–500 ns	——	——	———	——
500–625 ns	——	——	———	——
625–750 ns	——	——	———	——
750–875 ns	——	——	———	——
875 nS–1 μs	——	——	———	——

Table 1

5. Complete Table 1 for the circuit of Figure 6 based on the results shown in Figure 7.

6. What pins in Figure 6 are the select lines? (CBA , G1, G2, Y)

7. What pins in Figure 6 are the enable lines? (CBA , G1, G2, Y)

8. The outputs in Figure 6 are active-(LOW/HIGH).

9. Was the data in Figure 6 inverted? (Yes/No)

10. The enable inputs in Figure 6 are active-(LOW/HIGH).

11. What inputs in Figure 6 are dominant? (CBA , G1, G2, Y)

Lab 12: Demultiplexers

12.   Explain in appropriate detail how the circuit in Figure 6 would operate if either G2 inputs were at a logic-HIGH level.

_____

_____

_____

_____

13.   Save all files to Drive A as **demux3**, then exit the Graphic and Waveform Editors.

Part 4   Procedure

1.   Open the **demux3.gdf** and **demux3.scf** files that were created in Part 3 of this lab. Save these files as **demux4.gdf** and **demux4.scf**, respectively.

2.   Bring the Graphic Editor to the foreground.

3.   Disconnect the Data input symbol from the G1 input and delete the G2A input symbol.

4.   Connect the Data input symbol to the G2A input of the 74138.

5.   Connect an input symbol to the G1 input. Label this symbol **G1**, then save the Graphic Editor file.

6.   Bring the Waveform Editor to the foreground.

7.   Change the G2A waveform label to G1, invert the G1 waveform, then save the Waveform Editor file.

8.   Recompile and simulate the **demux4** circuit.

9.   Does the **demux4** circuit invert the data applied? (Yes/No)

10.   To enable the **demux4** circuit, G1 must be a logic-(LOW/HIGH).

11.   To enable the **demux4** circuit, G2B must be a logic-(LOW/HIGH).

12.   Obtain a hard copy of the Graphic and Waveform files. Label these hard copies **Part 4, Step 12A** and **Part 4, Step 12B**, respectively.

13.   Save all files to Drive A as **demux4**, then exit the Graphic and Waveform Editors.

Part 5   Procedure

1.   Open the Graphic and Waveform Editors in the Max+plus II software. Assign the project name **demux5**.

2.   Figure 8 illustrates a circuit containing an 8-line to 1-line multiplexer and a 1-line to 8-line demultiplexer that share common select inputs. Select proper components from the Max+plus II parts bins and create the circuit so that the Data Out is in phase with the Data In. Use a bus line for the select inputs but *not* for the data inputs or data outputs. Hard wire all enable inputs to turn on both ICs.

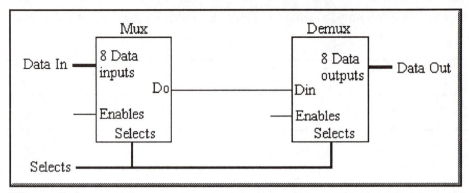

Figure 8

3.   Create eight data input signals to the multiplexer, each with a distinct bit pattern.

4.   Create and set the CBA bus to 000_2.

5.   Create eight data output signals to the demultiplexer.

6.   Compile, then simulate the circuit. Correct all errors before continuing.

7.   If successful, the waveform on output 0 of the demultiplexer should be identical to the waveform on input 0 of the multiplexer.

8.   Change the CBA value from 0 to 7, sequentially, to verify that each demultiplexer output matches the respective multiplexer input.

9.   Demonstrate the circuit you created to your instructor. Obtain the signature of approval on the answer page for this lab.

10.   Obtain a hard copy of the Graphic and Waveform files. Label these hard copies **Part 5, Step 10A** and **Part 5, Step 10B**, respectively.

11.   Save all files to Drive A as **demux5**, then exit the Graphic and Waveform Editors.

12.   Write a 1 to 2 page summary containing at least one embedded graphic pertaining to the results obtained from this lab.

13.   Place all papers for this lab in the following sequence, then submit the lab to your instructor for grading.

- Cover page
- Typed summary
- The completed answer page for this lab
- Hard copy of the Graphic Editor, **Part 4, Step 12A**
- Hard copy of the Waveform Editor, **Part 4, Step 12B**
- Hard copy of the Graphic Editor, **Part 5, Step 10A**
- Hard copy of the Waveform Editor, **Part 5, Step 10B**

Lab 12: Demultiplexers Answer Page

Name:_____

Part 1

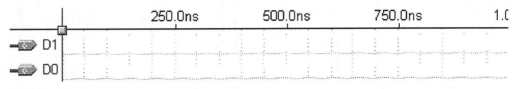

Figure 3

5.   D0   D1   6.   D0   D1

7.   LOW   HIGH   8.   LOW   HIGH

9.   Yes   No

Part 2

4.   (Y0 , Y1 , Y2 , Y3)

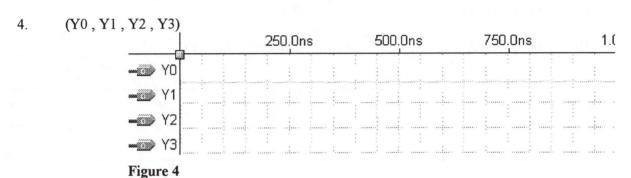

Figure 4

5.   (Y0 , Y1 , Y2 , Y3)   6.   (Y0 , Y1 , Y2 , Y3)

7.   (Y0 , Y1 , Y2 , Y3)   8.   Yes   No

Part 3

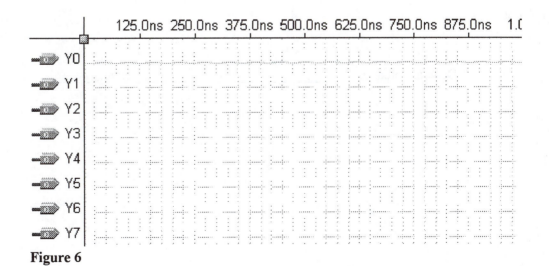

Figure 6

Time	G2B	G2A	C B A	Active Output
0–125 ns	——	——	—— —— ——	——
125–250 ns	——	——	—— —— ——	——
250–375 ns	——	——	—— —— ——	——
375–500 ns	——	——	—— —— ——	——
500–625 ns	——	——	—— —— ——	——
625–750 ns	——	——	—— —— ——	——
750–875 ns	——	——	—— —— ——	——
875 ns–1 μs	——	——	—— —— ——	——

Table 1

6.   (CBA , G1 , G2 , Y)   7.   (CBA , G1 , G2 , Y)

7.   LOW / HIGH   9.   Yes   No

10.   LOW / HIGH   11.   (CBA , G1 , G2 , Y)

12.   _____

_____

_____

Part 4

9.   Yes   No   10.   LOW / HIGH

11.   LOW / HIGH

Part 5

9.   Demonstrated to: _____ Date: _____

Grade: _____

Lab 13: Latches and Flip-Flops

Objectives:

1. Become familiar with the operation of the S-R Latch
2. Become familiar with the operation of the gated S-R Latch
3. Become familiar with the operation of the gated D-Latch
4. Become familiar with the operation of the D Flip-flop
5. Become familiar with the operation of the J-K Flip-flop

Materials Required:

Max+plus II software by Altera Corporation

Latches: S-R, $\overline{S}$-$\overline{R}$

Discussion:

A latch is a bistable multivibrator device. This means that the latch is an electronic circuit designed to exist in one of two possible states and is stable in either state. These two states are called SET and RESET (or CLEAR). This device typically has two outputs that are labeled Q and $\overline{Q}$. This labeling convention indicates that the two outputs are logically the inverse of each other (i.e., If Q = 1, then $\overline{Q}$ = 0).

By definition, a latch is SET (SET = 1, or more accurately, is active) when Q = 1 & $\overline{Q}$ = 0, and a latch is RESET (CLEAR, RESET = 0) when Q = 0 and $\overline{Q}$ = 1. Conversely, for "Active Low" inputs, the latch is set when $\overline{SET}$ = 0 and $\overline{RESET}$ = 1. To make this simple, remember: "Q follows S."

Part 1   Procedure

1. Open the Max+plus II software and assign the project name **sr-not**.

2. Open a new Graphic Editor and construct the circuit shown in Figure 1.

3. Open a new Waveform Editor and create the waveforms shown in Figure 2, then draw the corresponding output waveforms after simulation.

4. Referring to the output waveforms, complete the truth table, Table 1, for the $\overline{S}$-$\overline{R}$ latch.

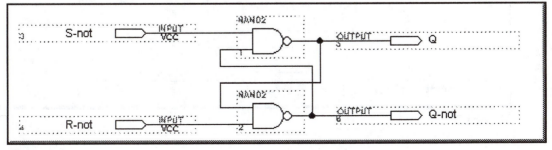

Figure 1

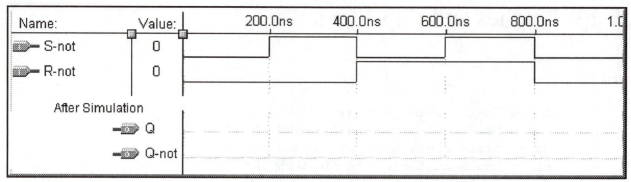

Figure 2

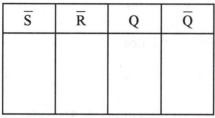

$\overline{S}$	$\overline{R}$	Q	$\overline{Q}$

Table 1

5. Write a paragraph explaining how the $\overline{S}\ \overline{R}$ latch operates, based on the function table and your waveforms.

_____

_____

_____

_____

6. Save all files to Drive A as **sr-not**, then exit the Graphics and Waveform Editors.

Part 2   Procedure

1. Open the Max+plus II software. Assign the project name **sr-latch**.

2. Open a new Graphic Editor and construct the circuit shown in Figure 3.

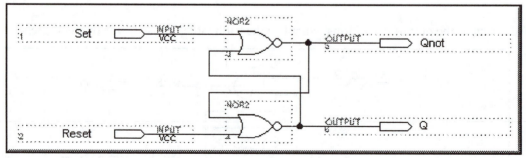

Figure 3

Lab 13: Latches and Flip-Flops

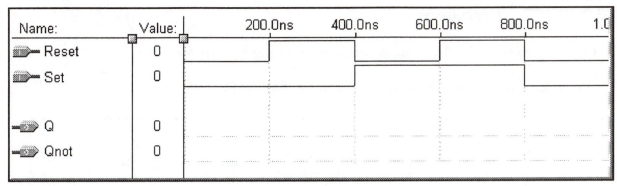

Figure 4

3.   Open a new Waveform Editor and create the waveforms shown in Figure 4 and draw the output waveforms after simulation.

4.   Referring to the waveforms in Figure 4, complete the following truth table for the S-R latch.

S	R	Q	$\overline{Q}$

Table 2

5.   Write a paragraph explaining how the S-R latch operates, based on the function table and your waveforms.

_____

_____

_____

_____

6.   Save all files to Drive A as **s-r-latch**, then exit the Graphic and Waveform Editors.

Latches: Gated S-R, Gated D

Discussion

The addition of a dual-input NAND gate to one of the inputs of a NAND gate version of the $\overline{S}$-$\overline{R}$ latch (Figure 1) and a second dual-input NAND gate to the second input of the latch provides the student with an S-R latch with four inputs. Assuming that two of the inputs are S and R, the remaining inputs may be interconnected to provide a circuit such as that in Figure 5. These two added gates are called "steering gates." The additional input provided by interconnection between the steering gates is called the "gate" or "enable" input. This input makes it possible for the clock to make time a factor in the operation of the basic S-R latch. In other words, the circuit is now synchronous, or "enabled" by the clock (Gate) signal.

Part 3   Procedure

1.   Open the Max+plus II software and assign the project name **gated-sr**.

2.   Open a new Graphic Editor and construct the circuit shown in Figure 5.

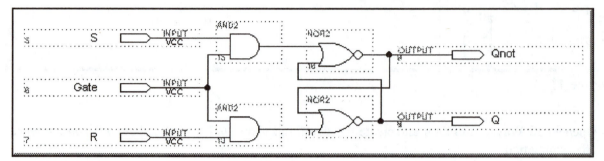

Figure 5

3.   Open a new Waveform Editor and create the waveforms shown in Figure 6.

4.   Draw output waveforms in Figure 6 after simulation.

5.   Referring to the waveforms in Figure 6, complete the following truth table for the gated S-R latch.

6.   Of the eight input combinations shown in the truth table, how many affect the latch output? _____.

7.   Of the input combinations that do not affect the latch output, one is unique because it did not allow the output to change. Which one is unique, and why is it unique?

_____

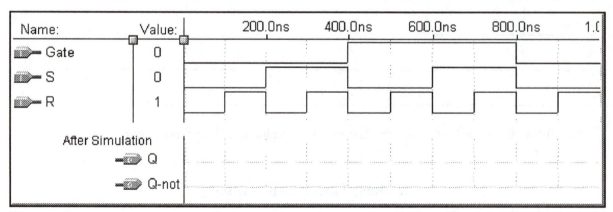

Figure 6

G	S	R	Q	$\bar{Q}$
0	X	X	___	___
1	___	___	___	___
1	___	___	___	___
1	___	___	___	___
1	___	___	___	___

Table 3

8. The output condition that resulted when all three inputs were HIGH (1) is called _____.

9. If all three inputs were in the HIGH state and changed to a LOW state at the same time, the latch would go through a condition called the_____ condition. Would the same condition occur if only the GATE input had gone LOW?   (Yes/No)

10. What would be the output state of the latch after it passed through the condition referred to in Step 8? _____ Why? _____

_____

11. To avoid the condition referred to in Step 7 and Step 8, the gated S-R latch will be modified by connecting an inverter between the S and R inputs. This ensures that the inputs would never be the same. The gated-D latch will be examined in Part 4.

12. Write a paragraph explaining how the gated S-R latch operates, based on the function table and your waveforms.

_____

_____

_____

13. Save all files to Drive A as **gated-sr**, then exit the Graphic and Waveform Editors.

Part 4   Procedure

1. Open the Max+plus II software and assign the project name **gated-d**.

2. Open a new Graphic Editor and construct the circuit shown in Figure 7.

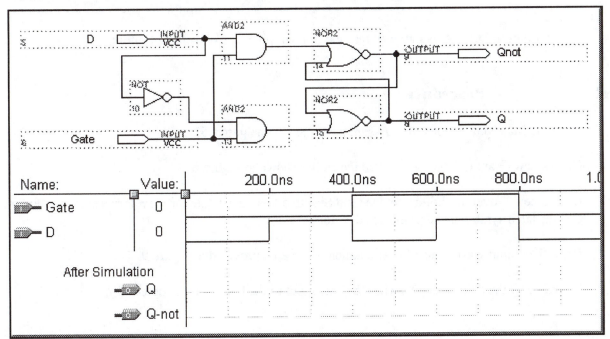

Figure 7

3. Open a new Waveform Editor and create the waveforms shown in Figure 7.

4. Referring to the waveforms in Figure 8, complete the following truth table for the gated-D latch.

G	D	Q	$\bar{Q}$
—	—	—	—
—	—	—	—
—	—	—	—
—	—	—	—

Table 4

5. How many inputs does your table show?_____. How many input combinations are possible with this latch?_____.

6. There is a saying that "Q follows D when the gate is 'active' in a gated-D latch." Does your truth table agree with this saying ?_____ Why or why not?

    _____

    _____

7. Does the invalid condition of S-R latches exist for the gated-D latch?   (Yes/No)

8. Write a paragraph explaining how the gated-D latch operates, based on the function table and your waveforms in Figure 7.

    _____

    _____

    _____

9. Save all files to Drive A as **gated-d**, then exit the Graphic and Waveform Editors.

Part 5   Procedure

1. Open the Max+plus II software. Assign the project name **gated-d2**.

2. Open a new Graphic Editor and create the circuit shown in Figure 8.

3. Open a new Waveform Editor, set the Grid Size to 50 ns, and create the waveforms shown in Figure 9. Use the latch symbol in the primitives directory.

4. Draw the output waveforms after simulation in the area provided in Figure 9.

5. Explain why the outputs are Xs when the gate input to the latches are a logic-LOW.

    _____

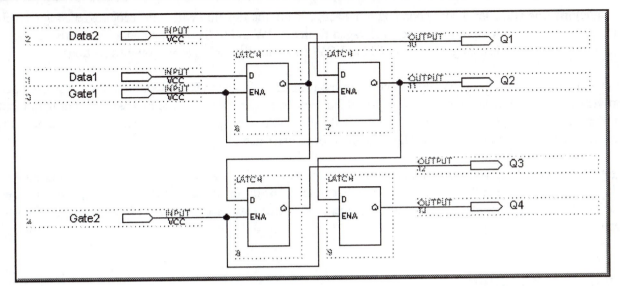

Figure 8

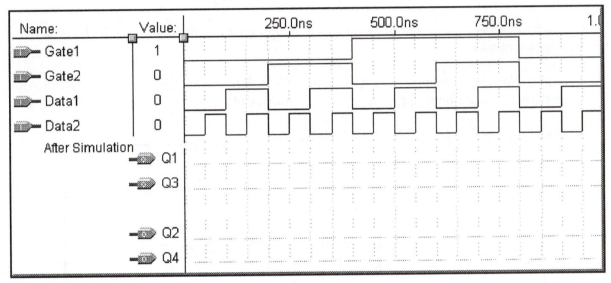

Figure 9

6. Q1 receives its data from _____ and Q2 receives its data from _____ .

7. Q3 receives its date from _____ and Q4 receives its data from _____ .

8. Why are all the Q outputs a logic-HIGH beyond 800 ns? _____

9. Save all files to Drive A as **gated-d2**, then exit the Graphic and Waveform Editors.

Flip-Flops: D-type

Discussion

The flip-flop differs from the gated latch in that the clock input of the flip-flop (FF) has an edge-detector circuit. This means that while the latch will change states to correspond to the logic levels on the input(s) whenever the gate (or enable) input is at the level corresponding to its active state, the flip-flop will only recognize the logic levels on the inputs when the clock input logic level is changed from a LOW to HIGH (leading edge or positive going transition), or the clock is changing from HIGH to LOW (trailing edge or negative going transition).

The D and J-K flip-flops are probably the most common flip-flops in use today. Both versions were developed as improvements on the S-R version. The D flip-flop did away with the "illegal" state by ensuring that both inputs would never be the same. This, however, left the D flip-flop with one input and the capability to monitor only one signal at a time. This fact makes the D flip-flop ideal for register use.

Edge-triggered devices have the advantage of rejuvenating input for only a few nanoseconds during the edge of the clock pulse, thus excluding "noise" inputs at all other times. The disadvantage is that the clock pulse must be "clean" or "sharp' square-wave. If the edge is jagged, the device may "see" several "edges" and trigger several times.

Part 6   Procedure

1.   Open the Max+plus II software. Assign the project name **d-fflop**.

2.   Open a new Graphic Editor and construct the circuit shown in Figure 10. Use the DFF symbol in the primitives directory.

3.   Open a new Waveform Editor, set the Grid Size to 50 ns, then create the waveforms shown in Figure 11. Draw the output waveforms in the space provided after simulation.

4.   List the times that the Q output goes to a logic-HIGH. _____

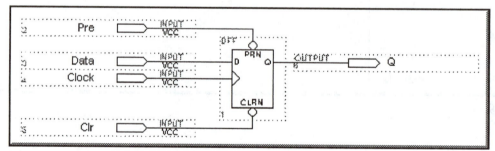

Figure 10

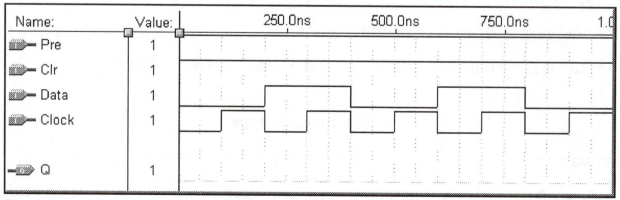

Figure 11

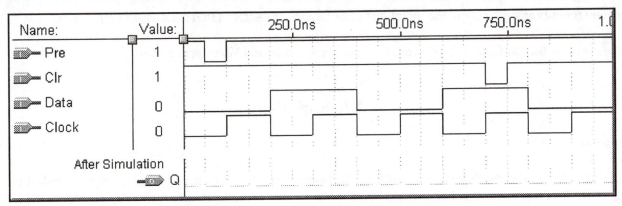

Figure 12

5.   List the times that the Q output goes to a logic-LOW. _____

6.   When output Q changes, Q follows the _____ when the _____ goes to a logic-
       (HIGH/LOW).

7.   Be sure the Snap to Grid in the Options menu is turned ON. Modify the Pre and Clr waveforms as shown
       in Figure 12. Draw output Q after simulation in the space provided in Figure 12.

8.   What input transition caused output Q to go to a logic-HIGH in the first 400 ns? _____

9.   At what time did output Q go to a logic-HIGH in the first 400 ns?   _____ ns

10.   Was this transition in output Q (during the first 400 ns) clock dependent? (Yes/No)

11.   Before 600 ns, Q went to a logic-LOW. This transition occurred at what time? _____ ns

12.   Was the first transition of Q from a logic-HIGH to a logic-LOW clock dependant?   (Yes/No)

13.   Why did Q go to a logic-LOW? _____

14.   A glitch occurred in the output waveform near 750 ns. Explain what caused this glitch.

       _____

       _____

15.   At what time did the glitch in the output waveform occur?   _____ ns

16.   The D Flip-Flop used in Figure 10 is (positive/negative) (edge/level) triggered.

17.   The D and clock inputs are (synchronous/asynchronous).

18.   Does the clock input have the same effect on the preset and clear inputs that it has on the D input?
       (Yes/No)

19.   The preset and clear inputs are (synchronous/asynchronous) inputs.

20.   From the timing diagram, the preset and clear inputs are (Active-HIGH/Active-LOW) inputs.

21.   Save all files to Drive A as **d-fflop**, then exit the Graphic and Waveform Editors.

J-K Flip-Flop

Discussion:

The J-K flip-flop turned the "illegal" state of the S-R flip-flop into the productive condition, or state, called the toggle state. This fact makes the J-K a useful flip-flop for making counter circuits.

Part 7   Procedure

1.   Open the Max+plus II software. Assign the project name **jk-fflop**.

2.   Open a new Graphic Editor, then import the **jkff** symbol from the **Prim** directory and connect input/output terminals with the labels shown in Figure 3.

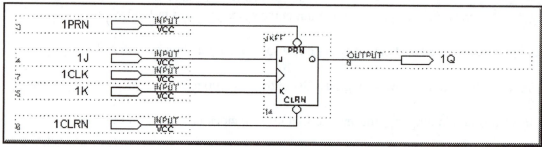

Figure 13

3.   Open a new Waveform Editor and create the waveforms shown in Figure 14.

4.   After simulating the circuit, draw the Q output waveform for the circuit constructed in the space provided in Figure 14.

5.   Evaluate the timing diagram you have just completed. According to the timing diagram, the **jkff** symbol is (leading/trailing) edge triggered.

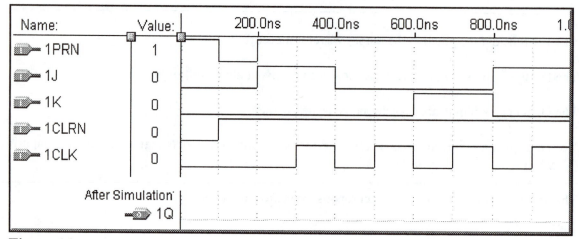

Figure 14

Time segment	1PRN	1J	1K	1CLRN	1CLK	1Q	MODE
0 to 100 ns							
100 to 200 ns							
200 to 300 ns							
300 to 400 ns							
400 to 500 ns							
500 to 600 ns							
600 to 700 ns							
700 to 800 ns							
800 to 900 ns							
900 ns to 1 µs							

Table 5

6.　Carefully examine the output waveform of Figure 13 with respect to the input waveforms and complete Table 4. For each time segment, identify the logic levels of the waveforms, then identify the flip-flop mode of operation.

7.　Revise the timing diagram as shown in Figure 15. Draw the new output after simulation.

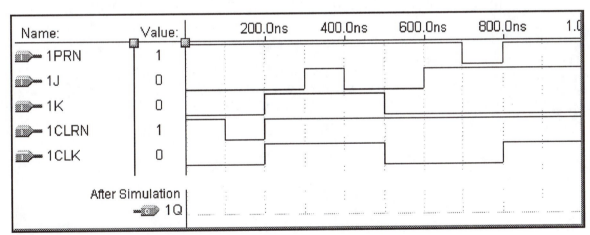

Figure 15

8.　At what time did the Q output waveform change from a logic-LOW to a logic-HIGH? _____ns

9.　What condition caused the Q output to change from a logic-LOW to a logic-HIGH? _____

10.　Explain why the J-K flip-flop Q output in Figure 15 did not change on either the leading or trailing edge of the clock.

_____

_____

11. According to the results displayed by the waveforms in Figure 14 and Figure 15, preset and clear inputs to the J-K flip-flop are (synchronous/asynchronous)

12. According to the results displayed by the waveforms in Figure 14 and Figure 15, the J, K, and clock inputs to the J-K flip-flop are (synchronous/asynchronous)

13. Which set of inputs to the flip-flop are dominant?   (synchronous/asynchronous)

14. Obtain a hard copy of the Graphic and Waveform Editor files. Label these hard copies **Part 7, Step 10A** and **Part 7, Step 10B**, respectively.

15. Demonstrate the circuit and waveforms for Part 8 of this lab to the instructor. Obtain the signature of approval directly on the answer page for this lab.

16. Save all files to Drive A as **JK-fflop**, then exit the Graphics and Waveform Editors.

17. Write a 1 to 2 page summary containing and referring to at least 1 embedded figure obtained from this lab.

18. Place all papers for this lab in the following sequence, then submit the lab to your instructor for grading.

   ■   Cover page
   ■   Typed summary
   ■   The completed answer page for this lab
   ■   Hard copy of the Graphic Editor, **Part 7, Step 10A**
   ■   Hard copy of the Waveform Editor, **Part 7, Step 10B**

Lab 13: Latches and Flip-Flops Answer Page

Name: _____

Part 1

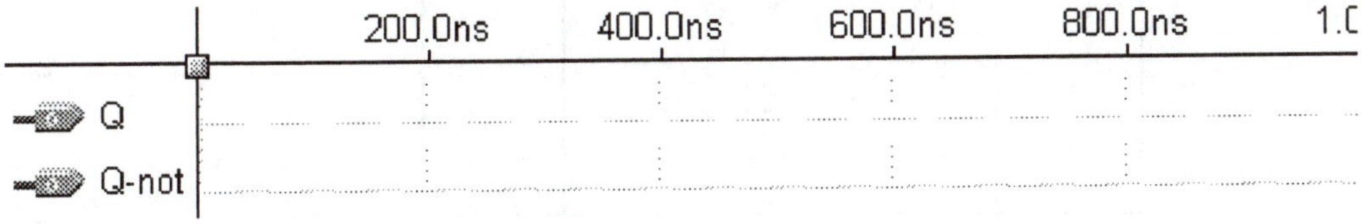

	200.0ns	400.0ns	600.0ns	800.0ns	1.0
Q					
Q-not					

Figure 2

5.

$\overline{S}$	$\overline{R}$	Q	$\overline{Q}$

Table 1

_____
_____
_____
_____
_____
_____

Part 2

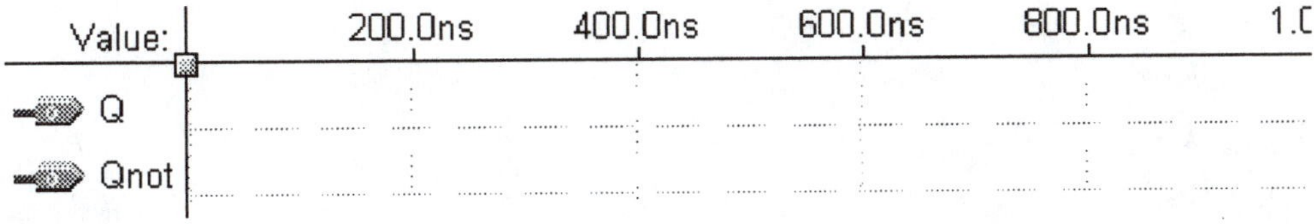

Value:	200.0ns	400.0ns	600.0ns	800.0ns	1.0
Q					
Qnot					

Figure 4

5.

S	R	Q	$\overline{Q}$

Table 2

_____
_____
_____
_____
_____
_____
_____

Part 3

Value:	200.0ns	400.0ns	600.0ns	800.0ns	1.0
Q					
Qnot					

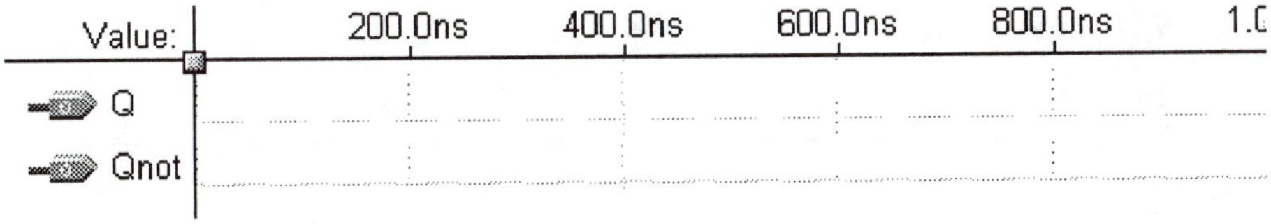

Figure 6

G	S	R	Q	$\overline{Q}$
0	X	X	——	——
1	——	——	——	——
1	——	——	——	——
1	——	——	——	——
1	——	——	——	——

Table 3

6. _____

7. _____

_____

_____

8. _____

9. _____   Yes   No

10. _____   Why? _____

_____

12. _____

_____

_____

Part 4

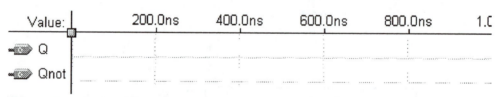

Figure 7

G	D	Q	$\overline{Q}$
——	——	——	——
——	——	——	——
——	——	——	——
——	——	——	——

Table 4

5. _____   _____

6. _____   _____

_____

_____

7.   Yes   No

8. _____

_____

_____

Part 5

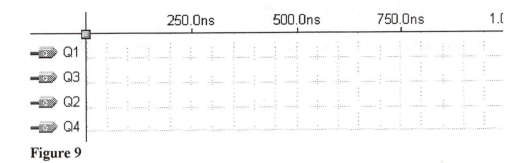

Figure 9

G	D	Q	$\overline{Q}$
___	___	___	___
___	___	___	___
___	___	___	___
___	___	___	___

Table 5

5. _____

_____

6. _____ _____

7. _____ _____

8. _____

Part 6

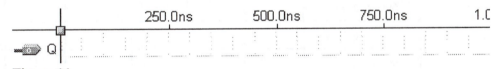

Figure 11

4. _____

5. _____

6. _____ _____ (HIGH/LOW)

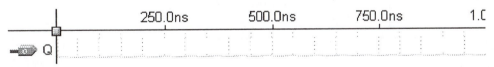

Figure 12

8. _____   9. _____   10.   Yes   No

11. _____   12.   Yes   No   13. _____

14. _____

_____

15. _____   16.   Positive/Negative   Edge/Level

17.   Synchronous/Asynchronous   18.   Yes   No

19.   Synchronous/Asynchronous   20.   Active-HIGH   Active-LOW

Part 7

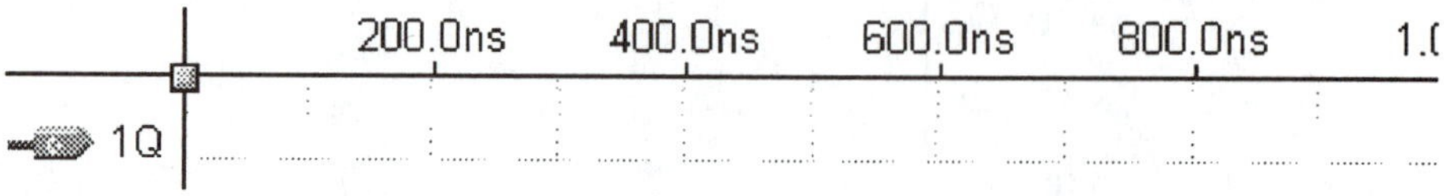

Figure 13

5.   Leading/Trailing

Time segment	1PRN	1J	1K	1CLRN	1CLK	1Q	MODE
0 to 100 ns							
100 to 200 ns							
200 to 300 ns							
300 to 400 ns							
400 to 500 ns							
500 to 600 ns							
600 to 700 ns							
700 to 800 ns							
800 to 900 ns							
900 ns to 1 μs							

Table 5

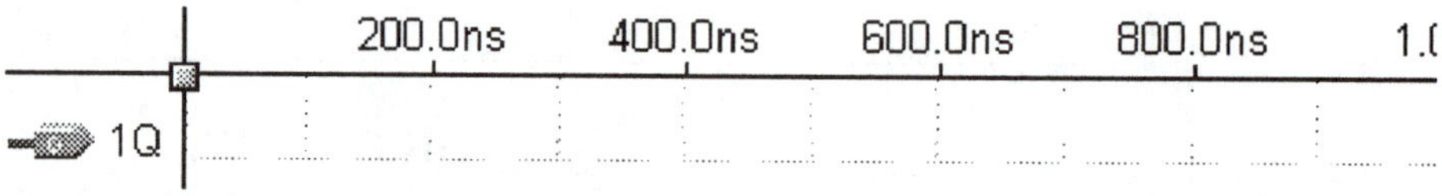

Figure 14

8. _____   9. _____

10. _____

_____

11.   Synchronous/Asynchronous   12.   Synchronous/Asynchronous

13.   Synchronous/Asynchronous

15.   Demonstrated to: _____   Date: _____

Grade: _____

Lab 14: Integrated Latches and Flip-Flops

Objectives:

1. Use the 7475 4-Bit Bistable Latch as a 2x2 bit memory
2. Analyze the 74373 Octal Transparent Latch for address latching
3. Compare the 7476 and 74LS76 Dual J-K flip-flops
4. Evaluate a computer output port for latched and unlatched data transfer

Materials List:

- ◆ Max+plus II software by Altera Corporation
- ◆ University Board by Altera Corporation (optional)
- ◆ Computer requirements:
  - Minimum 486/66 with 8 MB RAM
- ◆ Floppy disk

Discussion:

The latch is ideally suited for temporary storage of information between processing units and input/output devices. When the enable is "active", data on the input of the latch will pass to the Q output (transparent). When the enable becomes "inactive", the data on the Q outputs is "latched" and will be retained until the latch is again enabled or power is lost (volatile memory). The two latches discussed in this lab are the 7475 and 74373 integrated circuits.

The 7475 has four internal latches with two enable inputs. Enable E12 enables or inhibits Q1 and Q2. Enable 34 controls Q3 and Q4. Using separate enable signals allows independent control of Q1 and Q2 or Q3 and Q4. If the enables are tied together, then all four latches may be operated in parallel. Several wiring techniques of the 7475 will be examined.

The 74373 has 8 latches that share the same enable input. Microprocessors often will have multiplexed address and data lines sharing common pins. It is necessary to isolate the data an address lines external to the microprocessor. The 74373 will be used to "latch" onto the address lines, freeing up the address/data pins of the microprocessor to be used by data.

Flip-flops may also be used as temporary storage devices and are most appropriate for clock dependent circuits such as counters and registers. As demonstrated in Lab 13, flip-flops are edge triggered devices. Two J-K flip-flops discussed in this lab are the 7476 and 7476a (The 7476a is Altera's label for the 74LS76a).

The last circuit discussed in this lab uses latches to control data flow to an output port in a microprocessor system.

Tristate buffers will be used as needed to control the flow of data in circuits used in this lab.

Part 1 Procedure

1. Start the Max+plus II software. Assign the project name **latch75** and MAX7000S as the device family.

2. Open a new Graphic Editor and construct the circuit shown in Figure 1.

3. Open a new Waveform Editor, set the Grid Size to 50 ns, then create the waveforms shown in Figure 2.

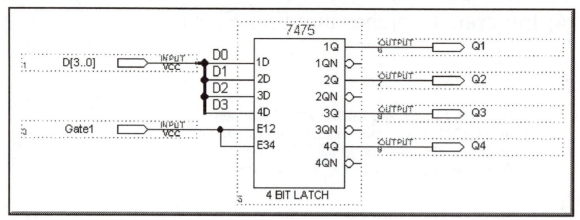

Figure 1

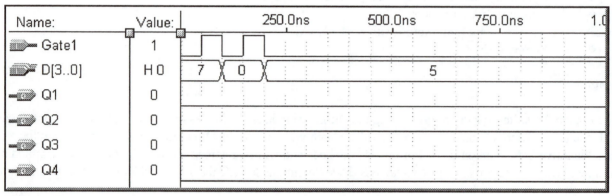

Figure 2

4.   Press the Compiler and Simulator buttons. Correct all errors before continuing.

5.   Draw the output waveforms created after simulation in the area provided in Figure 2.

6.   Based on the results observed, the Q outputs of the latch follow the data inputs when the gate is a logic- (LOW/HIGH).

7.   Explain why the Q outputs of the latch remained a logic-LOW even though the data was "5."

8.   Select the **Max+plus II** option (upper left) in the main menu. Select and run the Timing Analyzer in the list of options.

	Q1	Q2	Q3	Q4
D0				
D1				
D2				
D3				
GATE1				

Table 1

                              Lab 14: Integrated Latches and Flip-flops

9. Copy the time delays (in nanoseconds) shown in the Delay Matrix to Table 1.

10. Change the Gate1 signal to that shown in Figure 3.

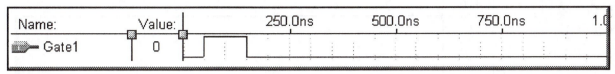

Figure 3

11. Press the simulate button.

12. Describe the differences between the outputs the Waveform Editor now displays as compared to the outputs shown in Figure 2.

_____

13. Latching onto the data occurs when the latch is shut off, thus memorizing the last data value applied to the latch just before the latch was shut off. At what time was the data latched when the gate signal of Figure 3 was applied? _____

14. Change the Gate1 waveform to that shown in Figure 4.

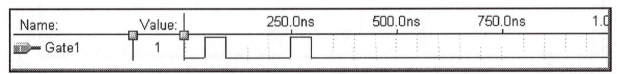

Figure 4

15. Press the Simulate button.

16. Why was the zero value of data ignored in the last set of outputs created by the simulator?

_____

17. Refer to Figure 4. At what time(s) did the 7475 "latch" on to the data? _____

18. If data applied to the latch changes logic levels while the Gate input is a logic-LOW, the Q output will
        A.   Change with the data
        B.   Remain constant

19. Which icon in the Tool bar shown in Figure 5 opens the Timing Analyzer?

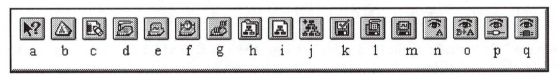

Figure 5

20. Save all files to Drive A as **latch75**, then exit the Graphic and Waveform Editors.

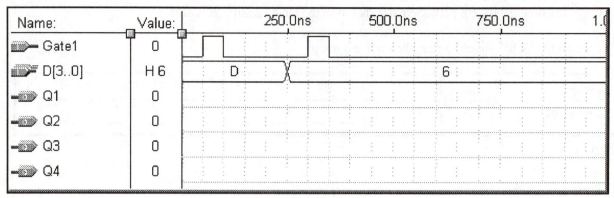

Figure 6

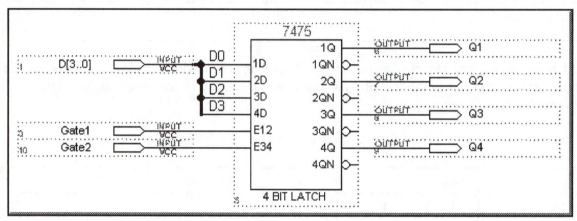

Figure 7

Part 2   Procedure

1.   Open the Max+Plus II software. Assign the project name **latch75a**.

2.   Open a new Graphic Editor and construct the circuit shown in Figure 6.

3.   Open a new Waveform Editor and create the waveforms shown in Figure 7.

4.   Run the Compiler and Simulator. DO NOT CORRECT ANY SIMULATOR WARNINGS.

5.   What warning did the Simulator report? _____

6.   Refer to Figure 7. At what time(s) did the 7475 latch onto the data applied?

7.   Convert D_H and 6_H to binary. $D_H =$ _____ $_2$ $6_H =$ _____ $_2$

8.   When the 7475 latched onto the D_H data, did the logic levels of Q2 and Q1 match the least two bit values of the data, D_H?   (Yes/No)

9.   When the 7475 latched onto the 6_H data, did the logic levels of Q2 and Q1 match the least two bit values of the data, D_H?   (Yes/No)

10.   Delete the Gate2 input from the Graphic Editor.

11.   Connect the E34 input of the latch to the Gate1 source.

12.   Press the Compiler and Simulator buttons. Correct all errors before continuing.

13.   Draw the resulting output waveforms in the area provided in Figure 7.

14.   Save all files to Drive A as **latch75a**, then exit the Graphic and Waveform Editors.

Part 3   Procedure

1.   Open the Max+plus II software. Assign the project name **latch373**.

2.   Open a new Graphic Editor and create the waveforms shown in Figure 8.

3.   Open a new Waveform Editor, set the Grid size to 100 ns, and create the waveforms shown in Figure 9.
       D[7..0] starts at 75 and increments by 174.

4.   Run the Compiler and Simulator. Correct all errors before continuing.

5.   Draw the resulting output waveforms in the area provided at the bottom of Figure 9.

6.   What time segment from 0 to 500 ns is the latch "ON" ? _____
       (When the Q outputs are transparent)

7.   What data was "latched" in the first 500 ns of time? _____

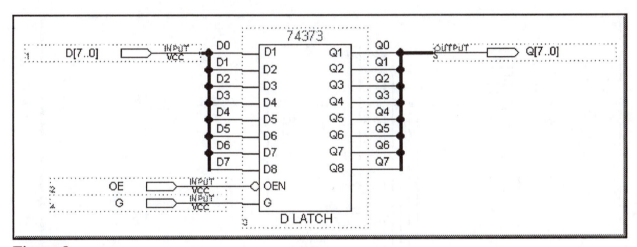

Figure 8

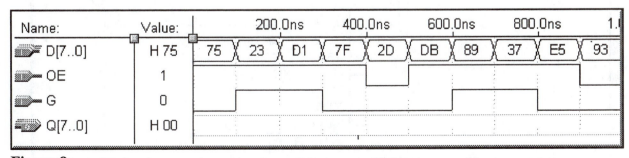

Figure 9

8.   In what time segment did this data appear on the outputs?   _____

9.   What data was "latched" in the second 500 ns time frame? (From 500 ns to 1 μs) _____

10.   What time segment did the this data appear on the outputs?   _____

11.   What do the ZZs in the output waveform represent? _____

12.   Save all files to Drive A as **latch373**, then exit the Graphic and Waveform Editors.

Part 4   Procedure

1.   Open the Graphics and Waveform Editors. Assign the project name **7476jk**.

2.   Open a new Graphic Editor and import the 7476 and 7476a symbols from the **mf** directory. Connect
        input/output terminals to both ICs with the labels shown in Figure 10.

3.   Open a new Waveform Editor, set the Grid Size to 50 ns, then create the waveforms shown in Figure 11.

4.   After compiling and simulating the circuit, draw the Q output waveform for the circuit constructed in the
        space provided in Figure 11.

5.   Evaluate the timing diagram you have just completed.   According to the timing diagram, the **7676** is
        (leading/trailing) edge triggered and the **7476a** is (leading/trailing) edge triggered.

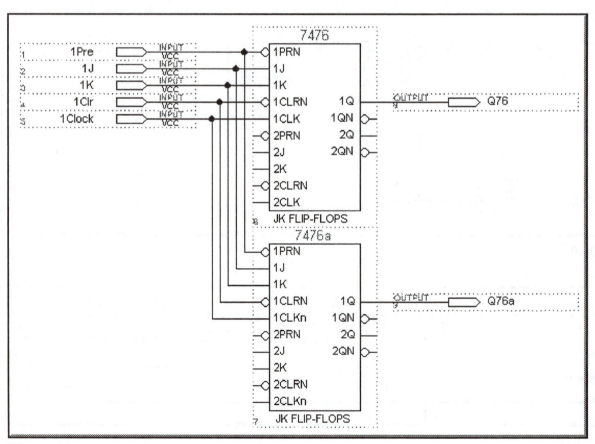

Figure 10

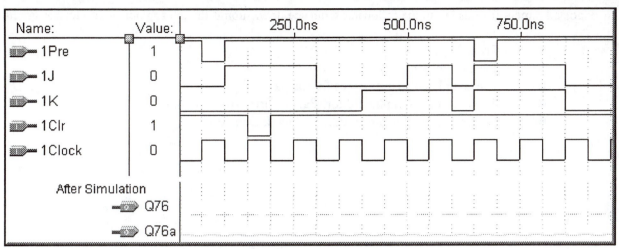

Figure 11

Time	Mode	7476 Q*		Time	Mode	7476a Q*
50 to 100 ns	_____	____		50 to 100 ns	_____	____
150 ns to 250 ns	_____	____		150 ns to 250 ns	_____	____
@ 250 ns	_____	____		@ 200 ns	_____	____
@ 450 ns	_____	____		@ 500 ns	_____	____
@ 550 ns	_____	____		@ 600 ns	_____	____
@ 750 ns	_____	____		@ 800 ns	_____	____
@ 850 ns	_____	____				

Table 1   * Record the value Q will become.

6. Carefully examine the output waveforms in Figure 11 with respect to the input waveforms and complete Table 1. For each time segment, identify the flip-flop mode of operation (Set, Reset, No Change, or Toggle) and the value the Q output will become for each flip-flop.

7. The PRE and CLR inputs to 7476 are (synchronous/asynchronous).

8. The PRE and CLR inputs to 74LS76, the 7476a used in Figure 10, are (synchronous/asynchronous).

9. Write a statement comparing the 7476 and 74LS76 (7476a) based on the results obtained in Part 3 of this lab.

    _____

    _____

10. Obtain a hard copy of the Graphic and Waveform Editors used to demonstrate Figure 12 in Part 4 of this lab. Label these hard copies **Part 4, Step 10A** and **Part 4, Step 10B**, respectively.

11. Save all files to Drive A as **7476jk** then exit the Graphic and Waveform Editors.

12. Demonstrate the circuit and waveforms for Part 8 of this lab to the instructor. Obtain the signature of approval directly on the answer page for this lab.

13. Write a 1 to 2 page summary containing and making reference to at least one embedded figure from this lab.

14. Place all papers for this lab in the following sequence, then submit the lab to your instructor for grading.

- Cover Page
- Typed summary
- The completed answer pages for this lab
- Printout of the Graphic Editor, **Part 4, Step 10A**
- Printout of the Waveform Editor, **Part 4, Step 10B**

Lab 14:   Integrated Latches and Flip-flops   Name: _____

Part 1

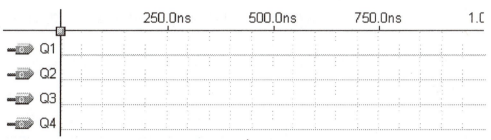

Figure 2

6.   LOW/HIGH

7.   _____

	Q1	Q2	Q3	Q4
D0				
D1				
D2				
D3				
GATE1				

Table 1

12.   _____

13.   _____

16.   _____

17.   _____   18.   _____   19.   _____

Part 2

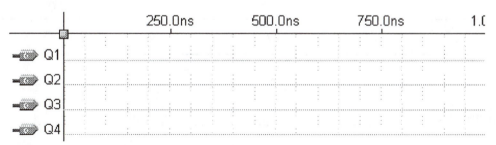

Figure 7

5.   _____   6. _____

7. D_H = _____ 6_H = _____   8. Yes   No   9.   Yes   No

Part 3

6. _____ 7. _____

8. _____ 9. _____

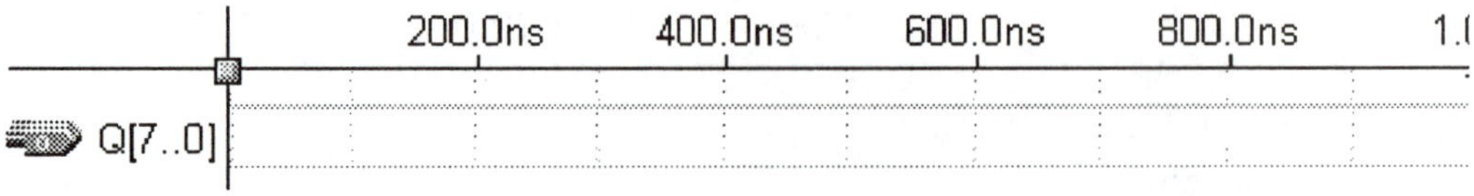

```
                    200.0ns    400.0ns    600.0ns    800.0ns    1.(
      ▣
  ▥ Q[7..0]
```

Figure 9

10. _____ 11. _____

Part 4

5. (7476) Leading/Trailing (7476a) Leading/Trailing

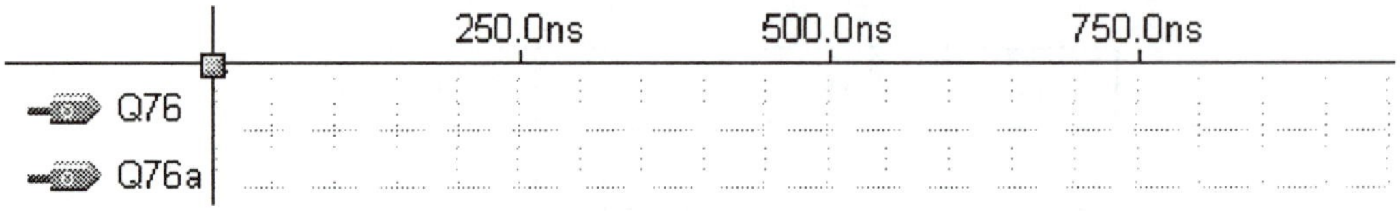

```
                250.0ns      500.0ns      750.0ns
      ▣
  ▥ Q76
  ▥ Q76a
```

Figure 11

Time	Mode	7476 Q*
50 to 100 ns	_____	_____
150 ns to 250 ns	_____	_____
@ 250 ns	_____	_____
@ 450 ns	_____	_____
@ 550 ns	_____	_____
@ 750 ns	_____	_____
@ 850 ns	_____	_____

Time	Mode	7476a Q*
50 to 100 ns	_____	_____
150 ns to 250 ns	_____	_____
@ 200 ns	_____	_____
@ 500 ns	_____	_____
@ 600 ns	_____	_____
@ 800 ns	_____	_____

Table 1 * Record the value Q will become.

7. Synchronous/Asynchronous 8. Synchronous/Asynchronous

9. _____

    _____

Demonstrated to: _____ Date: _____

Grade: _____

Lab 15: Asynchronous Counters

Objectives:

1. Create a 3-bit (Modulus 8) asynchronous binary counter using J-K flip-flops
2. Create a 3-bit (Modulus 5) asynchronous binary counter using J-K flip-flops
3. Use the Timing Analyzer to determine propagation delays
4. Construct a 4-bit binary counter using the 7493 integrated circuit
5. Construct a 4-bit decade counter using the 7490 integrated circuit
6. Study the effects of the preset and clear inputs with respect to the clock
7. Change the counter modulus using full or partial decoding

Materials List:

- Max+plus II software by Altera Corporation
- University Board by Altera Corporation (optional)
- Computer requirements:
  Minimum 486/66 with 8 MB RAM
- Floppy disk

Discussion:

J-K flip-flops with preset and clear inputs can be cascaded to create an *n*-bit binary or BCD counter.

The method of clocking each stage within the counter determines if the counter is asynchronously or synchronously clocked. Asynchronous clocking implies that each stage does *not* share the same clock, nor toggle at the same time, as the other flip-flops in the counter. Each flip-flop in an asynchronous counter is clocked by the Q output of the previous flip-flop. If the first stage toggles, it may cause the second stage to toggle, which in turn may cause the third stage to toggle, and so forth. Asynchronous counters, often called ripple counters, are the focus of this lab.

Synchronous counters are designed with all flip-flops responding to the same clock pulse, simultaneously. Synchronous counters are the focus of Lab 16.

The time it takes the Q output of the flip-flop to change with respect to a trigger event on the clock input is called the propagation delay time, t_p. For asynchronous counters, all propagation delay times for each stage are additive. For instance, if a binary counter has the count of 1111_2, it will change to 0000_2 on the next clock, and the delay for the output to change from a logic-HIGH to a logic-LOW will be 25 ns. Then the delay time for the counter to go from the Fh count to 0h count will be 100 ns.

The inherent characteristics of a J-K flip-flop wired in the toggle mode produces a square ware output frequency one-half the clock frequency. Several toggle flip-flops cascaded in asynchronous mode will create a 2^N frequency divider, where N represents the number of flip-flops, as illustrated in Figrue 1. In the example of Figure 1, the total frequency division is $2^N = 2^3 = \div 8$.

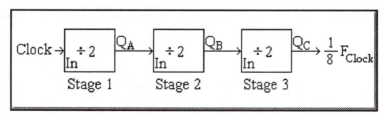

Figure 1

The modulus may be altered by using a decoder gate and wiring its output back to the clear inputs of each flip-flop. Since the clear input is asynchronous, or clock independent, the number the decoder is wired to decode will not be seen as part of the counter count sequence.

Part 1   Procedure

1.   Open the Max+plus II software. Assign the project name **counter1** and MAX7000S as the device family.

2.   Open a new Graphic Editor and create the 3-bit counter shown in Figure 2 using JKFF symbols.

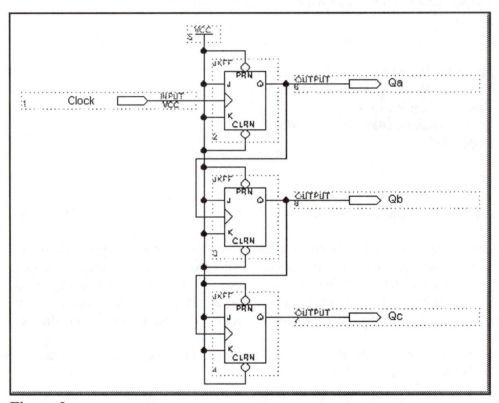

Figure 2

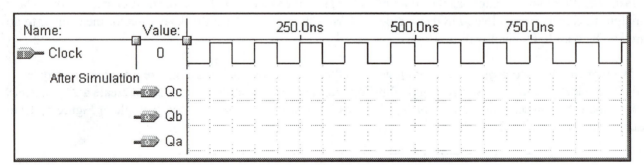

Figure 3

3.   Open a new Waveform Editor, set the Grid Size to 50 ns, and create the waveforms shown in Figure 3.

4.   Compile and simulate the circuit. Assuming zero errors, draw the resulting output waveforms in the area provided in Figure 3 above.

5. Copy the binary bit pattern for each time segment in Figure 3 into the respective cell block in Table 1, then convert the binary bit pattern to its octal equivalent.

Time Segment	Qc Qb Qa Bits (1 or 0)			Octal Value
100 to 150 ns	—	—	—	—
200 to 250 ns	—	—	—	—
300 to 350 ns	—	—	—	—
400 to 450 ns	—	—	—	—
500 to 550 ns	—	—	—	—
600 to 650 ns	—	—	—	—
700 to 750 ns	—	—	—	—
800 to 850 ns	—	—	—	—

Table 1

6. What direction does the circuit in Figure 2 count?   (Up/Down)

7. Based on your observation, the Q outputs of the circuit of Figure 2 change with respect to the (Leading/Trailing) edge of the clock applied to the circuit.

8. Turn off the Snap to Grid feature in the Options menu.

9. Press the Zoom-in button (the magnifying glass with a plus sign icon in the Draw tool bar) several times to magnify the waveforms to view only the time segment from 50 ns to 100 ns. Reposition the horizontal scroll bar as necessary to view this segment of the waveform.

10. Position the cursor on the 50 ns mark in the Waveform Editor. When you click on the 50 ns time, a vertical blue line will appear, and the Ref: box in the Waveform Editor (see Figure 4) will show 50 ns. The Time: box in the Waveform Editor shows the position of the mouse as the mouse is moved around the Waveform Editor.

Figure 4

11. Position the mouse pointer right on the blue vertical line on top of the Qa waveform, then click and hold the left mouse button down as you drag the mouse to the right. The section of the waveform you are dragging the mouse across will be highlighted (white waveform on black background) and the Interval: box will show the horizontal time of the highlighted area. Release the mouse button when the mouse pointer just touches the rising edge of the Qa waveform.

12. Record the propagation delay time it takes Qa to go from a logic-LOW to a logic-HIGH, T_{PLH}, with respect to the positive edge of the clock transition.

Qa delay at 50 ns : T_{PLH} = _____

13. Repeat Step 11 to determine the delay times for Qb and Qc with respect to the clock. Record the results below.

Qb delay at 50 ns : T_{PLH} = _____
Qc delay at 50 ns : T_{PLH} = _____

14. Position the cursor at 450 ns and determine the delay times for each waveform with respect to the clock transition.

Qa delay at 450 ns : T_{PLH} = _____
Qb delay at 450 ns : T_{PLH} = _____
Qc delay at 450 ns : T_{PLH} = _____

15. As you may have suspected, there is an easier method to determine delay times. Select the Max+plus II option in the main menu, then select the Timing Analyzer option (Figure 5).

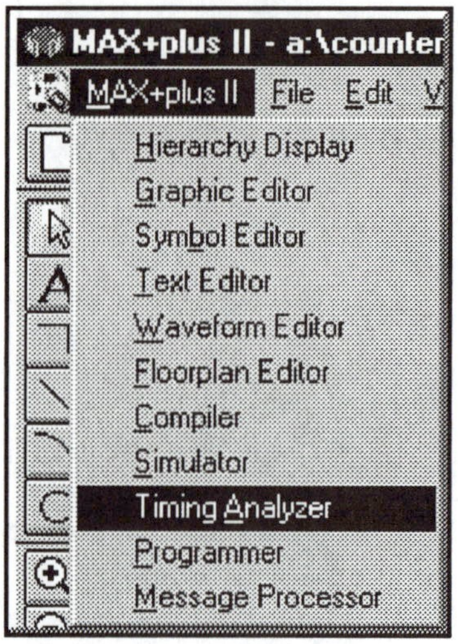

16. Press the Start button in the Timing Analyzer.

17. Press the OK button when the timing analysis is completed.

18. Maximize the Delay Matrix and record the delay times below.

	Qa	Qb	Qc
Clock			

Table 2

Figure 5

19. During the compilation, a report is generated and placed on your diskette. The report may be accessed using a word processor; however, at this time, you will be using the default text editor to view this report.

20. Recompile your **counter1** file. When finished, an icon labeled **rpt** appears directly below the Fitter box in the compiler window. Double click on this **rpt** icon (see Figure 6). You must have the Compiler window maximized to see the details within the compiler.

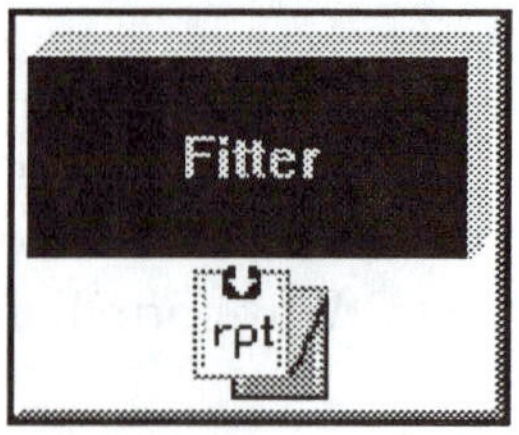

Figure 6

21. Scroll through the report file and answer the following questions.

   A. What pin was assigned to the clock input? _____
   B. How many input pins were used for your circuit? _____
   C. How many output pins were used for your circuit? _____
   D. How much was the IC utilized for the circuit of Figure 2? _____
   E. How many VCCIO pins were assigned to the chip? _____
   F. What is the acceptable voltage range for the VCCIO pins? _____
   G. What voltage is to be applied to the VCCINT pins? _____
   H. What name was assigned to the unused pins of the IC? _____
   I. What pins were labeled GND? _____
   J. What pin was Qa assigned? _____
   K. What pin was Qb assigned? _____
   L. What pin was Qc assigned? _____
   M. What was the total compilation time for this circuit? _____

22. Based on the waveforms drawn for Figure 3, the frequency of the clock was _____.

23. Based on the waveforms drawn for Figure 3, the frequency of Qa was _____.

24. Based on the waveforms drawn for Figure 3, the frequency of Qb was _____.

Lab 15: Asynchronous Counters

25. Based on the waveforms drawn for Figure 3, the frequency of Qc was _____.

26. Write a statement commenting on the frequency relationships of the outputs Qa, Qb, and Qc with respect to the clock frequency.

_____

_____

27. Save all files to Drive A as **counter1**, then exit the Graphic and Waveform Editors.

Part 2   Procedure

1. Open the Max+plus II software. Assign the project name **counter2**.

2. Open a new Graphic Editor and create the circuit shown in Figure 7.

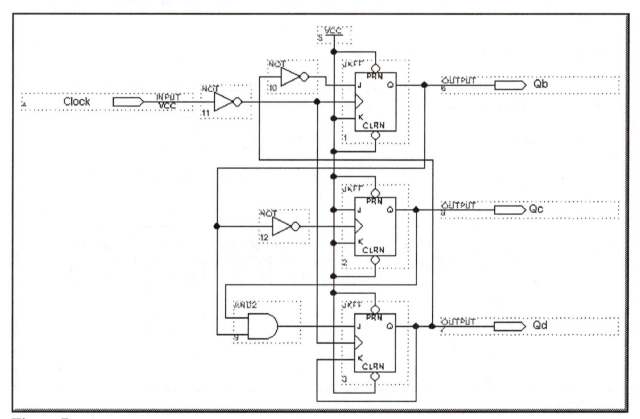

Figure 7

3. Open a new Waveform Editor, set the Grid Size to 75 ns, then construct the waveforms shown in Figure 8.

4. Compile and simulate the circuit. Assuming zero errors, draw the output waveforms in the space provided at the bottom of Figure 8.

5. Based on the resulting waveforms, the counter outputs are changing with respect to the clock's (rising/falling) edge.

6. Complete Table 3, identifying the octal value of the Q outputs, DCB, for the time segments listed.

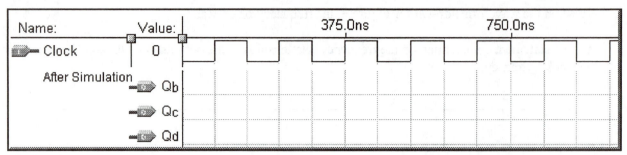

Figure 8

Time (ns)	40	110	180	260	340	400	480	560	640	710	790	860	940
DCB value													

Table 3

7.   Based on the waveforms and the DCB count sequence list in Table 3, the counter shown in Figure 7 counts ____ (Up/Down).

8.   What is the highest DCB count shown in Table 3?

9.   The counter modulus is defined as the total number of clocks it takes for the counter to count a complete count cycle. What is the modulus of the counter shown in Figure 2? _____

10.   What is the modulus of the counter shown in Figure 7? _____

11.   Set the Grid Size to 25 ns and make the necessary changes to the Waveform Editor file as shown in Figure 9.

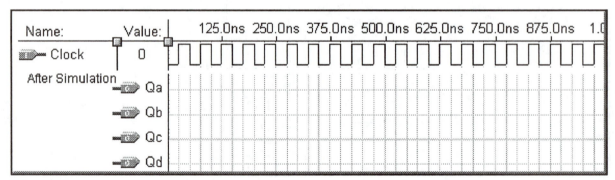

Figure 9

12.   Modify your Graphic Editor schematic to what is shown in Figure 10. Change the project name to **mod10** and save both Graphic and Waveform Editor files as **mod10**.

13.   Compile and simulate the circuit constructed. Correct all errors before continuing.

14.   Neatly draw the output waveforms in the area provided in Figure 9.

15.   Based on the results obtained for Figure 9, the counter outputs change on the ____ (rising/falling) edge of the applied clock.

Lab 15: Asynchronous Counters

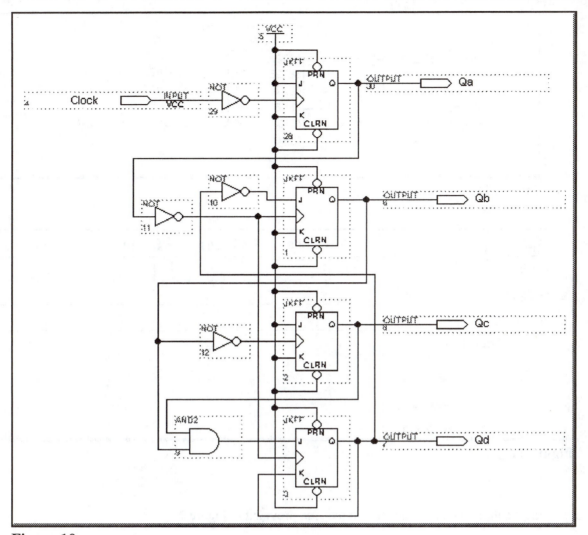

Figure 10

16.   Carefully examine the counter waveforms. What is the count sequence?

_____

17.   The modulus of an up counter may be determined by subtracting the low count from the high count, then add one to the difference. What is the modulus of the counter in Figure 10? _____

18.   Save all files to Drive A as **mod10**, then exit both Graphic and Waveform Editors.

Part 3   Procedure

1.   Open the Max+plus II software. Assign the project name **7490ctr**.

2.   Open a new Graphic Editor and construct the circuit shown in Figure 11.

3.   Open a new Waveform Editor, set the Grid Size to 40 ns, then create the waveforms shown in Figure 12.

4.   Compile, then run the simulator. Correct all errors before continuing.

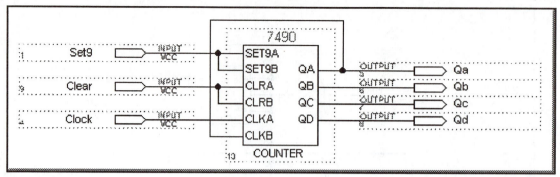

Figure 11

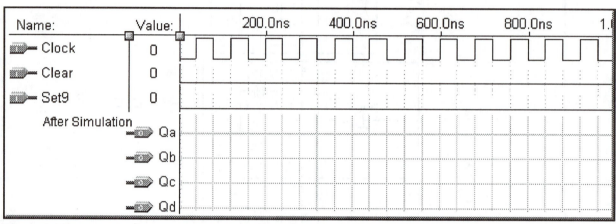

Figure 12

5.   Draw the resulting output waveforms in the area provided in Figure 12.

6.   Based on the waveforms for the 7490, the counter outputs change on the (rising/falling) edge of the applied clock.

7.   List the count sequence for the 7490.   _____

8.   Based on the waveforms, what is the modulus of the 7490? _____ (Note: This is called the natural modulus.)

9.   Highlight and change the logic level of the clear waveform from 400 ns to 600 ns to a high state.

10. Resimulate the waveforms.

11. Describe, in appropriate detail, the output waveforms for this counter based on the logic levels of the clear input.

_____

_____

_____

12. Based on the results of Step 10, the clear inputs are (asynchronous/synchronous) and are active-(LOW/HIGH).

13.   Change the SET9 waveform to a constant logic-HIGH.

14.   Highlight and set the clear input waveform to a constant logic-LOW level.

15.   Press the Simulator button.

16.   Based on the results of Step 15, the SET9 inputs are (asynchronous/synchronous) and are active-(LOW/HIGH).

17.   Describe, in appropriate detail, the effect the SET9 inputs have on this counter.

    _____

    _____

18.   Save all files to Drive A as **7490ctr**, then exit both Graphic and Waveform Editors.

Part 4   Procedure

1.   Open the Max+plus II software. Assign the project name **7493ctra**.

2.   Open a new Graphic Editor and construct the circuit shown in Figure 13.

3.   Open a new Waveform Editor, set the Grid Size to 30 ns, then create the waveforms shown in Figure 14.

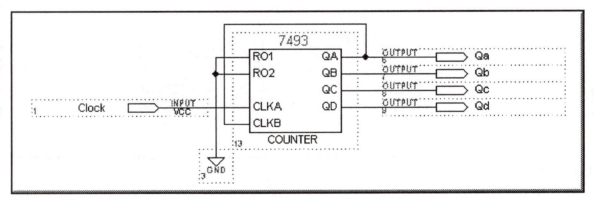

Figure 13

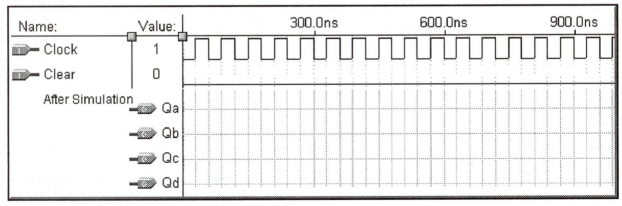

Figure 14

4.	Compile and simulate the circuit, then neatly draw the output waveforms in the space provided in Figure 14.

5.	The 7493 counter counts (Up/Down) from _____ to _____.

6.	The 7493 counter advances count on the (leading/trailing) edge of the clock signal.

7.	Set the clear input to a logic-HIGH from 600 ns to 1 μs.

8.	Resimulate the circuit and describe the effects of the clear input on the Q outputs.

_____

9.	Based on your observation of the effects of the clear input, the Clear input on the 7493 is (asynchronous/synchronous).

10.	Saving all files to Drive A as **7493ctra**, then exit both Graphic and Waveform Editors.

Part 5   Procedure

1.	Open the Max+plus II software. Assign the project name **7493ctrb**.

2.	Open a new Graphic Editor and construct the circuit shown in Figure 15.

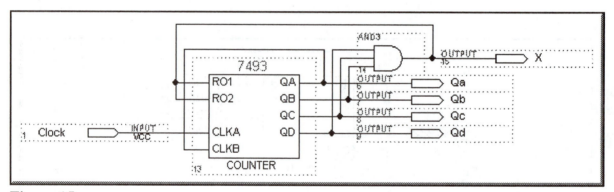

Figure 15

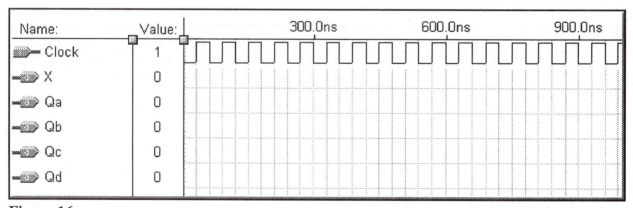

Figure 16

Lab 15: Asynchronous Counters

3.   Open a new Waveform Editor, set the Grid Size to 30 ns and create the waveforms shown in Figure 16.

4.   Draw the output waveform generated by the software after compilation and simulation.

5.   The 7493 as wired in Figure 15 counter counts (Up/Down) from _____ to _____.

6.   What count was detected by the decoder gate? _____

7.   Describe what action took place when the decoder ouput was "active."

        _____

8.   What is the natural modulus of the 7493? _____

9.   What is the modulus of the circuit shown in Figure 15? _____

10.   Save all files to Drive A as **7493ctrb**, then exit both Graphic and Waveform Editors.

Part 6   Procedure

1.   Open the Max+plus II software. Assign the project name **7493ctrc**.

2.   Open a new Graphic Editor. Use the 7493 IC and decoder gate to create a Mod 10 counter that gives a BCD count sequence.

3.   Open a new Waveform Editor and create a set of waveforms similar to Figure 16.

4.   Compile and simulate the circuit.

5.   Assuming zero errors, demonstrate the operational Mod 10 counter to the instructor. Obtain the signature of approval directly on the answer page for this lab.

6.   Obtain a hard copy of the Graphic and Waveform Editors. Label these hard copies **Part 6, Step 6a** and **Part 6, Step 6b**, respectively.

7.   Save all files to Drive A as **7493ctrc**, then exit both Graphic and Waveform Editors.

8.   Write a 1 to 2 page summary pertaining to the results obtained from this lab. Include at least one embedded graphic with corresponding waveforms after compilation and simulation.

9.   Place all papers for this lab in the following sequence, then submit the lab to your instructor for grading.
        - Cover page
        - Typed summary
        - The completed answer page for this lab
        - Print out of the Graphic Editor, **Part 6, Step 6a**
        - Print out of the Waveform Editor, **Part 6, Step 6b**

Lab 15: Asynchronous Counters Answer Page   Name: _____

Part 1

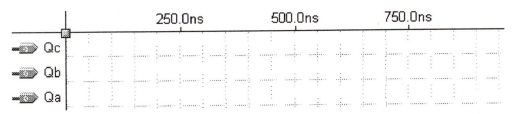

Figure 3

Time Segment	Qc Qb Qa Bits (1 or 0)	Octal Value
100 to 150 ns	— — —	—
200 to 250 ns	— — —	—
300 to 350 ns	— — —	—
400 to 450 ns	— — —	—
500 to 550 ns	— — —	—
600 to 650 ns	— — —	—
700 to 750 ns	— — —	—
800 to 850 ns	— — —	—

Table 1

6.   UP / DOWN

7.   Leading / Trailing

12. Qa delay at 50 ns : T_{PLH} = _____

13. Qb delay at 50 ns : T_{PLH} = _____

Qc delay at 50 ns : T_{PLH} = _____

14.   Qa delay at 450 ns : T_{PLH} = _____
Qb delay at 450 ns : T_{PLH} = _____
Qc delay at 450 ns : T_{PLH} = _____

	Qa	Qb	Qc
Clock			

Table 2

21. A. _____

B. _____

C. _____

D. _____   E. _____   F. _____   G. _____

H. ____ _____   I. _____   J. _____   K. _____

L. _____   M. _____

1.   _____   23. _____   24. _____   25. _____

26.   _____

_____

Part 2

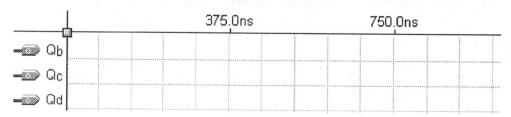

Figure 8

5.   (rising/falling)

Time (ns)	40	110	180	260	340	400	480	560	640	710	790	860	940
DCB value													

Table 3

7.   (Up/Down)   8. _____   9. _____   10. _____

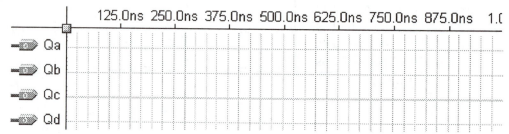

Figure 9

15.   (rising/falling)

16.   _____

17.   _____

Part 3

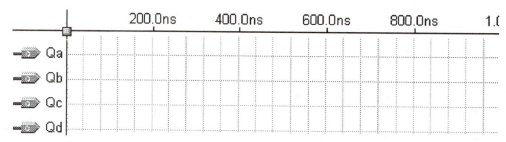

Figure 12

6.   (rising/falling)   7.   _____

8.   _____   11.   _____

_____

_____

12.   (asynchronous/synchronous) (LOW/HIGH)

16.   (asynchronous/synchronous) (LOW/HIGH)

17.   _____

      _____

Part 4

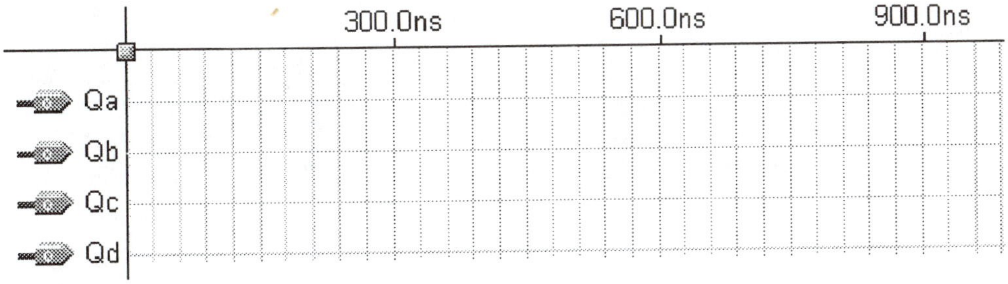

Figure 14

5.   (Up/Down) from _____ to _____.   6.   (leading/trailing)

8.   _____

9.   (asynchronous/synchronous)

Part 5

5.   (Up/Down) from _____ to _____.   6.   _____

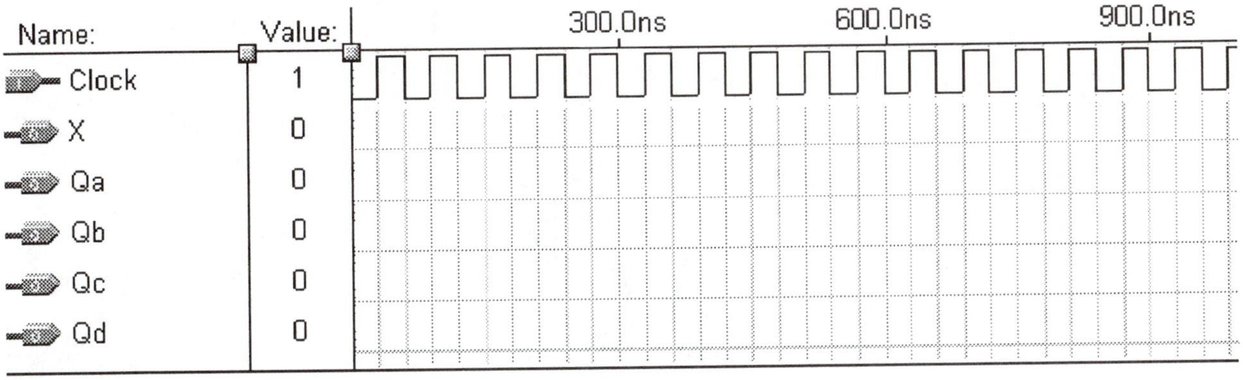

Figure 16

7.   _____

8.   _____   9.   _____

Part 6

5.   Demonstrated to: _____ Date: _____

Grade: _____

Lab 16: Synchronous Counters

Objectives:

1. Create a 3-bit (Modulus 8) synchronous binary counter using J-K flip-flops
2. Create a 4-bit (Modulus 16) synchronous binary counter using J-K flip-flops
3. Use the Timing Analyzer to determine propagation delays
4. Construct a 4-bit decade counter using the 74190 integrated circuit
5. Construct a 4-bit binary counter using the 74191 integrated circuit
6. Cascading two counters, making a Mod 100 or Mod 256 counter
7. Change the counter modulus using full or partial decoding

Materials List:

♦ Max+plus II software by Altera Corporation
♦ University Board by Altera Corporation (optional)
♦ Computer requirements:
   Minimum 486/66 with 8 MB RAM
♦ Floppy disk

Discussion:

One disadvantage of asynchronous counters is that propagation delays are additive, making asynchronous counters low frequency devices. Synchronous counters eliminate this problem for all flip-flop clock inputs that are tied to the same source, as a result all flip-flops are triggered at the same time. With asynchronous counters, the clock of each flip-flop was clocked by the previous Q output. With synchronous counters, the Q output of previous stages determines the mode of flip-flop operation as either toggle or no-change when the next clock arrives. For the toggle condition, both J and K inputs are a logic-HIGH. For the no-change condition, J and K inputs are both a logic-LOW.

The preset and clear inputs of the flip-flops may be used to load a number into the counter or to clear the counter to zero. These asynchronous inputs are disabled for Part 1 and Part 2 of this lab by wiring all PRE and CLR inputs to Vcc. The PRE and CLR inputs will be demonstrated once counter ICs are introduced.

The 74190 and 74191 integrated circuits will be the focus of this lab. Both chips have identical pin assignments and identical control functions. The counter enable, CTEN, input is active-LOW and is considered to be an synchronous input since CTEN affects the synchronous J and K inputs to the first flip-flop in the counter. The presettable inputs, D,C,B, and A, are controlled by the asynchronous LOAD input, which is also active-LOW. The counters may count UP or DOWN as determined by the logic state applied to the D/U input. The 74190 is a BCD, 0 to 9, counter whereas the 74191 is a 4-bit binary counter, 0 to F. Both CTEN and LOAD are active-LOW.

As with the asynchronous counter, full and partial decoding will be demonstrated as the modulus of the 74191 counter changes. A decoder glitch in the output waveforms will appear any time a decoder is used to change the modules.

Part 1   Procedure

1. Open the Max+plus II software. Assign the project name **sync-ctr**.

2. Open a new Graphic Editor and construct the circuit shown in Figure 1.

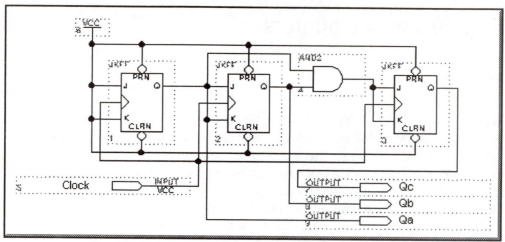

Figure 1

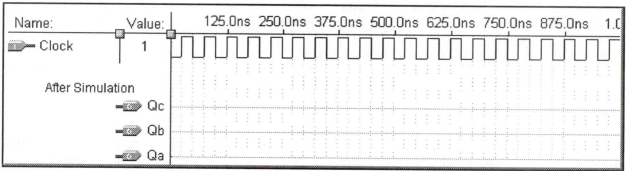

Figure 2

3. Open a new Waveform Editor, set the Grid Size to 25 ns, then create the waveforms shown in Figure 2.

4. Run the Compiler and Simulator. Draw the resulting output waveforms in the area provided in Figure 2.

5. What direction does the circuit in Figure 2 count? (Up/Down)

6. Based on your observation, the Q outputs of the circuit of Figure 2 change with respect to the (Leading/Trailing) edge of the clock applied to the circuit.

7. Copy the binary bit pattern for each time segment in Figure 3 into the respective cell block in Table 1, then convert the binary bit pattern to its octal equivalent.

Time Segment	Qc Qb Qa Bits (1 or 0)	Octal Value
0 to 25 ns	__ __ __	___
25 to 75 ns	__ __ __	___
75 to 125 ns	__ __ __	___
125 to 175 ns	__ __ __	___
175 to 225 ns	__ __ __	___
225 to 275 ns	__ __ __	___
275 to 325 ns	__ __ __	___
325 to 375 ns	__ __ __	___

Table 1

Lab 16: Synchronous Counters

8.   Open the Timing Analyzer and press the Start button in the Delay Matrix window.

9.   Record the delay times in Table 2 for the Q outputs with respect to the clock signal.

Qa Delay	Qb Delay	Qc Delay

Table 2

10.   Recompile your **sync-ctr** file. When finished, an icon labeled **rpt** appears directly below the Fitter box in the Compiler window. Double click on this **rpt** icon (see Figure 3). You must have the Compiler window maximized to see the details within the compiler.

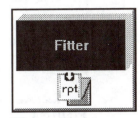

Figure 3

11.   Scroll through the report file and answer the following questions.

    A.   What pin was assigned to the clock input? _____
    B.   How many input pins were used for your circuit? _____
    C.   How many output pins were used for your circuit? _____
    D.   How much was the IC utilized for the circuit of Figure 2? _____
    E.   How many VCCIO pins were assigned to the chip? _____
    F.   What is the acceptable voltage range for the VCCIO pins? _____
    G.   What voltage is to be applied to the VCCINT pins? _____
    H.   What name was assigned to the unused pins of the IC? _____
    I.   What pins were labeled GND? _____
    J.   What pin was Qa assigned? _____
    K.   What pin was Qb assigned? _____
    L.   What pin was Qc assigned? _____
    M.   What was the total compilation time for this circuit? _____

12.   Based on the waveforms drawn for Figure 2, the frequency of the clock was _____.

13.   Based on the waveforms drawn for Figure 2, the frequency of Qa was _____.

14.   Based on the waveforms drawn for Figure 2, the frequency of Qb was _____.

15.   Based on the waveforms drawn for Figure 2, the frequency of Qc was _____.

16.   Write a statement commenting on the frequency relationships of the outputs Qa, Qb, and Qc with respect to the clock frequency.

_____

_____

17.   Save all files to Drive A as **sync-ctr**, then exit the Graphic and Waveform Editors.

Part 2   Procedure

1.   Open the Max+plus II software. Assign the project name **sync-ctr**.

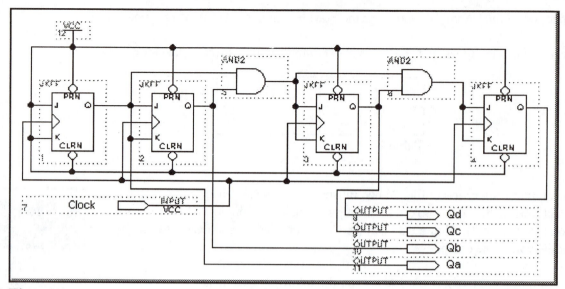

Figure 4

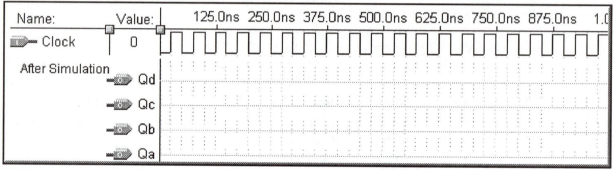

Figure 5

2.   Open a new Graphic Editor and construct the circuit shown in Figure 4 using the **jkff** symbol.

3.   Open a new Waveform Editor, set the Grid Size to 25 ns, then create the waveforms shown in Figure 5.

4.   Run the compiler and simulator. Draw the resulting output waveforms in the area provided in Figure 5.

5.   Copy the binary bit pattern for each time segment in Figure 3 into the respective cell block in Table 3, then convert the binary bit pattern to its octal equivalent.

Time Segment	Qd Qc Qb Qa Bits (1 or 0)	Octal Value	Time Segment	Qd Qc Qb Qa Bits (1 or 0)	Octal Value
0 to 25 ns	__ __ __ __	____	375 to 425 ns	__ __ __ __	____
25 to 75 ns	__ __ __ __	____	425 to 475 ns	__ __ __ __	____
75 to 125 ns	__ __ __ __	____	475 to 425 ns	__ __ __ __	____
125 to 175 ns	__ __ __ __	____	525 to 475 ns	__ __ __ __	____
175 to 225 ns	__ __ __ __	____	575 to 525 ns	__ __ __ __	____
225 to 275 ns	__ __ __ __	____	625 to 675 ns	__ __ __ __	____
275 to 325 ns	__ __ __ __	____	675 to 625 ns	__ __ __ __	____
325 to 375 ns	__ __ __ __	____	725 to 775 ns	__ __ __ __	____

Table 3

6.   What direction does the circuit in Figure 4 count?   (Up/Down)

7.   Based on your observation, the Q outputs of the circuit of Figure 4 change with respect to the (Leading/Trailing) edge of the clock applied to the circuit.

8.   Open the Timing Analyzer and press the Start button in the Delay Matrix window.

9.   Examine the time delays shown in the Delay Matrix window and explain how the addition of the fourth stage affected the total propagation delay of the counter as compared to the 3-stage counter of Figure 2.

_____

10.   Scroll through the report file and answer the following questions.

   A.   What pin was assigned to the clock input? _____
   B.   How many input pins were used for your circuit? _____
   C.   How many output pins were used for your circuit? _____
   D.   How much was the IC utilized for the circuit of Figure 2? _____
   E.   What pin was Qa assigned? _____
   F.   What pin was Qb assigned? _____
   G.   What pin was Qc assigned? _____
   H.   What pin was Qd assigned? _____
   I.   What was the total compilation time for this circuit? _____

11.   Based on the waveforms shown in Figure 5, what is the clock frequency? _____

12.   Based on the waveforms shown in Figure 5, what is the frequency of Qd? _____

13.   Divide your answer to Question 11 by your answer to Question 12. The quotient is _____.

14.   The modulus of the counter is the total number of clocks required for the counter to count through its count cycle. What is the modulus of the circuit constructed in Figure 4? _____

15.   Save all files to Drive A as **mod16ctr**, then exit the Graphic and Waveform Editors.

Part 3   Procedure

1.   Open the Max+plus II software. Assign the project name **mod10ic**.

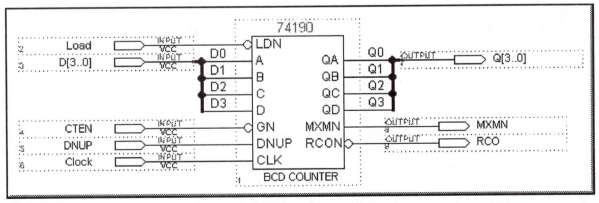

Figure 6

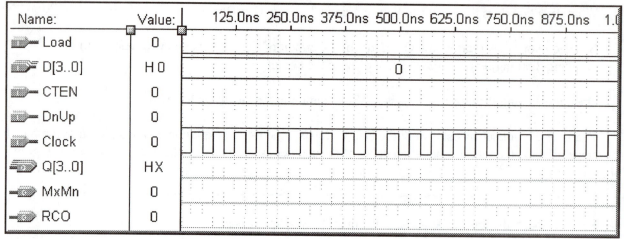

Figure 7

2.   Open the Graphic Editor and construct the circuit shown in Figure 6 using the 74190 symbol.

3.   Open the Waveform Editor and create the waveforms as shown in Figure 7.

4.   Run the compiler and simulator. Correct all errors before continuing.

5.   What count appears on the Q[3..0] output? _____

6.   Highlight the D[3..0] waveform and press the Group Waveform Overwrite icon
        (see Figure 8) in the Draw tool bar.

Figure 8

7.   Assign the Group Value: 3.

8.   Press the Simulate button.

9.   What count appears on the Q[3..0] output? _____

10.   Change the section of the load waveform from 500 ns to 1 μs to a logic-HIGH level.

11.   Press the Simulate button.

12.   What count appears on the Q[3..0] output from 0 to 500 ns? _____

13.   What count appears on the Q[3..0] output from 500 ns to 1 μs? _____

14.   Based on the results obtained from Steps 4 through 14, the load input to the 74190 is
        (synchronous/asynchronous).

15.   Based on the results obtained from Steps 4 through 14, the load input to the 74190 is active-
        (LOW/HIGH).

16.   Change the load waveform to a constant logic-HIGH level from 0 ns to 1 μs.

17.   Press the Simulate button.

18.   Draw the resulting output waveforms in the area provided in Figure 7.

19. Demonstrate the circuit you created to your instructor. Obtain the signature of approval directly on the answer page for this lab.

20. Obtain a hard copy of the Graphic and Waveform files. Label these hard copies **Part 3, Step 21A** and **Part 3, Step 21B**.

21. Save all files to Drive A as **mod10ic**, then exit the Graphic and Waveform Editors.

22. Write a 1 to 2 page summary pertaining to the results obtained from this lab. Include embedded graphics as part of your summary.

23. Place all papers for this lab in the following sequence, then submit the lab to your instructor for grading.

- Cover page
- Typed summary
- The completed answer page for this lab
- Printout of the Graphic Editor, **Part 3, Step 21A**
- Printout of the Waveform Editor, **Part 3, Step 21B**

Part 1

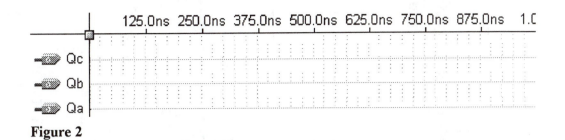

Figure 2

5. _____ (UP/DOWN)   6. _____ (Leading/Trailing)

Time Segment	Qc Qb Qa Bits (1 or 0)	Octal Value
0 to 25 ns	— — —	—
25 to 75 ns	— — —	—
75 to 125 ns	— — —	—
125 to 175 ns	— — —	—
175 to 225 ns	— — —	—
225 to 275 ns	— — —	—
275 to 325 ns	— — —	—
325 to 375 ns	— — —	—

Table 1

Qa Delay	Qb Delay	Qc Delay

Table 2

11. A. _____

B. _____

C. _____

D. _____

11. (Cont.)

E. _____   F. _____   G. _____   H. _____

I. _____   J. _____   K. _____   L. _____

M. _____

12. _____   13. _____   14. _____   15. _____

16. _____

_____

Part 2

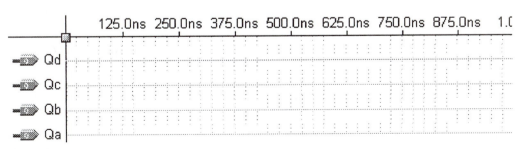

Figure 5

Time Segment	Qd Qc Qb Qa Bits (1 or 0)	Octal Value	Time Segment	Qd Qc Qb Qa Bits (1 or 0)	Octal Value
0 to 25 ns	__ __ __ __	___	375 to 425 ns	__ __ __ __	___
25 to 75 ns	__ __ __ __	___	425 to 475 ns	__ __ __ __	___
75 to 125 ns	__ __ __ __	___	475 to 425 ns	__ __ __ __	___
125 to 175 ns	__ __ __ __	___	525 to 475 ns	__ __ __ __	___
175 to 225 ns	__ __ __ __	___	575 to 525 ns	__ __ __ __	___
225 to 275 ns	__ __ __ __	___	625 to 675 ns	__ __ __ __	___
275 to 325 ns	__ __ __ __	___	675 to 625 ns	__ __ __ __	___
325 to 375 ns	__ __ __ __	___	725 to 775 ns	__ __ __ __	___

Table 3

6.   (UP/DOWN)   7.   (Leading/Trailing)

9.   _____

10.   A. _____   B. _____   C. _____

D. _____   E. _____   F. _____

G. _____   H. _____   I. _____

11.   _____   12.   _____   13. _____

14.   _____

Part 3

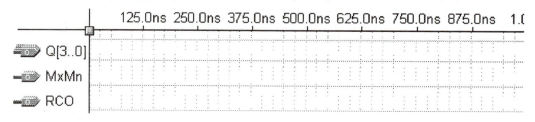

Figure 7

6.   _____   10.   _____   13.   _____   14.   _____

15.   synchronous/asynchronous   16.   LOW/HIGH

20.   Demonstrated to: _____ Date: _____

Grade: _____

Lab 17: Shift Registers

Objectives:

1. Construct and demonstrate the serial shifting of data through D-type flip-flops
2. Analyze the 74194 constructed as a serial right or serial left shift register
3. Construct and demonstrate parallel shifting of data through several 74194s
4. Construct and analyze a parallel in, serial out shift register
5. Construct and analyze a serial in, parallel out shift register

Materials List:

♦ Max+plus II software by Altera Corporation
♦ University Board by Altera Corporation (optional)
♦ Computer requirements:
  Minimum 486/66 with 8 MB RAM
♦ Floppy disk

Discussion:

Figure 1 shows a basic 4-bit shift register using four transparent D-type flip-flops with synchronous clocking. Data applied to the D input of flip-flop A will appear on the Q output of flip-flop A when a rising edge of the clock appears. Since Qa is the data input to flip-flop B, the content that was in flip-flop A will be transferred to flip-flop B at the same time data was entered into flip-flop A. This data shifting is illustrated in Figure 2.

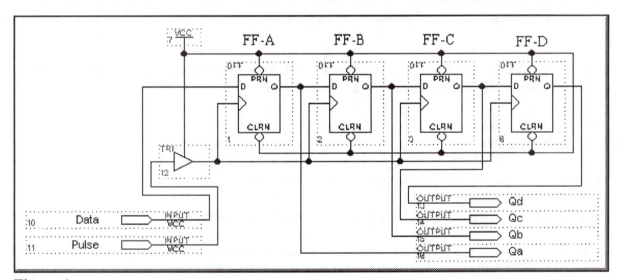

Figure 1

Initially, at time t_0, all flip-flops contain logic-LOWs and the data is a logic-HIGH. When the rising edge of the clock occurs at time t_1, the high state of the data is moved into flip-flop A. The content that was in flip-flop A was transferred to flip-flop B, the content that was in flip-flop B was transferred to flip-flop C, the content that was in flip-flop C was transferred to flip-flop D, and the content that was in flip-flop D was shifted out to the next stage, if one exists. Since all flip-flops initially contained zeros, the shifting may not be obvious, but now the flip-flops contain 1_H, 0001_2.

Notice the data shifting that takes place at the second rising edge of the clock at time t_2. Since the data input is a logic-HIGH, that data is shifted into flip-flop A. The logic-HIGH that was in flip-flop A shifted to flip-flop B. Of

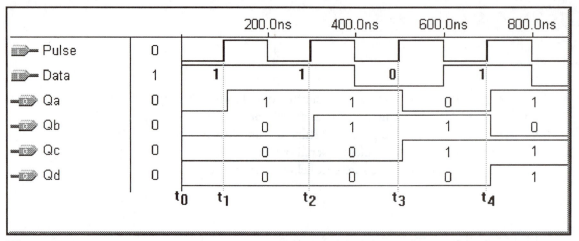

Figure 2

course, the contents of flip-flop C moved to flip-flop D and the contents in flip-flop D moved on to the next stage. The flip-flops now contain 3_H, 0011_2.

On the third clock pulse at time t_3, the logic-LOW at the data input is transferred to flip-flop A. As the original contents of each flip-flop is transferred to the next, the flip-flops now contain 6_H, 0110_2. At t_4, flip-flop A receives a logic-HIGH and the data in each flip-flop is shifted to the next flip-flop, resulting in D_H, 1101_2, now stored in "memory." It takes one clock pulse to shift one data bit one flip-flop position. This equates to 4 clock pulses to shift one nibble of data through four flip-flops.

Note the final contents of the four flip-flops contain 1101_2, the same sequence of the bits applied on the data input. Data shifting from the least significant flip-flop (A) to the most significant flip-flop (D in this case) is called right shifting.

The 74194 is a 4-bit shift register that may be wired to serial shift data either right or left, or parallel shift four bits, simultaneously. Various shifting techniques will be studied using the 74194.

Part 1   Procedure

1.   Open the Max+plus II software. Assign the project name **reg-1**.

2.   Open a new Graphic Editor and construct the circuit shown in Figure 1.

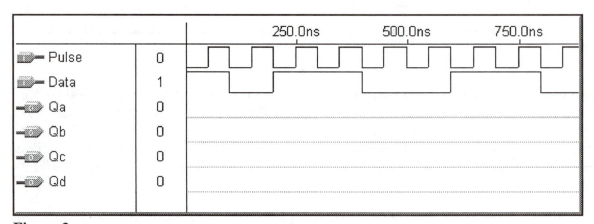

Figure 3

3. Open a new Waveform Editor, set the Grid Size to 50 ns, and create the waveforms shown in Figure 3.

4. Run the compiler and simulator. Correct all errors before continuing.

5. Neatly and accurately draw the output waveforms in the area provided in Figure 3.

6. Record the bit pattern of the Data waveform, copying the logic level of the data that is present just before the rising edge of each clock pulse (8 bits required).

    Data sequence applied: _____ $_2$

7. Complete Table 1, showing the data shifting through the flip-flops after each rising edge of the clock pulse. Read "Bit D" as the most significant bit when converting the bit pattern to hexadecimal.

Data Applied	Flip-flop A B C D	Clock Pulse	Contents (in HEX)
_____ $_2$ (from Step 6)	0 0 0 0	Initial	0_H
	_ _ _ _	1st	_____
	_ _ _ _	2nd	_____
	_ _ _ _	3rd	_____
	_ _ _ _	4th	_____
	_ _ _ _	5th	_____
	_ _ _ _	6th	_____
	_ _ _ _	7th	_____
	_ _ _ _	8th	_____

Table 1

8. Save all files to Drive A as **reg-1**, then exit the Graphic and Waveform Editors.

Part 2   Procedure

1. Open the Max+plus II software. Assign the project name **reg-2**.

2. Open a new Graphic Editor and construct the circuit shown in Figure 4.

3. Open the Waveform Editor, set the Grid Size to 50 ns, and create the waveforms shown in Figure 5.

4. Run the compiler and simulator. Correct all errors before continuing.

5. Refer to the function table for the 74194, Table 2, for the shift register and explain why the outputs are a constant logic-LOW.

    _____

6. Highlight and set the S0 waveform to a logic-HIGH.

7. Press the Simulate button.

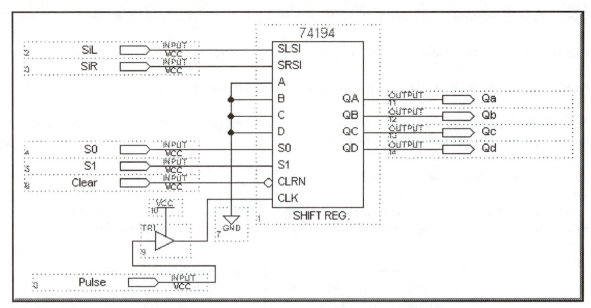

Figure 4

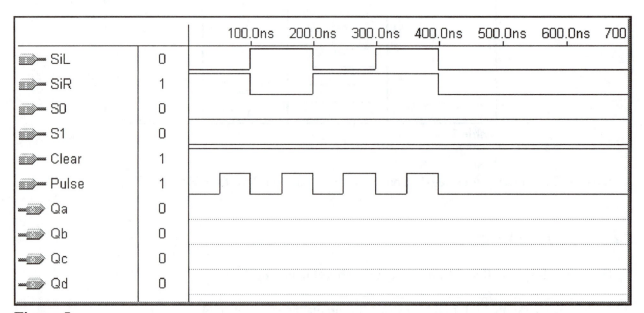

Figure 5

Inputs									Outputs			
Clear	Mode S1 S0		Clock	Serial Left Right		Parallel A B C D				Qa Qb Qc Qd		
Clear	S1	S0	Clock	Left	Right	A	B	C	D	Qa	Qb	Qc	Qd
L	X	X	X	X	X	X	X	X	X	L	L	L	L
H	X	X	L	X	X	X	X	X	X	Qao	Qbo	Qco	Qdo
H	X	X	↑	X	X	a	b	c	d	a	b	c	d
H	L	H	↑	X	H	X	X	X	X	H	Qan	Qbn	Qcn
H	L	H	↑	X	L	X	X	X	X	L	Qan	Qbn	Qcn
H	H	L	↑	H	X	X	X	X	X	Qbn	Qcn	Qdn	H
H	L	L	↑	L	X	X	X	X	X	Qbn	Qcn	Qdn	L
H	L	L	X	X	X	X	X	X	X	Qao	Qbo	Qco	Qdo

Table 2   Function table for the 74194

8. Refer to the function table for the 74194 and explain how the inputs are affecting the outputs for the 74194 register.

_____

9. Neatly and accurately draw the resulting output waveforms in the area provided in Figure 5.

10. Complete Table 3 showing the shifting pattern for the register when S1 = 0 and S0 = 1.

Clock	SiR Data	A B C D	Hex value
Initial	____	0 0 0 0	0_H
1st	___	___ ___ ___ ___	_____
2nd	___	___ ___ ___ ___	_____
3rd	___	___ ___ ___ ___	_____
4th	___	___ ___ ___ ___	_____

Table 3

11. Highlight and set the S0 waveform to a logic-LOW.

12. Highlight and set the S1 waveform to a logic-HIGH.

13. Press the Simulate button.

14. Refer to the function table for the 74194 and explain how the inputs are affecting the outputs for the 74194 register.

_____

15. Neatly and accurately draw the resulting output waveforms in the area provided in Figure 6.

16. Complete Table 4 showing the shifting pattern for the register when S1 = 1 and S0 = 0.

17. Based on the results shown in Figure 6, the shift register is wired for (RIGHT/LEFT) shift.

18. Highlight and set the clear waveform to a logic-LOW.

19. Press the Simulate button.

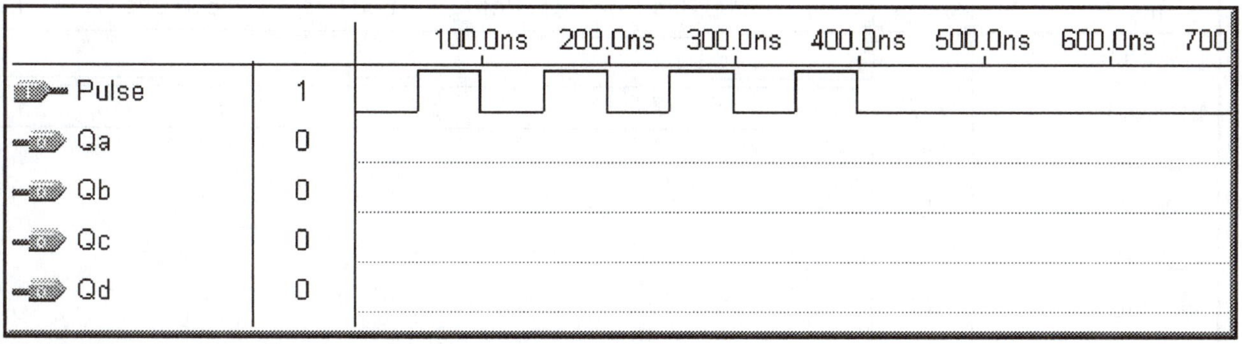

Figure 6

Clock	SiL Data	D C B A	Hex value
Initial	___	0 0 0 0	0_H
1st	___	___ ___ ___ ___	___
2nd	___	___ ___ ___ ___	___
3rd	___	___ ___ ___ ___	___
4th	___	___ ___ ___ ___	___

Table 4

20.   Based on the results obtained and the function table, which input is dominant? (SiR , SiL, Clear)

21.   Save all files to Drive A as **reg-2**, then exit the Graphic and Waveform Editors.

Part 3   Procedure

1.   Open the Max+plus II software. Assign the project name **reg-3**.

2.   Open a new Graphic Editor and construct the circuit shown in Figure 7.

3.   Open the Waveform Editor, set the Grid Size to 100 ns, and create the waveforms shown in Figure 8.

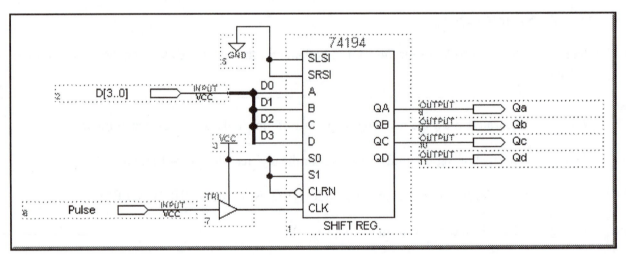

Figure 7

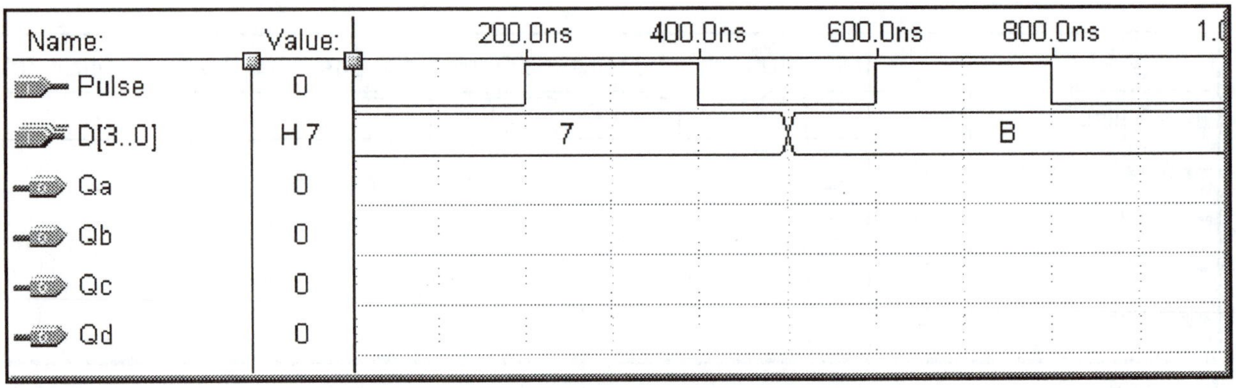

Figure 8

4.   Run the compiler and simulator. Correct all errors before continuing.

5.   Neatly and accurately draw the resulting output waveforms in the area at the bottom of Figure 8.

6.   At what time(s) did the data on the DCBA inputs get loaded into the 74194? _____ ns

7.   What mode of operation is the 74194 shown in Figure 7 wired for? _____

8.   How many clock pulses did it take to load 7_H into the four flip-flops contained within the 74194?
      _____

9.   Save all files to Drive A as **reg-3**, then exit the Graphic and Waveform Editors.

Part 4   Procedure

1.   Open the Max+plus II software. Assign the project name **reg-4**.

2.   Open a new Graphic Editor and construct the circuit shown in Figure 9.

3.   Open a new Waveform Editor, set the Grid Size to 100 ns, and create the waveforms shown in Figure 10.

4.   Run the compiler and simulator. Correct all errors before continuing.

5.   Neatly and accurately draw the resulting waveforms in the area provided at the bottom of Figure 10.

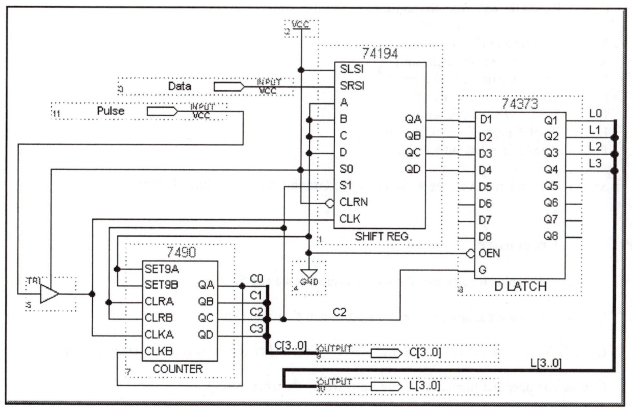

Figure 9

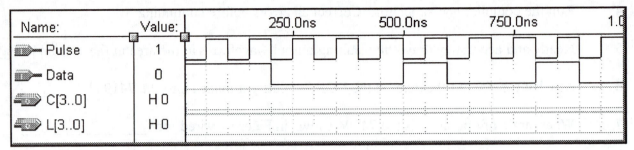

Figure 10

6. Identify the count sequence of the counter. _____

7. What number is decoded by the counter? _____

8. When C2 of the counter is a logic-LOW, the 74194 is wired as a _?_ register.
    A. Serial shift right
    B. Serial shift left
    C. Parallel in

9. When C2 of the counter goes to a logic-HIGH, the 74373
    A. Shuts off
    B. Latches onto the register data
    C. Passes the data from the register

10. When C2 of the counter goes to a logic-LOW due to counter reset, the 74373
    A. Shuts off
    B. Latches onto the register data
    C. Passes the data from the register

11. The circuit shown in Figure 9 is a
    A. Serial in/serial out right shift
    B. Serial in/serial out left shift
    C. Serial in right/parallel out
    D. Serial in left/parallel out
    E. Parallel in/serial out right shift
    F. Parallel in/serial out left shift

12. Save all files to Drive A as **reg-4**, then exit the Graphic and Waveform Editors.

Part 5   Procedure

1. Open the Max+plus II software. Assign the project name **reg-5**.

2. Open a new Graphic Editor and construct the circuit shown in Figure 11.

3. Open the Waveform Editor, set the Grid Size to 50 ns, and create the waveforms shown in Figure 12.

4. Run the compiler and simulator. Correct all errors before continuing.

5. Neatly and accurately draw the output waveforms in the area provided at the bottom of Figure 12.

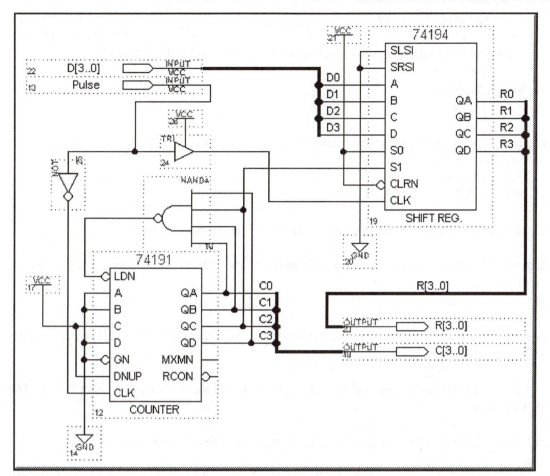

Figure 11

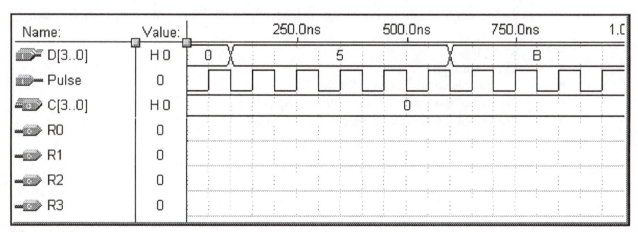

Figure 12

6. Based on the waveforms, the counter advances on the (positive/negative) edge of the pulse.

7. Based on the waveforms, the register shifts data on the (positive/negative) edge of the pulse.

8. What number is decoded in the counter circuit? _____

9. What number is loaded in the counter circuit? _____

10. What is the modulus of the counter? _____

11. What is the mode of operation for the register when the counter is on the 4 count?
    A. Si/So right shift
    B. Si/So left shift
    C. Parallel shift

12. What mode of operation is the register when the counter is not on the 4 count?
    A. Si/So right shift
    B. Si/So left shift
    C. Parallel shift

13. What is the data inputted to the register when the counter is counting from 3 to 0? _____

14. The majority of the time, the register is serially shifting data. Which register output would be used during serial shift mode?
    A. Qa   B. Qb   C. Qc   D. Qd

15. Demonstrate the circuit you created to your instructor. Obtain the signature of approval directly on the answer page for this lab.

16. Obtain a hard copy of the Graphic and Waveform files. Label these hard copies **Part 5, Step 16A** and **Part 5, Step 16B**.

17. Save all files to Drive A as **reg-5**, then exit the Graphic and Waveform Editors.

18. Write a 1 to 2 page summary pertaining to the results obtained from this lab. Explain the operation of Figure 11 and include the circuit and simulated waveforms as embedded graphics in your summary.

19. Place all papers for this lab in the following sequence, then submit the lab to your instructor for grading.

    ■ Cover page
    ■ Typed summary
    ■ The completed answer page for this lab
    ■ Printout of the Graphic Editor, **Part 5, Step 16A**
    ■ Printout of the Waveform Editor, **Part 5, Step 16B**

Lab 17: Shift Registers Answer Page Name: ____________________

Part 1

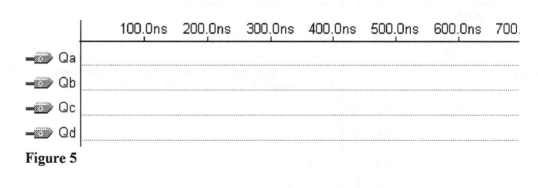

250.0ns
500.0ns
750.0ns
Qa
Qb
Qc
Qd

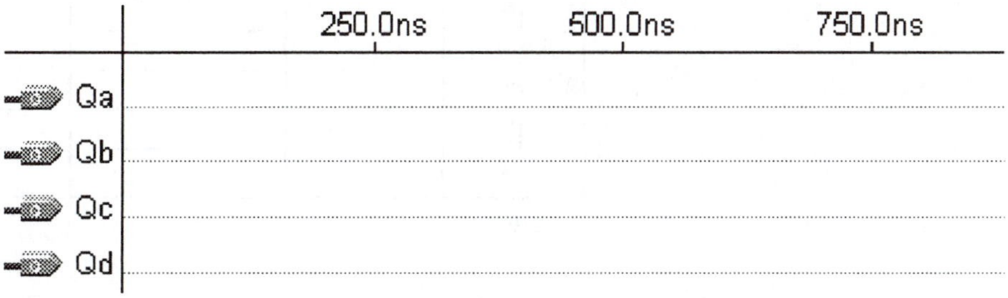

Figure 3

6. ____________[2]

Data Applied	Flip-flop A B C D	Clock Pulse	Contents (in HEX)
________[2]	0 0 0 0	Initial	0_H
(from Step 6)	__ __ __ __	1st	____
	__ __ __ __	2nd	____
	__ __ __ __	3rd	____
	__ __ __ __	4th	____
	__ __ __ __	5th	____
	__ __ __ __	6th	____
	__ __ __ __	7th	____
	__ __ __ __	8th	____

Table 1

Part 2

100.0ns
200.0ns
300.0ns
400.0ns
500.0ns
600.0ns
700.
Qa
Qb
Qc
Qd

Figure 5

5. ____

8. ____

Clock	SiR Data	A B C D	Hex value
Initial	——	0 0 0 0	0$_H$
1st	——	—— —— —— ——	——
2nd	——	—— —— —— ——	——
3rd	——	—— —— —— ——	——
4th	——	—— —— —— ——	——

Table 3

14. _____

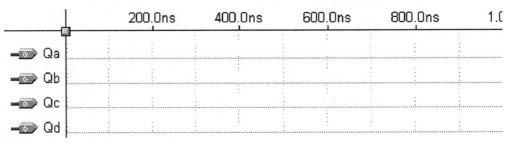

Figure 6

Clock	SiL Data	A B C D	Hex value
Initial	——	0 0 0 0	0$_H$
1st	——	—— —— —— ——	——
2nd	——	—— —— —— ——	——
3rd	——	—— —— —— ——	——
4th	——	—— —— —— ——	——

Table 4

17. RIGHT/LEFT

20. SiR   SiL   Clear

Part 3

Figure 8

6. _____ ns   7. _____   8. _____

Part 4

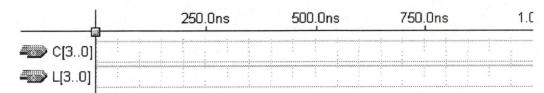

Figure 10

6. _____   7.   _____

8.   A B C   9.   A B C   10.   A B C   11.   A B C D E F

Part 5

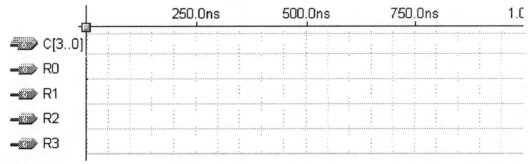

Figure 12

6.   Positive/Negative   7.   Positive/Negative   8.   _____

9.   _____   10.   _____   11.   A B C

12.   A B C   13.   _____   14.   A B C D

15.   Demonstrated to: _____ Date: _____

Grade: _____

Lab 18: Johnson and Ring Counters

Objectives:

1. Construct and evaluate the bit shift pattern of a ring counter
2. Use a ring counter to multiply and divide by two
3. Construct and evaluate the shift pattern of a Johnson counter

Materials list:

- Max+plus II software by Altera Corporation
- University Board by Altera Corporation (optional)
- Computer requirements:
    Minimum 486/66 with 8 MB RAM
- Floppy disk

Discussion:

Johnson and ring counters are circuits made from shift registers. To make a ring counter, wire the serial output back to the serial input. To make a Johnson counter, wire the serial output through an inverter, then the output of the inverter is wired back to the serial input of the register. Of course, if the serial input is used to load new data into the register, then the feedback signal and the serial input signal are to be multiplexed so only one signal source will be used at a time. This lab will use a 2-line to 1-line multiplexer for data selection. If data is first parallel (not serial) loaded into the register, then the multiplexer would not be needed.

Ring counters allow one to read the contents of a shift register without destroying the contents of the register. As the data is outputted, it is also fed back to the serial input. Since a register shifts data one flip-flop position on each clock, a 4-bit shift register will take four clock pulses to load (and output) four bits of data. This nondestructive readout of the ring counter may be a useful feature when programming in assembly language.

Right shift ring counters may also be used to multiply the contents of the register by two, as long as the most significant bit in the register is a logic-LOW. Left shift ring counters may divide the contents of the register by two, as long as the least significant bit is a logic-LOW. The respective bits should be checked before multiplying or dividing or else an overflow may occur. An overflow condition exists if the answer is too large to fit into the register. For instance, the maximum number that an 8-bit register can hold is FF_H. Multiplying $7F_H$ (01111111_2) by 2 (10_H) will give FE_H (11111110_2) as an answer; 80_H times 2 will yield 01_H due to feeding back a logic-HIGH. This will become more apparent while completing the lab.

The bit pattern of Johnson and ring counters will be examined, as well as each counter modules.

Part 1   Procedure

1. Open the Max+plus II software. Assign the project name **ring1**.

2. Open the Graphic Editor and construct the circuit shown in Figure 1.

3. Open the Waveform Editor, set the Grid Size to 30 ns, and create the waveforms shown in Figure 2.

4. Press the Compiler and Simulator buttons. Correct all errors before continuing.

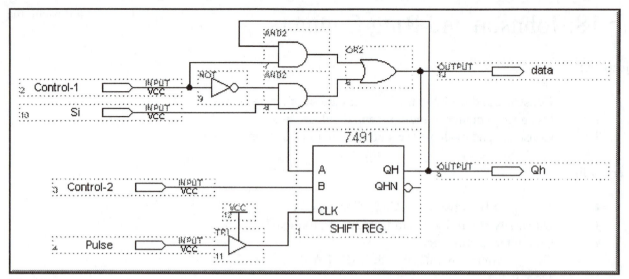

Figure 1

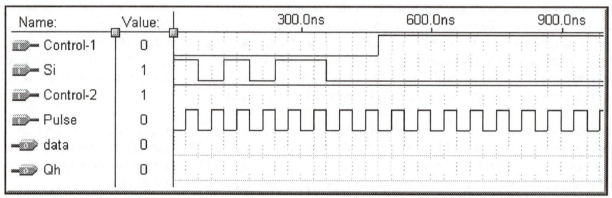

Figure 2

5.   The shift register initial contents can be observed as data are shifted in and out of the register. How many clock pulses did it take to load new data into the register in Figure 1? _____

6.   What was the initial contents of the register?   _____

7.   What was the data bit sequence (answer in binary) loaded into the register? _____ 2

8.   When the control-1 input is a logic-LOW, the data entering the "A" input of the register is from
        a.   The serial output, Qh.   b.   The serial input, Si.

9.   At what time in Figure 1 does the control-1 input go to a logic-HIGH?   _____ns

10.   When the control input goes to a logic-HIGH, the data entering the "A" input of the register is from
        a.   The serial output, Qh.   b.   The serial input, Si.

11.   Once data has been serial loaded into the register, how many clock pulses does it take before the data reappears in the register as a ring counter?   _____

12. Assume the register of Figure 1 contains $b7_H$. Complete Table 1 showing the data shifting through the register wired as a ring counter.

Clock	Binary Pattern H G F E D C B A	Hex Value
Initial contents	— — — — — — — —	$b7_H$
1st	— — — — — — — —	____ H
2nd	— — — — — — — —	____ H
3rd	— — — — — — — —	____ H
4th	— — — — — — — —	____ H
5th	— — — — — — — —	____ H
6th	— — — — — — — —	____ H
7th	— — — — — — — —	____ H
8th	— — — — — — — —	____ H
9th	— — — — — — — —	____ H

Table 1

13. Save all files to Drive A as **ring1**, then exit the Graphic and Waveform Editors.

Part 2   Procedure

1. Open the Max+plus II software. Assign the project name **ring2**.

2. Open the Graphic Editor and construct the circuit shown in Figure 3.

3. Open the Waveform Editor, set the Grid Size to 30 ns, and create the waveforms shown in Figure 4.

4. Press the Compiler and Simulator buttons. Correct all errors before continuing.

5. Draw the resulting output waveforms in the area provided at the bottom of Figure 4.

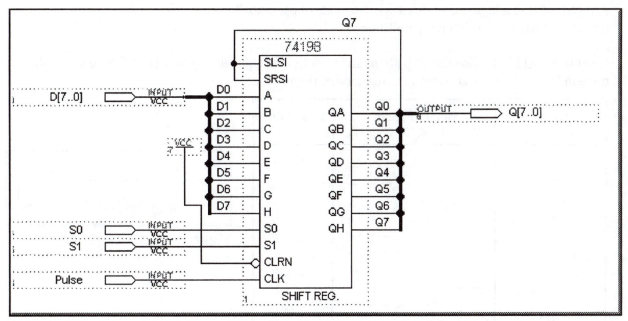

Figure 3

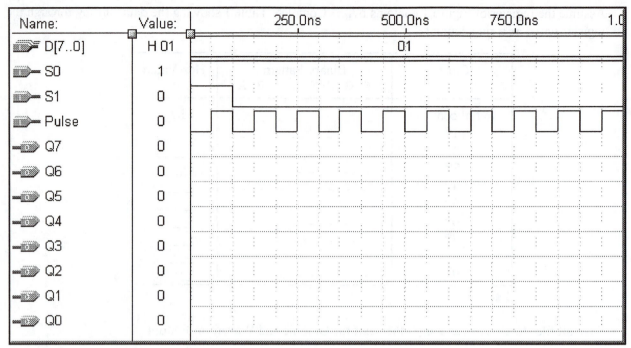

Figure 4

6. The 74198 shifts data on the (leading/trailing) edge of the clock pulse.

7. What was the initial contents of the 74198 register before the first clock transition? _____

8. Initially at 0 ns, S0 = ____ and S1 = ____. According to the function table for the 74198, the mode inputs are for: (serial shift right/serial shift left/parallel input) .

9. On the first clock transition, the data loaded into the register was _____.

10. At what time did S1 go to a logic-LOW? _____

11. After S1 went to a logic-LOW, what was the mode of operation?
    (serial shift right/serial shift left/parallel input)

12. Complete Table 2 showing the bit pattern (and hexadecimal equivalents) as data of Figure 4 was shifted through the 74198 register wired as a ring counter (Figure 5).

Clock	Binary Pattern H G F E D C B A	Hex Value
1st	– – – – – – – –	01_H
2nd	– – – – – – – –	_____H
3rd	– – – – – – – –	_____H
4th	– – – – – – – –	_____H
5th	– – – – – – – –	_____H
6th	– – – – – – – –	_____H
7th	– – – – – – – –	_____H
8th	– – – – – – – –	_____H
9th	– – – – – – – –	_____H
10th	– – – – – – – –	_____H

Table 2

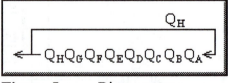

Figure 5   Ring counter

13. Note the pattern developed by the hexadecimal count. For the most part, as long as the MSB (most significant bit) was a logic-LOW, this serial shifting pattern demonstrates a _?_ function.
   a.   times 2   b.   divide by 2   c.   logic

14. Change the data to 24_H, then press the Simulate button.

15. Complete Table 3 showing the binary and hexadecimal pattern based on 24_H.

Clock	Binary Pattern H G F E D C B A	Hex Value
1st	_ _ _ _ _ _ _ _	24_H
2nd	_ _ _ _ _ _ _ _	_____H
3rd	_ _ _ _ _ _ _ _	_____H
4th	_ _ _ _ _ _ _ _	_____H
5th	_ _ _ _ _ _ _ _	_____H
6th	_ _ _ _ _ _ _ _	_____H
7th	_ _ _ _ _ _ _ _	_____H
8th	_ _ _ _ _ _ _ _	_____H
9th	_ _ _ _ _ _ _ _	_____H
10th	_ _ _ _ _ _ _ _	_____H

Table 3

16. On the first clock pulse, 24_H was loaded into the register. How many clock pulses did it take to swap the two nibbles of date (the 2 and the 4) to get 42_H? _____

17. Add Q[7..0] as an output waveform to the Waveform Editor file. Compare the pattern shown in Q[7..0] waveform to your recorded results in Table 3. Are they identical? (Yes/No)

18. For the most part, as long as the MSB (most significant bit) in Table 3 was a logic-LOW, this serial shifting pattern demonstrated a _?_ function.
   a.   times 2   b.   divide by 2   c.   logic

19. Save all files to Drive A as **ring2**, then exit the Graphic and Waveform Editors.

Part 3   Procedure

1. Open the Max+plus II software. Assign the project name **johnson1**.

2. Open the **ring1.gdf** file that is located on your disk in Drive A.

3. Modify your Graphic Editor file to match Figure 6.

4. Save the file as **johnson1** to your disk in Drive A.

5. Open the Waveform Editor, set the Grid Size to 20 ns, and create the waveforms shown in Figure 7.
   - The control-1 line goes high at 320 ns.
   - Si is a logic-HIGH from 0 to 40 ns, 80 to 120 ns, and 160 to 240 ns.

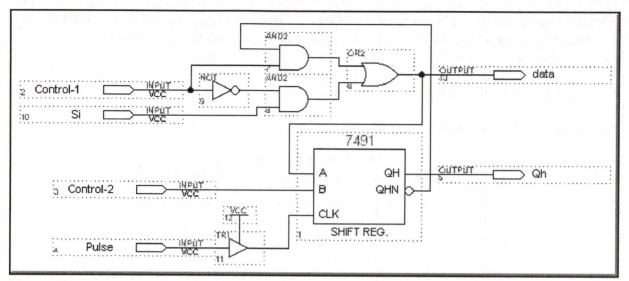

Figure 6

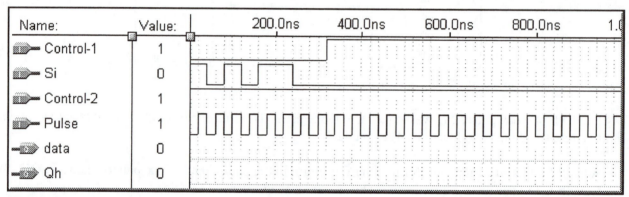

Figure 7

6. Compile and simulate the circuit. Correct all errors before continuing.

7. The waveforms you obtain after simulation should look similar to the waveforms in Figure 8. The data (highlighted) appearing on input A of the register won't start appearing on the output, Q_H, until 300 ns later. At 300 ns when the control-1 input goes to a logic-HIGH, the inverted Q_H output supplies the data and won't be seen on Q_H until 640 ns.

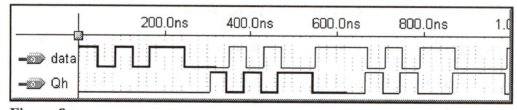

Figure 8

8. Since the 7491 only has one output, the shifting pattern may be difficult to see from the waveforms. Complete Table 4 showing the data being loaded into the 7491 as clock pulses are applied. On the first clock pulse, bit 7 of the data will appear on Q_A, what was on Q_A will be moved to Q_B and so on. On the second clock pulse, bit 6 will appear on Q_A, moving the remaining bits in the IC one flip-flop position towards Q_H.

Lab 18: Johnson and Ring Counters

Clock	Q_H Q_G Q_F Q_E Q_D Q_C Q_B Q_A	10101100_2
Initial	0 0 0 0 0 0 0 0	
1st	— — — — — — — —	⇐ bit 7
2nd	— — — — — — — —	⇐ bit 6
3rd	— — — — — — — —	⇐ bit 5
4th	— — — — — — — —	⇐ bit 4
5th	— — — — — — — —	⇐ bit 3
6th	— — — — — — — —	⇐ bit 2
7th	— — — — — — — —	⇐ bit 1
8th	— — — — — — — —	⇐ bit 0

Table 4

9. Once the IC has been serially loaded, the control-1 input goes to a logic-HIGH, switching the circuit to a Johnson counter. The inverted Q_H output becomes the serial input data to flip-flop A. Complete Table 5 showing the data shifting through the Johnson counter (Figure 9) as clock pulses are applied. Assume the IC contains AC_H at the start of this count sequence.

Clock	Q_H Q_G Q_F Q_E Q_D Q_C Q_B Q_A	Hex Equiv.
Initial	— — — — — — — —	AC_H
1st	— — — — — — — —	___H
2nd	— — — — — — — —	___H
3rd	— — — — — — — —	___H
4th	— — — — — — — —	___H
5th	— — — — — — — —	___H
6th	— — — — — — — —	___H
7th	— — — — — — — —	___H
8th	— — — — — — — —	___H
9th	— — — — — — — —	___H
10th	— — — — — — — —	___H
11th	— — — — — — — —	___H
12th	— — — — — — — —	___H
13th	— — — — — — — —	___H
14th	— — — — — — — —	___H
15th	— — — — — — — —	___H
16th	— — — — — — — —	___H

Table 5

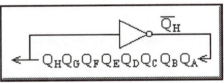

Figure 9   Johnson Counter

10. Compare the bit pattern after the 8th clock pulse to the initial contents, AC_H. Compare the bit pattern after the first clock pulse to the pattern after the 9th clock pulse. Write a brief statement describing the relationship of the bit pattern the IC will contain after 8 clock pulses, regardless of the initial content of the IC.

_____

_____

11. Save all files to Drive A as **johnson1**, then exit the Graphic and Waveform Editors.

Part 4 Procedure

1. Open the Max+plus II software. Assign the project name **johnson2**.

2. Open the **ring2.gdf** file located on your diskette in Drive A. Modify the circuit as shown in Figure 10, then save the file as **johnson2.gdf**.

3. Open the **ring2.scf** file located on your disk in Drive A. Modify the waveforms shown in Figure 11, then save the file as **johnson2.scf**.

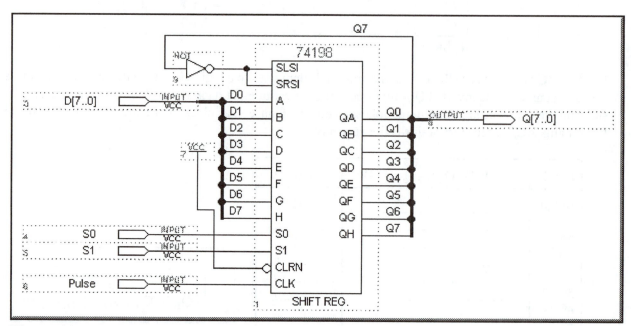

Figure 10

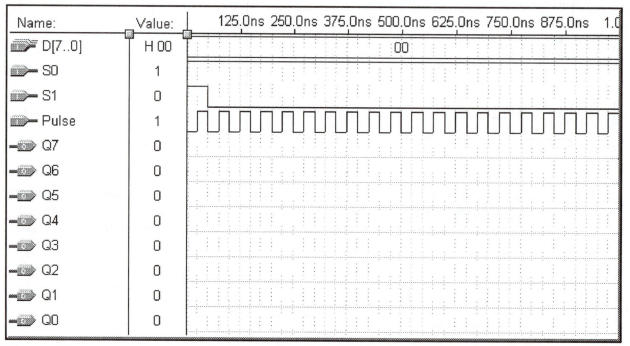

Figure 11

4. Press the Compiler and Simulator buttons. Correct all errors before continuing.

5. Draw the resulting output waveforms in the area provided at the bottom of Figure 11.

6. What was the number loaded into the resister during the Pi mode? _____

7. Complete Table 5 showing the bit pattern and hex equivalents as clock pulses are applied to the Johnson counter of Figure 10.

Clock	Q_H Q_G Q_F Q_E Q_D Q_C Q_B Q_A	Hex equiv.
1st	— — — — — — — —	_____H
2nd	— — — — — — — —	_____H
3rd	— — — — — — — —	_____H
4th	— — — — — — — —	_____H
5th	— — — — — — — —	_____H
6th	— — — — — — — —	_____H
7th	— — — — — — — —	_____H
8th	— — — — — — — —	_____H
9th	— — — — — — — —	_____H
10th	— — — — — — — —	_____H
11th	— — — — — — — —	_____H
12th	— — — — — — — —	_____H
13th	— — — — — — — —	_____H
14th	— — — — — — — —	_____H
15th	— — — — — — — —	_____H
16th	— — — — — — — —	_____H
17th	— — — — — — — —	_____H

Table 5

8. Modify the waveforms and circuit as described below:
- Set S0 from 50 ns to 1 μs to a logic-LOW
- Set S1 to a constant logic-HIGH from 0 ns to 1 μs
- Change the Q7 label on the wire to the inverter to Q0

4. Press the Compiler and Simulator buttons. Correct all errors before continuing.

5. Describe how the modifications to the circuit affected the circuit operation.

_____

6. List the new count sequence (in hexadecimal) of the Johnson counter.

_____H _____H _____H _____H _____H _____H _____H _____H

_____H _____H _____H _____H _____H _____H _____H _____H

7. Demonstrate your circuit and waveforms to your professor. Obtain the signature of approval directly on the answer page for this lab.

8. Obtain a hard copy of the Graphic and Waveform Editor files. Label these hard copies **Part 4, Step 13A** and **Part 4, Step 13B**, respectively.

9. Save all files to Drive A as **johnson2**, then exit the Graphic and Waveform Editors.

10. Write a 1 to 2 page summary based on the 74198 wired as a Johnson and Ring counter. Provide a set of waveforms and discuss the results obtained after simulation.

11. Submit the following for review:
    - Cover page
    - Completed answer page for this lab
    - Hard copy of the Graphic Editor from **Part 4, Step 13A**
    - Hard copy of the Waveform Editor from **Part 4, Step 13B**

Lab 18: Johnson and Ring Counters Answer Page

Name: _____

Part 1

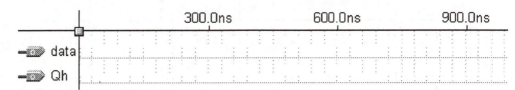

Figure 2

5. _____

6. _____

7. _____ 2

8.　　A　　B

9. _____ ns

10.　　A　　B

11. _____

Clock	Binary pattern H G F E D C B A	Hex value
Initial contents	— — — — — — — —	b7$_H$
1st	— — — — — — — —	___$_H$
2nd	— — — — — — — —	___$_H$
3rd	— — — — — — — —	___$_H$
4th	— — — — — — — —	___$_H$
5th	— — — — — — — —	___$_H$
6th	— — — — — — — —	___$_H$
7th	— — — — — — — —	___$_H$
8th	— — — — — — — —	___$_H$
9th	— — — — — — — —	___$_H$

Table 1

Part 2

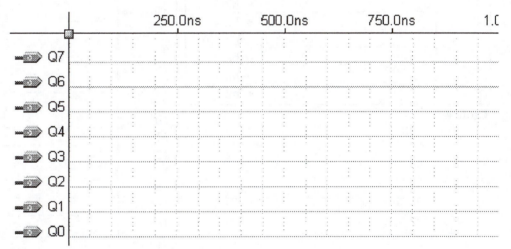

Figure 4

6.　　Leading/Trailing　　　　7. _____

8.　　S0=____　S1 =____　　(serial shift right/serial shift left/parallel input)

9. _____　　　　10. _____

11.　　(Serial shift right/serial shift left/parallel input)　　　13.　　A　　B　　C

Clock	Binary pattern H G F E D C B A	Hex value
1st	— — — — — — — —	01$_H$
2nd	— — — — — — — —	____$_H$
3rd	— — — — — — — —	____$_H$
4th	— — — — — — — —	____$_H$
5th	— — — — — — — —	____$_H$
6th	— — — — — — — —	____$_H$
7th	— — — — — — — —	____$_H$
8th	— — — — — — — —	____$_H$
9th	— — — — — — — —	____$_H$
10th	— — — — — — — —	____$_H$

Table 2

Clock	Binary pattern H G F E D C B A	Hex value
1st	— — — — — — — —	24$_H$
2nd	— — — — — — — —	____$_H$
3rd	— — — — — — — —	____$_H$
4th	— — — — — — — —	____$_H$
5th	— — — — — — — —	____$_H$
6th	— — — — — — — —	____$_H$
7th	— — — — — — — —	____$_H$
8th	— — — — — — — —	____$_H$
9th	— — — — — — — —	____$_H$
10th	— — — — — — — —	____$_H$

Table 3

16. _____   17. Yes/No   18. A   B   C

Part 3

Part 4

Clock	Q_H Q_G Q_F Q_E Q_D Q_C Q_B Q_A	10101100$_2$
Initial	0 0 0 0 0 0 0 0	
1st	— — — — — — — —	⇐ bit 7
2nd	— — — — — — — —	⇐ bit 6
3rd	— — — — — — — —	⇐ bit 5
4th	— — — — — — — —	⇐ bit 4
5th	— — — — — — — —	⇐ bit 3
6th	— — — — — — — —	⇐ bit 2
7th	— — — — — — — —	⇐ bit 1
8th	— — — — — — — —	⇐ bit 0

Table 4

Clock	Q_H Q_G Q_F Q_E Q_D Q_C Q_B Q_A	Hex equiv.
Initial	— — — — — — — —	AC$_H$
1st	— — — — — — — —	____$_H$
2nd	— — — — — — — —	____$_H$
3rd	— — — — — — — —	____$_H$
4th	— — — — — — — —	____$_H$
5th	— — — — — — — —	____$_H$
6th	— — — — — — — —	____$_H$
7th	— — — — — — — —	____$_H$
8th	— — — — — — — —	____$_H$
9th	— — — — — — — —	____$_H$
10th	— — — — — — — —	____$_H$
11th	— — — — — — — —	____$_H$
12th	— — — — — — — —	____$_H$
13th	— — — — — — — —	____$_H$
14th	— — — — — — — —	____$_H$
15th	— — — — — — — —	____$_H$
16th	— — — — — — — —	____$_H$

Table 5

10. _____

_____

_____

_____

_____

Part 4 Cont.

10. _____

11. ____$_H$ ____$_H$ ____$_H$ ____$_H$ ____$_H$ ____$_H$ ____$_H$ ____$_H$

____$_H$ ____$_H$ ____$_H$ ____$_H$ ____$_H$ ____$_H$ ____$_H$ ____$_H$

12. Demonstrated to: _____ Date: _____ Grade: _____

234 Lab 18: Johnson and Ring Counters

Lab 19: Tristate Logic

Objective:
    1.   Examine the characteristics of the tristate logic
    2.   Use tristate logic on bus lines
    3.   Create bidirectional I/O pins

Materials List:
    ♦   Max+plus II software by Altera Corporation
    ♦   University board by Altera Corporation   (Optional)
    ♦   Computer requirements:
                Minimum 486/66 with 8 MB RAM

Discussion:
In computers, it is often necessary for several devices to share a common data bus for transmitting or receiving data to and from various devices. Buffers, based on tristate logic, are designed to isolate one circuit from another. When the device is "ON," the output will be either a logic-HIGH or a logic-LOW, depending on the inputs to that device. When the device is "OFF," the output will exhibit a high impedance state.

The symbol of a tristate gate is distinguished from others by the addition of an input to the side of the gate. Figure 1 shows several common tristate gates that may be created inside an integrated circuit.   The Max+plus II software includes a tristate buffer (D) that may be connected in series with an output to create various tristate functions. It is important that only one tristate output is active at a time when several of these devices share common signal lines (buses).

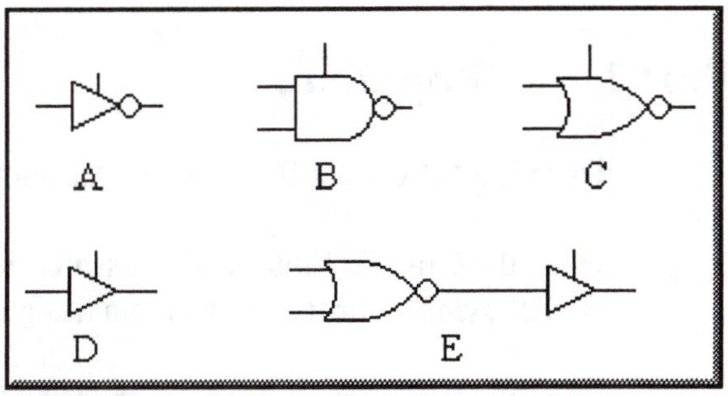

This lab utilizes the basic tristate buffer (Figure 1 D) to develop uni- or bi-directional bus control that may be used in microprocessor-based applications.

Figure 1

Part 1

1.   Open the Max+plus II software. Assign the project name **buffer1** and MAX7000S as the device family.

2.   Open the Graphic Editor and construct the circuit shown in Figure 2.

3.   Open the Waveform Editor, set the Grid Size to 25 ns, and create the waveforms shown in Figure 3.

4.   Press the Compiler and Simulator buttons. Correct all errors before continuing.

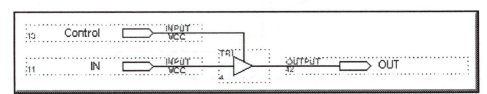

Figure 2

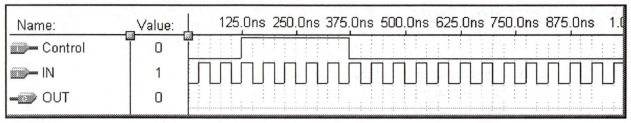

Name:	Value:	125.0ns 250.0ns 375.0ns 500.0ns 625.0ns 750.0ns 875.0ns 1.0
Control	0	
IN	1	
OUT	0	

Figure 3

5.   Draw the resulting output waveform in the area provided at the bottom of Figure 3.

6.   There are three logic states when using a tristate logic: a logic-LOW, a logic-HIGH, and a high impedance, Z_H, state. Which logic state is represented by the output from 0 ns to 125 ns? _____

7.   Which logic state(s) is represented by the output from 125 ns to 375 ns? _____

8.   Based on the recorded results, the tristate input to the buffer shown in Figure 2 is active-(LOW/HIGH)

9.   Save the files to Drive A as **buffer1**, then exit the Graphic and Waveform Editors.

Part 2   Procedure

1.   Open the Max+plus II software. Assign the project name **buffer2**.

2.   Open the Graphic Editor and construct the circuit shown in Figure 4. Use bus lines as shown and use the BIDIR symbol for the INOUT pin designator on the right side of the top buffer.

3.   Open the Waveform Editor, set the Grid Size to 25 ns, and create the waveforms shown in Figure 5.

4.   Press the Compiler and Simulator buttons. Correct all errors before continuing.

5.   Draw the resulting output waveform in the area provided at the bottom of Figure 5.

6.   When the Control 1 input is a logic-LOW, which buffer is turned ON? (Top/Bottom)

7.   Why is INOUT a high impedance state? _____

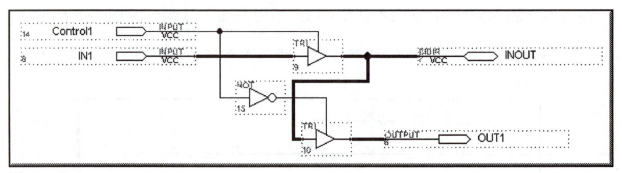

Figure 4

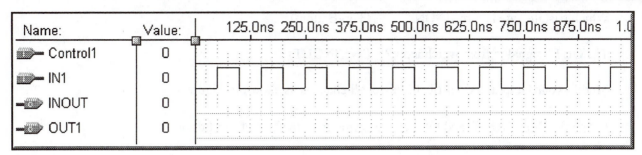

Figure 5

8.   Describe the signal that appeared on the OUT1 pin connector. _____

_____

9.   Set the Control 1 signal to a constant logic-HIGH.

10.   Press the Simulate button.

11.   Which output now has valid data?   (INOUT/OUT1)

12.   Make the following changes to the Waveform Editor file:
- Place the Control 1 signal to a constant logic-LOW
- Change the I/O type of the INOUT signal to an input Pin
- Change the grid size to 100 ns, highlight the INOUT signal, press the Overwrite Count Value button, then press OK. The INOUT signal should now be a square wave with a pulse width of 100 ns.

13.   Press the Simulator button.

14.   Draw the resulting output waveforms in Figure 6.

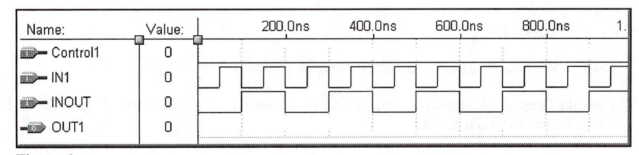

Figure 6

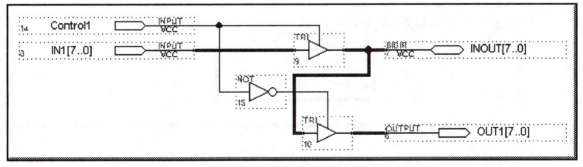

Figure 7

15. Which tristate gate is turned "ON."   (Top/Bottom)

16. The OUT1 signal is from which input?   (IN1/INOUT)

17. Modify your Graphic Editor file to reflect all changes as shown in Figure 7.

18. Delete the IN1, INOUT, and OUT1 waveforms from the Waveform Editor.

19. Set the Grid Size to 100 ns and add the waveforms as shown in Figure 8. (Notice Control 1 = 1.)

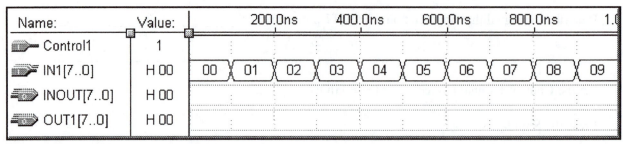

Name:	Value:	200.0ns	400.0ns	600.0ns	800.0ns	1.0
Control1	1					
IN1[7..0]	H 00	00 X 01 X 02 X 03 X 04 X 05 X 06 X 07 X 08 X 09				
INOUT[7..0]	H 00					
OUT1[7..0]	H 00					

Figure 8

20. Press the Compiler and Simulator buttons. Correct all errors before continuing.

21. Draw the resulting output waveforms in the area provided at the bottom of Figure 8.

22. Since the tristate buffer symbol may be used with single or multiple inputs and outputs, the need for specialty buffer chips like the 74240, 74241, and 74244 are not needed for circuit designs using the Max+plus II software. However, these buffer chips may be necessary to isolate the EPM7128LC84 chip from heavy current demanding loads.

23. Save all files to your disk in Drive A as **buffer2**, then exit the Graphic and Waveform Editors.

Part 3   Procedure

1. Open the Max+plus II software. Assign the project name **buffer3**.

2. Open the Graphic Editor and construct the circuit shown in Figure 9. Use BIDIR symbols for the INOUTA and INOUTB signals.

3. Open the Waveform Editor and create the waveforms shown in Figure 10.

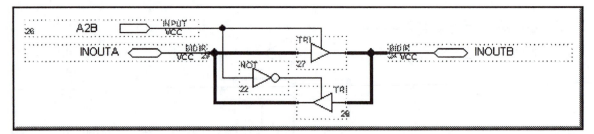

Figure 9

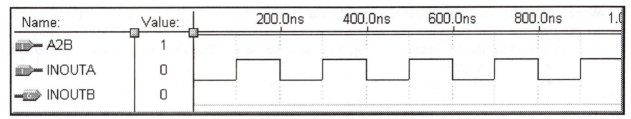

Figure 10

4. Press the Compiler and Simulator buttons. Correct all errors before continuing.

5. Draw the resulting output waveform in the area provided at the bottom of Figure 10.

6. What error message (if any) would be displayed if the control line was a logic-LOW when the circuit was simulated?

    _____

7. Modify the waveforms as shown in Figure 11.

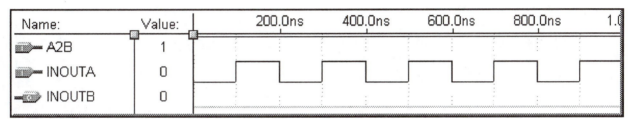

Figure 11

8. Press the simulator button, and draw the resulting output waveform in the area provided at the bottom of Figure 11.

9. When the control input A2B is a logic-LOW, data flow from input (INOUTA/INOUTB) to output (INOUTA/INOUTB).

10. When the control input A2B is a logic-HIGH, data flow from input (INOUTA/INOUTB) to output (INOUTA/INOUTB).

11. When using a TRI buffer, you must observe the following rules[1]:

    • A TRI buffer may drive only one BIDIR or BIDIRC pin. You must use a BIDIR or BIDIRC pin if feedback is included after the TRI buffer.
    • If a TRI buffer feeds logic, it must also feed a BIDIR or BIDIRC pin unless it is part of a tri-state bus. If it feeds a BIDIR or BIDIRC pin, it may not feed any other outputs.

12. Obtain a hard copy of your modified circuit and simulated waveforms with the R/W control input. Label these hard copies **Part 3, Step 12A** and **Part 3, Step 12B**.

13. Demonstrate the results obtained from the circuit designed to your instructor. Obtain the signature of approval on the answer page for this lab.

14. Save both editor files to Drive A as **buffer3**, then exit the Graphic and Waveform Editors.

---

1   From the MaxPlus II Help screen for the TRI Primitive. Altera Corporation.

15. Write a summary pertaining to the results obtained from this lab.

16. Place all papers for this lab in the following sequence, then submit the lab to your instructor for grading.
    - Cover page
    - Typed summary
    - The completed answer page for this lab
    - Hard copy of the Graphic Editor, **Part 3, Step 12A**
    - Hard copy of the Waveform Editor, **Part 3, Step 12B**

Lab 19: Buffers and Line Drivers Answer Page

Name: ____________________

Part 1

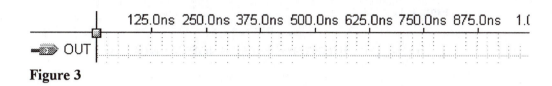

Figure 3

6. __________ 7. __________ 8. LOW/HIGH

Part 2

6. Top/Bottom

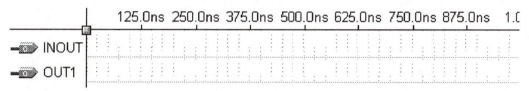

Figure 5

7. ____

8. ____

11. INOUT/OUT

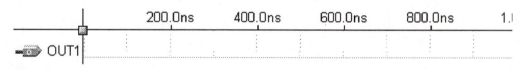

Figure 6

15. Top/Bottom 16. IN1/INOUT

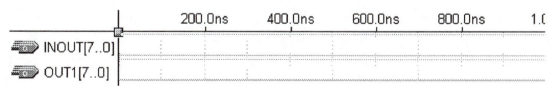

Figure 8

Part 3

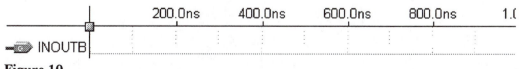

Figure 10

6. ____

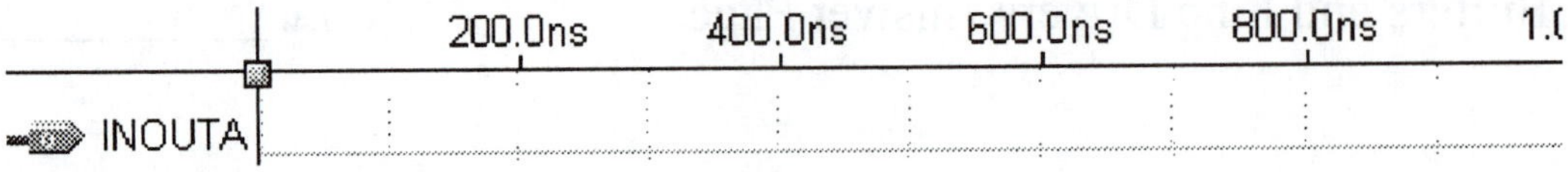

Figure 11

9.   input (INOUTA/INOUTB) to output (INOUTA/INOUTB)

10.   input (INOUTA/INOUTB) to output (INOUTA/INOUTB)

13.   Demonstrated to: _____ Date: _____

Grade: _____

Lab 19: Tristate Logic

Lab 20: Memory Addressing

Objectives:

1.   Learn the basic operation of RAM (Random Access Memory)
2.   Construct a circuit to read from or write to any address in a RAM
3.   Control read/write cycles and memory addressing with the EPM7128LC84

Materials List:

- Max+plus II software by Altera Corporation
- Circuit card with the EPM7128SLC84 chip
- Computer requirements:
   Minimum 486/66 with 8 MB RAM
- (1) 6116 - 2 K× 8 memory (or equivalent)
- (8) 1 KΩ resistors
- Floppy disk
- (2) 0.1 µFd capacitors
- (2) 0.01 µFd capacitors

- Power supply
- Breadboard
- (8) LEDs
- (10) toggle switches
- (2) pushbutton switches
- (1) NE555
- (3) 4.7 KΩ resistors
- (1) 33 KΩ resistors
- (2) 47 KΩ resistors

Discussion:

The memory integrated circuit that you will use in this lab is the 6116 (or equivalent), which is a 2 K x 8 static RAM. 2 K × 8 implies 2048 memory addresses, 2^{11}, with 8 bits of data storage at each address. Because the 6116 is a static device, the data stored in the memory elements is stable and does not require refresh, as with DRAM (Dynamic RAM). Also, data read is nondestructive and will be the same data that was written to that location.

The pin configuration, logic symbol, and pin names are shown in Figrue 1. The eleven address inputs, A_0 to A_{10}, provide the 2048 (2^{11}) addresses. The eight data input/output lines, I/O_1 to I/O_8, will be connected to a bidirectional data bus to write or read data to each address specified by the bit pattern on A_0 to A_{10}. The chip select, CS, input enables the memory when CE is a logic-LOW. The CE input must be a logic-LOW for either the read or write operations. Data is written into memory when the Write Enable, WE, input is a logic-LOW. Data is read when Write Enable is a logic-HIGH and the Output Enable, OE, is a logic-LOW. The data out is tristate logic, allowing for more than one memory IC to be connected to the data bus. The memory chip operation is illustrated in the following table with respect to the control line logic levels.

Mode	CS	WE	OE	I/O_0 to I/O_8
Off	H	X	X	Z_H
Write	L	L	X	Data inputs
Read	L	H	L	Data outputs
Read	L	H	H	Z_H

Table 1

The general configuration of the 16348 (2 K × 8) bits in the 6116 is illustrated in Figure 2. Each of the squares represents a memory location for one bit. Thus, the eight squares under the "0" column indicates that these eight bits are accessed simultaneously (for read or write) when binary address 00000000000_2 is applied to address lines A_0 to A_{10}. Also, the eight squares under the "1" column are simultaneously accessed when the binary address

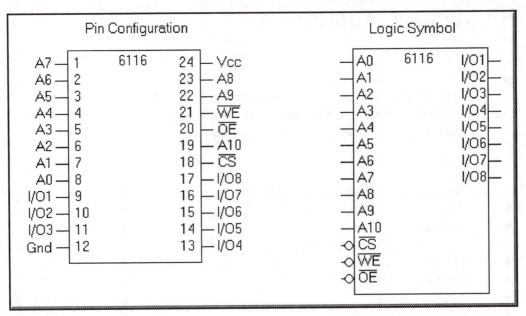

Figure 1

Pin Names	
A_0 to A_{10}	Address Inputs
WE	Write Enable
CS	Chip Select
OE	Output Enable

Table 2

Pin Names	
I/O_1 to I/O_8	Data Input/Output
Vcc	Power (+5 V)
Gnd	Ground

00000000001_2 is applied. The remaining locations, 2 through 2047, are accessed by binary addresses 00000000010_2 to 11111111111_2 (0002_H to $7FFF_H$). The address applied to A_0 to A_{10} identifies the location where the contents at that location is the data.

The eight I/O lines in Figure 2 are data lines used for writing data to the memory or reading data from memory. Other RAM memory may have separate data input and data output lines. How memory is structured depends solely on the internal design of the device.

To prevent this lab from becoming tedious and repetitious, only a portion of the 2048 addresses will be accessed for read and write for Part 1. For Part 2, you will build a mod 2048 counter to access all memory addresses and use an 8-bit Johnson counter to supply data to these addresses. To prevent contention in Part 1, where more than one active output share a common load, a 74244 (octal tristate buffer) will be used to isolate the "data" switches from the memory chip during the read mode. In Part 2, tristate buffers will be used to prevent contention during read and write operations.

Finally, in Part 3 and Part 4, you will program the EPM7128SLC84 IC and interface the circuit card containing the chip to a 6116 memory chip. Part 3 is based on **memory.gdf** and **memory.scf** created in Part 1 of this lab. Part 4 is based on **memory2.gdf** and **memory2.scf** as constructed in Part 2.

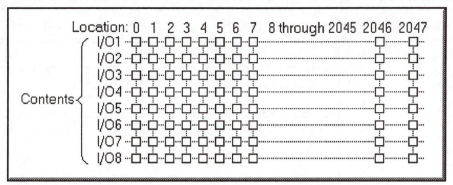

Figure 2

Part 1   Procedure

1.   Open the Max+plus II software. Assign the project name **memory**.

2.   Open the Graphic Editor and create the circuit shown in Figure 3.

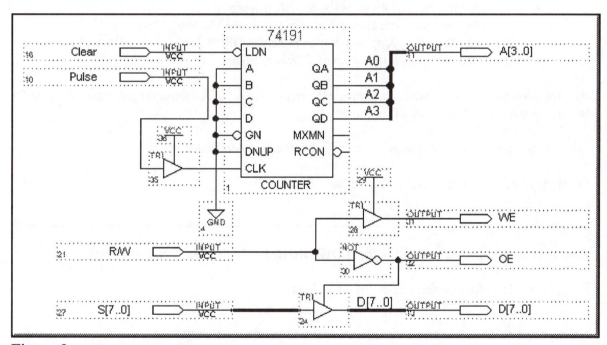

Figure 3

3.   Open the Waveform Editor, turn off the Snap to Grid feature in the Options menu, and create the waveforms shown in Figrue 4 following these setup instructions.

- Set the Grid Size to 6 ns
- Set the clear waveform to a constant logic-HIGH
- Highlight 0 to 6 ns, set this section of the clear waveform to a logic-LOW
- Highlight 498 to 504 ns, set this section of the clear waveform to a logic-LOW
- Set the Grid Size to 20 ns
- Highlight the pulse waveform
- Press the Clock Overwrite button in the Draw tool bar, then press the OK button
- Set the Grid Size to 500 ns
- Highlight the R/W waveform

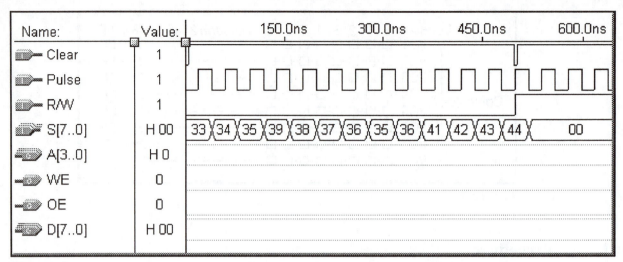

Figure 4

- Press the Clock Overwrite button in the Draw tool bar, then press the OK button
- Set the Grid Size to 40 ns
- Highlight the first 40 ns of the S[7..0] waveform
- Press the Overwrite Group Value button in the Draw tool bar
- Enter 33 as the group value, then press the OK button
- Complete the S[7..0] values as shown in Figure 4

4. Run the compiler and simulator. Assuming zero errors, draw the resulting output waves (0 ns to 650 ns) in the area provided at the bottom of Figure 4.

5. What is the counter count sequence as displayed in the Graphic Editor? _____

6. What prevented the counter from reaching the "F" count?

   _____

7. Data appears on the data bus during the (LOW/HIGH) level of the R/W control signal.

8. Describe the D[7..0] waveform from 500 ns to 1 μs.

   _____

9. The data was given in standard ASCII code. Identify the character of each ASCII code shown in Table 3. Refer to your textbook or research the library for the ASCII table.

ASCII	Character
33	
34	
35	
39	
38	
37	
36	

ASCII	Character
35	
36	
41	
42	
43	
44	

Table 3

10. WE and OE will be connected to the active-LOW WE and OE control inputs of a 6116 memory chip. During the time segment 0 to 500 ns as shown in the Waveform Editor, data will be (written to/read from) memory.

11. During the time segment 500 ns to 1 μs as shown in the Waveform Editor, data will be (written to/read from) memory.

12. Obtain a hard copy of the Graphic and Waveform Editor files. Label these hard copies **Part 1, Step 12A**. and **Part 1, Step 12B**, respectively.

13. Save all files to Drive A as **memory**, exit the Graphic and Waveform Editors.

Part 2   Procedure

1. Open the Max+plus II software. Assign the project name **memory1**.

2. Open the Graphic Editor and create the circuit shown in Figure 5.

3. Open the Waveform Editor and create the waveforms shown in Figure 6 following these setup instructions.

   - Set the Grid Size to 10 ns
   - Highlight the pulse waveform
   - Press the Clock Overwrite button in the Draw tool bar, then press the OK button
   - Highlight the pulse waveform
   - Press the Clock Overwrite button in the Draw tool bar, then press the OK button
   - Set the Grid Size to 3 ns
   - Set the clear waveform to a constant logic-HIGH
   - Highlight and set the first 3 ns of the clear waveform to a logic-LOW
   - Highlight then set the first 6 ns of the S1waveform to a logic-HIGH

4. Run the compiler and simulator. Assuming zero errors, draw the resulting output waves (0 ns to 90 ns) in the area provided at the bottom of Figure 6.

5. What is the count sequence of the three 74191 ICs? _____

6. What is the count sequence of the 74198 register as wired in Figure 5?

   _____

7. What mode of operation is the shift register when S1 is a logic-HIGH? _____

8. What mode of operation is the shift register when S1 is a logic-LOW? _____

9. The clear input to the circuit of Figure 5 is (synchronous/asynchronous).

10. As long as the counter counts and data from the 74194 starts to repeat itself, you may proceed with the next step, otherwise correct all mistakes and repeat Steps 2 through 9 of Part 2.

11. Obtain a hard copy of the Graphic and Waveform Editor files. Label these hard copies **Part 2, Step 11A** and **Part 2, Step 11B**, respectively.

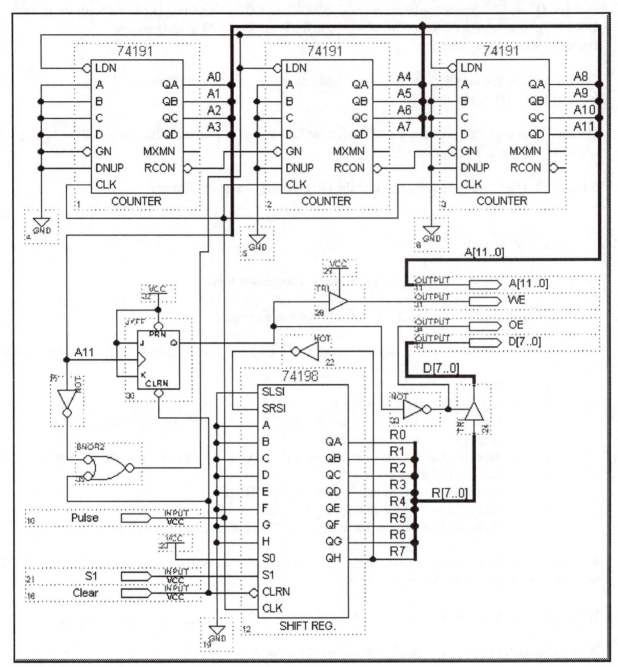

Figure 5

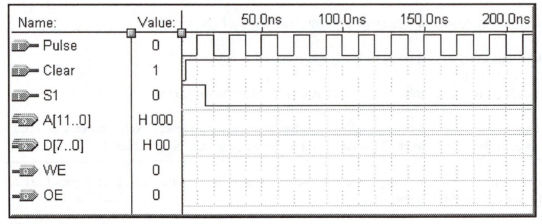

Figure 6

248 Lab 20: Memory Addressing

12. Save all files to Drive A as **memory1**, then exit the Graphic and Waveform Editors.

Part 3   Procedure

1. Connect the circuit card with the EPM7128SLC84 chip to the computer's printer port. If the computer has a software key attached to LPT1, connect the card to the parallel port, LPT2. See your instructor to determine the correct connection port.

2. Open the Max+plus II software. Assign the project name **memory**.

3. Open the **memory.gdf** file created in Part 1 of this lab.

4. Open the **memory.scf** file created in Part 1 of this lab.

5. Run the compiler and simulator. Correct all errors before continuing.

6. Select Programmer in the Max+plus II menu item (left of the File option).

7. The software should automatically detect the board, providing the switches on the board are in the correct settings. It is best to follow the board manufacturer's notes on programming the 7128 chip since the procedure will be different for each board. Appendix C at the end of this lab contains typical instructions for programming the EPM7128SLC84. Program your chip following the procedure outlined in Appendix C. Potential problems that inhibit programming the IC are:

   - Not all required wires in the interface cable are connected
   - The speed of transmission between the computer and board is too fast
   - The cable from the computer to the board is too long
   - Your need the patch program from Altera
   - Your computer misidentified the board, assuming the board is a printer
   - Lack of power to the EPM7128SLC84
   - Poor ground
   - For problems not mentioned above, see your professor for suggestions.

8. Assuming the board was successfully programmed, construct the circuit shown in Figure 7. Refer to the **memory.rpt** file on your disk that was created during compilation for pin assignments of the EPM7128SLC84 IC. You may also want to place LEDs at the A3, A2, A1, and A0 address lines to monitor the address as you proceed to program the 6116.

9. Pin 2 of the NE555 one shot is an active-LOW trigger input. When pressed, the Q output (pin 3) becomes unstable for a period of time before returning to a logic-LOW. Calculate the time the one shot is unstable. Unstable time: _____

10. The CS input of the 6116 is active-LOW. This switch will be used to turn on the 6116 to complete the read or write operation.

11. The clear input (see Figure 3) of the 74191 is active-LOW. Set the clear switch to the GND side, then place this switch to the Vcc side. This action loads the counter with zero (DCBA inputs), and provides address 00000000000_2 to the 6116.

12. Set the R/W switch to the GND position for writing data to memory.

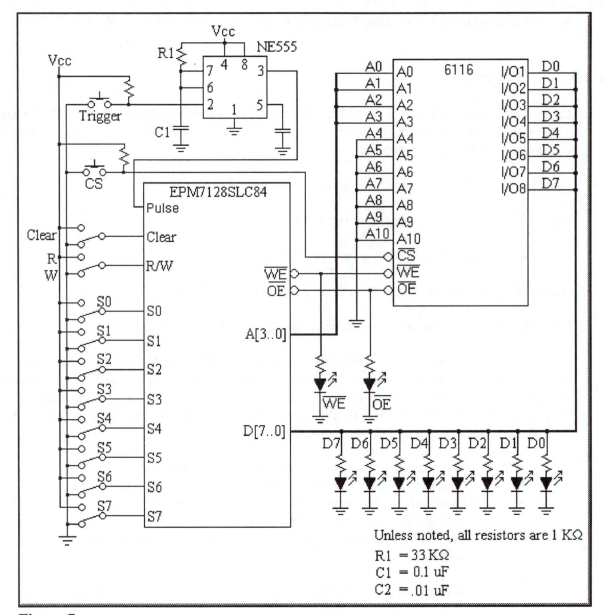

Figure 7

13. Set switches S7 through S0 for 33_H. Note, the LEDs D7 through D0 should show 33_H.

14. Press and release the CS switch.

15. 33_H was loaded into the 6116 at address 00000000000_2.

16. Press and release the trigger switch. The counter advances to 1_H, creating address 00000000001_2.

17. Set switches S7 through S0 for 34_H. Note, the LEDs D7 through D0 should show 34_H.

18. Press and release the CS switch.

19. 34_H was loaded into the 6116 at address 00000000001_2.

20. Press and release the trigger switch. The counter advances to 2_H, creating address 00000000010_2.

21. Repeat Steps 16, 17, 18, and 19 to program the data shown in Table 4 to the addresses shown. Place the R/W switch to a logic-HIGH. This places the 6116 in read mode. Note that switches S7 through S0 no longer have an effect on the LEDs.

Address	Data	Address	Data
00000000010_2	35_H	00000001001_2	20_H
00000000011_2	39_H	00000001010_2	41_H
00000000100_2	38_H	00000001011_2	42_H
00000000101_2	37_H	00000001100_2	43_H
00000000110_2	36_H	00000001101_2	44_H
00000000111_2	35_H	00000001110_2	45_H
00000001000_2	36_H	00000001111_2	46_H

Table 4

22. Place the clear switch to its GND side, then place it back to the Vcc side to set address zero.

23. Verify that the contents of the 6116 matches Table 4. Press the CS switch to read data and press the trigger switch to advance to the next address.

24. Demonstrate the programmed EPM7128SLC84 and 6116 to your instructor. Obtain the signature of approval directly on the answer page.

25. Exit the Graphic and Waveform Editors.

Part 4   Procedure

1. Connect the circuit card with the EPM7128SLC84 chip to the computer's printer port. If the computer has a software key attached to LPT1, connect the card to the parallel port, LPT2. See your instructor to determine the correct connection port.

2. Open the Max+plus II software. Assign the project name **memory1**.

3. Open the **memory1.gdf** and **memory1.scf** files created in Part 2 of this lab.

4. Run the compiler and simulator.

5. Select Programmer in the Max+plus II menu item (left of the File option).

6. Proceed to program the EPM7128SLC84 chip following the instructions in Appendix C or refer to the circuit board manufacturer's programming instructions.

7. Assuming the board was successfully programmed, construct the circuit shown in Figure 8. Refer to the **memory1.rpt** file on your disk that was created during compilation for pin assignments of the EPM7128SLC84 IC. You may want to place LEDs at the A10 through A0 address lines to monitor the address as the 6116 is programmed with the data generated by the 74194.

8. The 555 is wired as a(n) (bistable, astable, monostable) multivibrator.

9. Calculate the frequency of the oscillator.   f = _____

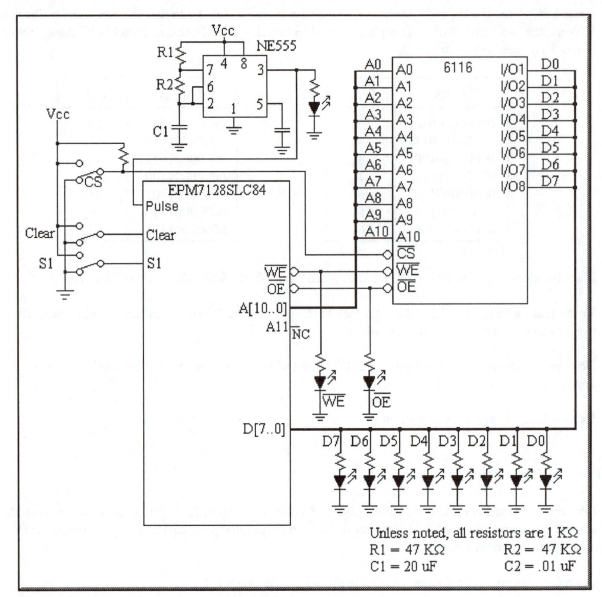

Figure 8

10. Calculate the time it takes to store data at all memory addresses within the 6116. _____

11. Explain the effect of switch CS.

    _____

    _____

12. In order for data to be loaded into various memory addresses, the clear switch must be set to a (logic-LOW/logic-HIGH).

13. Demonstrate the programmed EPM7128SLC84 and 6116 to your instructor. Obtain the signature of approval directly on the answer page.

14. Exit the Graphic and Waveform Editors.

15.	Write a 1 to 2 page summary containing charts and/or graphics pertaining to the results obtained from this lab.

16.	Place all papers for this lab in the following sequence, then submit the lab to your instructor for grading.

- Cover page
- Typed summary
- The completed answer page for this lab
- Hard copy of the Graphic Editor, **Part 1, Step 12A**
- Hard copy of the Waveform Editor, **Part 1, Step 12B**
- Hard copy of the Graphic Editor, **Part 2, Step 11A**
- Hard copy of the Waveform Editor, **Part 2, Step 11B**

Name: _____

Part 1

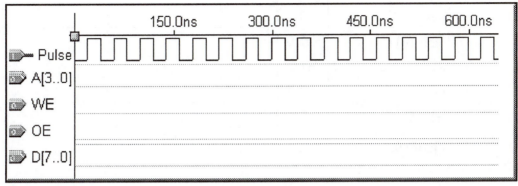

Figure 4

5. _____

6. _____

7. (LOW/HIGH)

8. _____

ASCII	Character
33	
34	
35	
39	
38	
37	
36	

ASCII	Character
35	
36	
41	
42	
43	
44	

Table 3

9. Written to/read from

10. Written to/read from

Part 2

5. _____

6. _____

7. _____

8. _____

9. synchronous/asynchronous

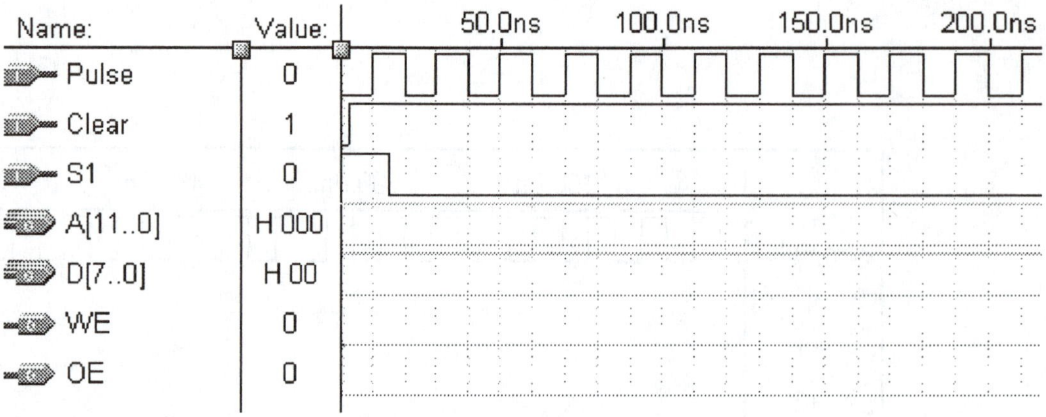
Name:
Value:
50.0ns
100.0ns
150.0ns
200.0ns
Pulse
0
Clear
1
S1
0
A[11..0]
H 000
D[7..0]
H 00
WE
0
OE
0

Figure 6

Part 3

8. ______________

23. Demonstrated to: ________________________________ Date: ____________________

Part 4

8. ______________

9. f = __________________________

10. ______________

11. ____

____

12. Logic-LOW/Logic-HIGH

13. Demonstrated to: ________________________________ Date: ____________________

Grade: ___________

Lab 21: The D/A Convertor

Objectives:
1. Convert digital quantities to analog voltages using the DAC0808 D/A convertor
2. Build a digital controlled analog amplifier
3. Program the MAX7000S to produce different bit patterns to apply to the D/A convertor for creating ramp and trapezoidal waveforms

Materials List:
- (1) 220 Ω resistor
- (4) 4.7 KΩ resistors
- (3) 10 KΩ resistors
- (5) 20 KΩ resistors
- (1) 20 µF electrolytic capacitor
- (2) Quad SPDT switches
- Power supply
- Bench generator
- (1) DAC0808 D/A convertor

- (1) 741 operational amplifier
- (2) 0.1 µF capacitors
- Max+plus II software
- Computer requirements:
    Minimum 486/66 with 8 MB RAM
- ISP circuit card with the Altera
    EPM7128SLC84 chip
- Oscilloscope
- Digital voltmeter

Discussion:
The D/A convertor converts digital quantities to an analog voltage. The simplest D/A convertor with load resistor is shown in Figure 1. This resistive D/A convertor is dependent on the relationship of each input resistor with respect to each other. Ideally, the most significant input, input D for the circuit shown, will have a resistance "R" and the next significant input, input C, will have a value of "2R," input B will have a resistance of "4R," and input A has a resistance of "8R."

If standard resistor values are used, R_B will probably be 39 KΩ and R_A will be 68 KΩ or 86 KΩ. Either way, the accuracy of the convertor will be affected since the relationship of the resistors are no longer R, 2R, 4R, and 8R. The use of potentiometers may increase accuracy but also increases costs. Additionally, the value of R_L should be at least ten times that of R_A so that the load doesn't affect the resistive network as various DCBA codes are applied.

Assume the DCBA code 0001_2 is applied to the inputs of Figure 1, with a logic-LOW representing 0 volts and a logic-HIGH representing 5 volts.

Fig 2 shows the equivalent circuit with input A wired to Vcc and inputs B, C, and D wired to ground. The equivalent resistance of the 10 K, 20 K, and 40 K resistors is 5714 Ω in series with the 80 KΩ resistor yields 0.333 V at the output. If 0010_2 was applied to Figure 1, the 80 KΩ and 40 KΩ resistors in Figure 2 would be swapped, giving 0.667 volts on e_o.

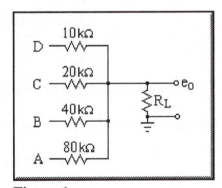

Figure 1

The ladder R/2R circuit in Figure 3 and Thevenin's equivalent in Figure 4 has an advantage over the resistive network in that only two resistor values are required. If the DCBA code 0001_2 is applied to the inputs of the R/2R network, the output voltage will be 0.3125 V. A voltage on input D will have a greater effect of the output that a voltage applied to inputs C, B, or A.

Once the step voltage is determined, 0.333 V for Figure 1 or 0.3125 V for Figure 2, the output voltage for any DCBA code applied may be calculated by multiplying the decimal equivalent of the number applied by the step voltage. Otherwise, doubling the binary value doubles the output voltage. If the input binary number increases by a factor of four, the output increases by a factor of four.

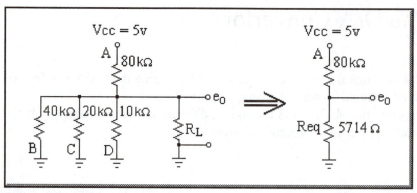

Figure 2

The bit resolution, *N*, is the total number of binary digits in the convertor. For both Figure 1 and Figure 3, the bit resolution is 4.

The voltage resolution, sometimes called the step voltage, E_{STEP}, may be calculated by the following equation:

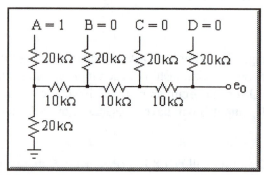

Figure 3

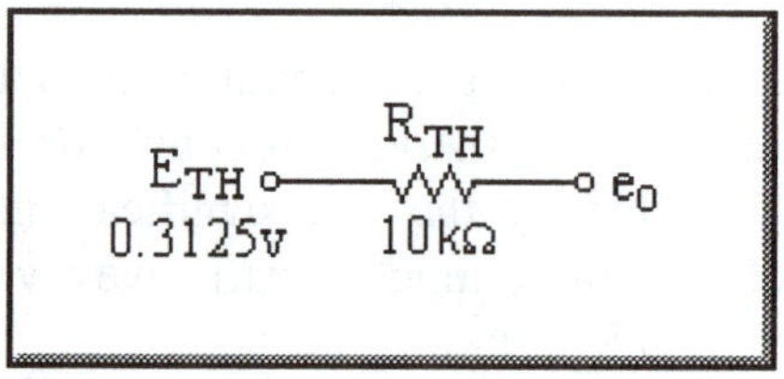

$$E_{TH} \circ\!\!-\!\!\!\overset{R_{TH}}{\wedge\!\wedge\!\wedge}\!\!-\!\!\circ e_0$$
$$0.3125v \quad 10k\Omega$$

Figure 4

For the resistive network:

$$step = \frac{V_{OH} - V_{OL}}{2^N - 1} \qquad (1)$$

For the ladder R/2R network:

$$step = \frac{V_{OH} - V_{OL}}{2^N} \qquad (2)$$

(Source output voltage for a logic-HIGH, V_{OH}, or a logic-LOW, V_{OL}.)

For any D/A convertor, the output voltage for any given input number may be determined by:

$$OUT = E_{STEP} \times \text{Number Applied (IN DECIMAL)} \qquad (3)$$

In integrated form, D/A convertors come in various bit sizes from 8 to 16 bits. This lab focuses mainly on the 8-bit DAC0808 D/A convertor by National Semiconductors. Product specification sheets are available on-line at http://www.national.com. Enter DAC0808 in the search engine on National's site to locate the specific data sheets for the digital-to-analog convertor used in this lab.

The DAC0808 (Fig 5) has a bit resolution of 8 and operates with a maximum of +18 and – 18 VDC. The DAC0808 has an internal R/2R ladder D/A convertor so equations 2 and 3 may be used to calculate the step voltage and output voltage for any binary number applied. Full scale output current (max 2 mA), I_{FS}, is determined by the selection of V_{REF} and R_{REF} attached to pin 14 of the IC. If V_{REF} is 5 V and R_{REF} is 4.7 K, I_{FS} will be

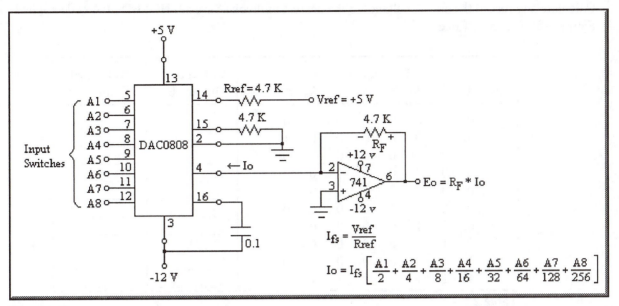

Figure 5

1.064 mA. The 1.064 mA current flowing through the 4.7 K feedback resistor of the inverting operational amplifier shown in Figure 5 produces +5 V on the amplifier output. The operational amplifier protects the D/A convertor from load variations.

The output current, and thus output voltage of the operational amplifier, may be determined for any binary number applied to the D/A convertor using the binary weighted equation shown in the lower right of Figure 5. As long as the feedback resistor, R_F, in the inverting amplifier is identical to the reference resistor at pin 14 of the D/A convertor, equations 2 and 3 may also be used to determine the output voltage of Figure 5.

Part 1   Procedure

1. Construct the circuit shown in Figure 3. Wire the data inputs D, C, B, and A to switches providing 5 V for a logic-HIGH and 0 V for a logic-LOW.

2. Calculate the output voltage to the nearest millivolt of Figure 3 for the different DCBA input combinations. Record your calculated answers in Table 1.

3. Complete Table 1 by recording the measured output voltage for each DCBA input code shown in Table 1.

Part 2   Procedure

1. Construct the D/A convertor circuit shown in Figure 5.

DCBA Code	Calculated Output	Measured Output
0 0 0 0		
0 0 0 1		
0 0 1 0		
0 0 1 1		
0 1 0 0		
0 1 0 1		
0 1 1 0		
0 1 1 1		
1 0 0 0		
1 0 0 1		
1 0 1 0		
1 0 1 1		
1 1 0 0		
1 1 0 1		
1 1 1 0		
1 1 1 1		

Table 1

2.	Calculate and record the output voltage (to the nearest millivolt) for each HGFEDCBA code applied to Figure 5 as shown in Table 2.

D/A Inputs								Calculated Output, Eo	Measured Output, Eo
(MSB) A_1	A_2	A_3	A_4	A_5	A_6	A_7	A_8 (LSB)		
0	0	0	0	0	0	0	0	_____	_____
0	0	0	0	0	0	0	1	_____	_____
0	0	0	0	0	0	1	0	_____	_____
0	0	0	0	0	1	0	0	_____	_____
0	0	0	0	1	0	0	0	_____	_____
0	0	0	1	0	0	0	0	_____	_____
0	0	1	0	0	0	0	0	_____	_____
0	1	0	0	0	0	0	0	_____	_____
1	0	0	0	0	0	0	0	_____	_____
1	1	1	1	1	1	1	1	_____	_____

Table 2

3.	Set the data switches of Figure 5 to each bit combination shown in Table 2 and record the measured output voltages.

4.	As the binary pattern increases in magnitude, the output voltage (decreases/increases).

5.	Do not disassemble your circuit.

# Part 3	Procedure

1.	Add the 0.1 µF capacitor and 4.7 K resistor to ground as shown in Figure 6 to your circuit of Figure 5.

2.	Set the bench signal generator for a 10 KHz sine wave with a low voltage amplitude.

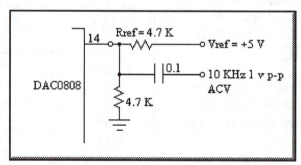

Figure 6

3.	Set all data switches for full scale, FF_H, output of the D/A convertor.

4.	Monitor the ACV at the output of the operational amplifier using an oscilloscope.

5.	Vary the bench signal generator output amplitude until the observed sine wave at the amplifier output is 8 V peak to peak.

6.	Use the oscilloscope to measure and record the bench signal generator sine wave output amplitude that yielded the 8 V p-p signal at the output of the operational amplifier.	_____ V (p-p)

D/A Inputs								Measured Eo ACV	Measured Eo, DCV
(MSB) A_1 A_2 A_3 A_4 A_5 A_6 A_7 A_8 (LSB)									
1 1 1 1 1 1 1 1								_____	_____
0 1 1 1 1 1 1 1								_____	_____
0 0 1 1 1 1 1 1								_____	_____
0 0 0 1 1 1 1 1								_____	_____
0 0 0 0 1 1 1 1								_____	_____
0 0 0 0 0 1 1 1								_____	_____
0 0 0 0 0 0 1 1								_____	_____
0 0 0 0 0 0 0 1								_____	_____
0 0 0 0 0 0 0 0								_____	_____

Table 3

7.   Monitor and record the output of the operational amplifier with the digital voltmeter measuring DCV and the oscilloscope measuring ACV as each input switch is set to a logic-LOW. Be sure to change the meter and scope sensitivity settings for accurate readings as each switch is toggled to a logic-LOW.

8.   You should notice that the amplitude of the AC signal at the output of the operational amplifier is determined by the digital bit pattern applied to the D/A convertor. A computer operator inserts a CD-ROM or DVD-ROM into a player, increases the on-screen volume control, which in turn increases the digital code applied to an D/A convertor, and the analog sound coming out of the speaker increases.

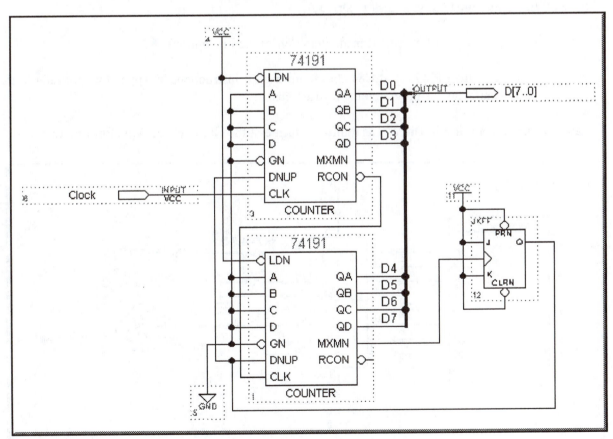

Figure 7

Part 4   Procedure

A ramp signal, either positive stepping or negative stepping, can be created by applying the output of a binary counter to the digital inputs of a D/A convertor.

1.   Connect the circuit card with the EPM7128SLC84 chip to the computer's printer port. If the computer has a software key attached to LPT1, connect the card to the parallel port, LPT2. See your instructor to determine the correct connection port.

2.   Open the Max+plus II software. Assign the project name **dabinctr** and MAX7000S as the device family.

3.   Open the Graphic Editor and construct the circuit shown in Figure 7.

4.   Open the Waveform Editor, set the Grid Size to 20 ns, and create the waveforms shown in Figure 8.

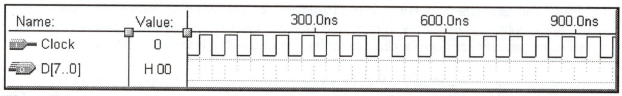

Figure 8

5.   Press the Compiler and Simulator buttons.   Correct all errors before continuing.

6.   Save all files as **dabinctr** to your disk in Drive A.

7.   Select Programmer in the Max+plus II menu item (left of the File option).

8.   Proceed to program the EPM7128SLC84 chip following the instructions in Appendix C or refer to the circuit board manufacturer's programming instructions.

9.   Save all files to your disk in Drive A as **dabinctr**, then exit the Graphic and Waveform Editors.

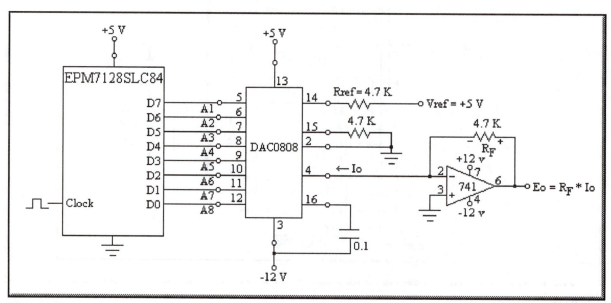

Figure 9

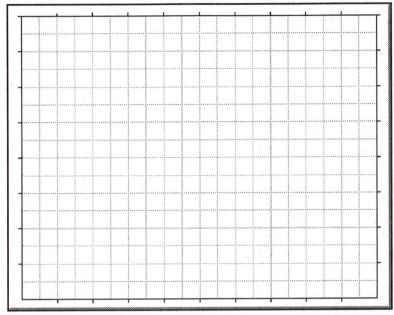

a. Show ground reference

b. $+E_{PEAK} =$ _____V

c. $-E_{PEAK} =$ _____V

d. Time for 1 cycle: _____

e. Frequency of output: _____

Figure 10

10.   Assume the board was successfully programmed, construct the circuit shown in Figure 9. Refer to the **dabinctr.rpt** file on your disk that was created during compilation for pin assignments of the EPM7128SLC84 IC.

11.   Apply a 10 KHz square wave clock (with a zero volt DC offset) to the circuit card containing the EPM7128LC84 chip. See the board manufacturer's programming notes for switch settings when applying an external clock signal.

12.   Monitor the output of the operational amplifier with an oscilloscope, then neatly and accurately sketch the resulting output waveform in Figure 10. Identify the amplitude and time base for the waveform sketched.

Part 5   Procedure

Assume we want to create a 100% modulated waveform with an amplitude of 0 V to 5 V. Let's also take 16 samples of the modulated waveform in one complete cycle. This equates to one sample every 22.5 degrees (360 ÷ 16). From the sketch of the modulated waveform, see Figure 11, we can see the envelope of the waveform appears to be two sine waves, one on a 1.25 VDC reference and the other on a 3.75 VDC reference. Also notice that every other sample is taken from top envelope of the modulated waveform.

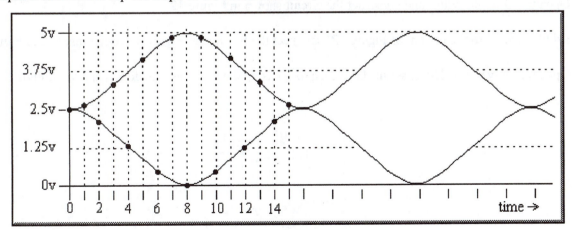

Figure 11

1. Calculate the amplitude of each point on the waveform using the equation: $E_{IT} = E_{PEAK} \sin\theta + E_{REF}$. The peak voltage for each sine wave is 1.25 V. The DC reference for the top sine wave is 3.75 V and the DC reference for the bottom sine ware is 1.25 V. Complete the calculations in Table 4 to determine the magnitude of each point on the waveforms.

Time	Degree	$E_{IT}=E_{PK}\sin\theta+E_{REF}$ (Step 1)	÷ E_{STEP} (Step 2)	Hex equivalent	Binary hgfedcba
0	90	1.25 V × sin90+1.25 = _____ V	_____	_____	_____
1	292.5	1.25 V × sin292.5+3.75= _____ V	_____	_____	_____
2	135	1.25 V × sin135+1.25= _____ V	_____	_____	_____
3	337.5	1.25 V × sin337.5+3.75= _____ V	_____	_____	_____
4	180	1.25 V × sin180+1.25= _____ V	_____	_____	_____
5	22.5	1.25 V × sin22.5+3.75= _____ V	_____	_____	_____
6	225	1.25 V × sin225+1.25= _____ V	_____	_____	_____
7	67.5	1.25 V × sin67.5+3.75= _____ V	_____	_____	_____
8	270	1.25 V × sin270+1.25= _____ V	_____	_____	_____
9	112.5	1.25 V × sin112.5+3.75= _____ V	_____	_____	_____
10	315	1.25 V × sin315+1.25= _____ V	_____	_____	_____
11	157.5	1.25 V × sin157.5+3.75= _____ V	_____	_____	_____
12	0	1.25 V × sin0+1.25= _____ V	_____	_____	_____
13	202.5	1.25 V × sin202.5+3.75= _____ V	_____	_____	_____
14	45	1.25 V × sin45+1.25= _____ V	_____	_____	_____
15	247.5	1.25 V × in247.+3.75= _____ V	_____	_____	_____

Table 4

2. Calculate E_{STEP} for the DAC0808 using Equation 2, then divide each amplitude recorded for Step 1 in Table 4 by the voltage resolution of the DAC0808 D/A convertor. Record the answers in the fourth column in Table 4.

3. Convert each answer recorded for Step 2 to hexadecimal and show the binary equivalents. Record these conversions in Table 4.

4. If the binary equivalents are applied to the D/A convertor inputs at a given rate, the waveform shown in Figure 11, theoretically, will be created.

5. Open the Max+plus II software. Assign the project name **am-mod** and assign MAX7000S as the device family.

6. Open the Graphic Editor and construct the circuit shown in Figure 12.

7. Add Figure 13 to the bottom of Figure 12. Connect the bus line in Figure 13 to the bus line in Figure 12.

8. Open the Waveform Editor, set the Grid Size to 30 ns, and create the waveforms shown in Figure 14.

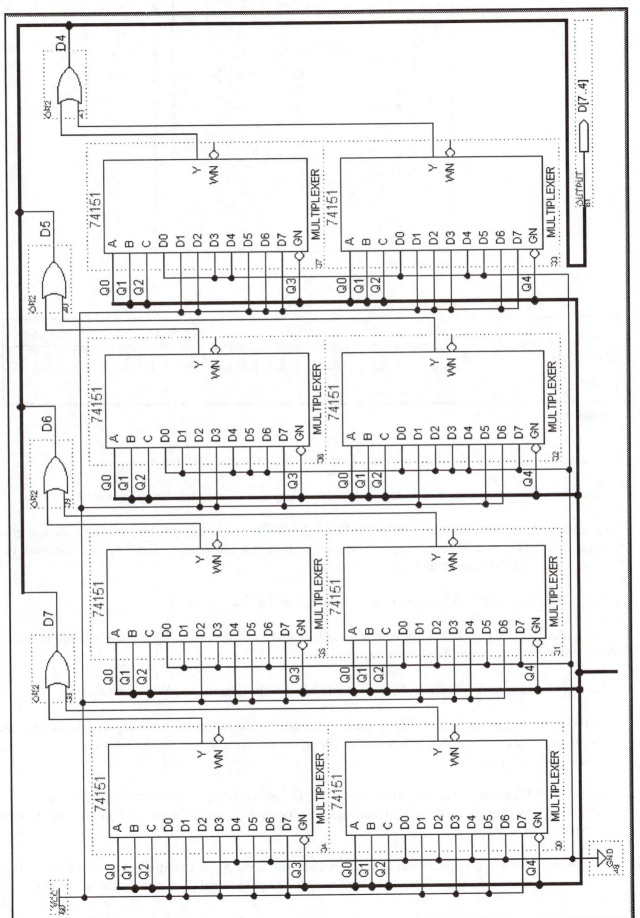

Figure 12

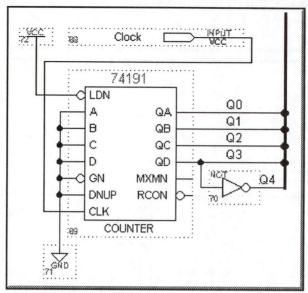

Figure 14

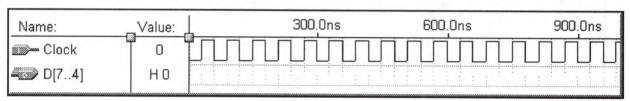

Figure 13

9. Press the Compiler and Simulator buttons. Correct all errors before continuing.

10. Neatly and accurately draw the resulting output waveform in the area provided in Figure 14.

11. Connect the circuit card with the EPM7128SLC84 chip to the computer's printer port. If the computer has a software key attached to LPT1, connect the card to the parallel port, LPT2. See your instructor to determine the correct connection port.

12. Select Programmer in the Max+plus II menu item (left of the File option).

13. Proceed to program the EPM7128SLC84 chip following the instructions in Appendix C or refer to the circuit board manufacturer's programming instructions.

14. Save all files to your disk in Drive A as **am-mod**, then exit the Graphic and Waveform Editors.

15. Assuming the board was successfully programmed, construct the circuit shown in Figure 15. Refer to the **am-mod.rpt** file on your disk that was created during compilation for pin assignments of the EPM7128SLC84 IC.

16. Apply a 10 KHz square wave clock (with a zero volt DC offset) to the circuit card containing the EPM7128LC84 chip. See the board manufacturer's programming notes for switch settings when applying an external clock signal.

17. Monitor the output of the operational amplifier with an oscilloscope, then neatly and accurately sketch the resulting output waveform in Figure 16. Do identify the amplitude and time base for the waveform sketched.

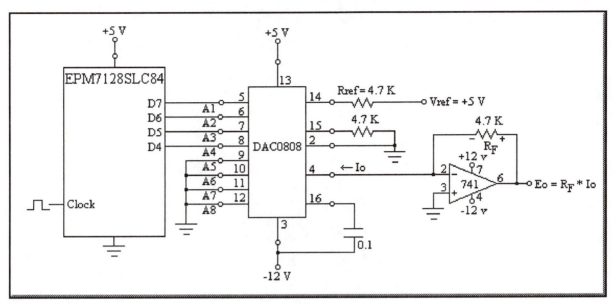

Figure 15

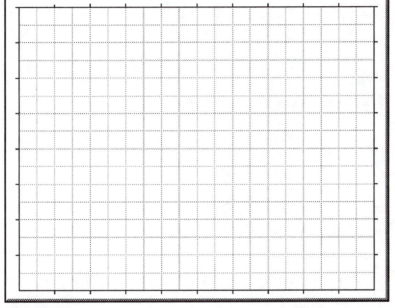

Figure 16

a. Show ground reference

b. $+E_{PEAK} = $ _____ V

c. $-E_{PEAK} = $ _____ V

d. Time for 1 cycle: _____

e. Frequency of output: _____

18. Demonstrate your functional circuit and displayed waveforms to your instructor. Obtain the signature of approval directly on the answer page for this lab.

19. Write a 1 to 2 page summary of this lab. Include a paragraph based on each part of the lab and an embedded graphic of the waveforms for Figure 14.

20. Submit the following for grading:
   - Cover page
   - Typed summary
   - The completed answer page for this lab

Lab 21: The D/A Convertor Answer Page Name: ____________________

Part 1

DCBA code	Calculated Output	Measured Output
0 0 0 0		
0 0 0 1		
0 0 1 0		
0 0 1 1		
0 1 0 0		
0 1 0 1		
0 1 1 0		
0 1 1 1		
1 0 0 0		
1 0 0 1		
1 0 1 0		
1 0 1 1		
1 1 0 0		
1 1 0 1		
1 1 1 0		
1 1 1 1		

Table 1

Part 2

D/A inputs A_1 A_2 A_3 A_4 A_5 A_6 A_7 A_8	Calculated Eo	Measured Eo
0 0 0 0 0 0 0 0		
0 0 0 0 0 0 0 1		
0 0 0 0 0 0 1 0		
0 0 0 0 0 1 0 0		
0 0 0 0 1 0 0 0		
0 0 0 1 0 0 0 0		
0 0 1 0 0 0 0 0		
0 1 0 0 0 0 0 0		
1 0 0 0 0 0 0 0		
1 1 1 1 1 1 1 1		

Table 2

4. Decreases/Increases

Part 3

6. ______________ V p-p

D/A inputs A_1 A_2 A_3 A_4 A_5 A_6 A_7 A_8	Calculated Eo	Measured Eo
0 0 0 0 0 0 0 0		
0 0 0 0 0 0 0 1		
0 0 0 0 0 0 1 0		
0 0 0 0 0 1 0 0		
0 0 0 0 1 0 0 0		
0 0 0 1 0 0 0 0		
0 0 1 0 0 0 0 0		
0 1 0 0 0 0 0 0		
1 0 0 0 0 0 0 0		
1 1 1 1 1 1 1 1		

Table 4

Part 4

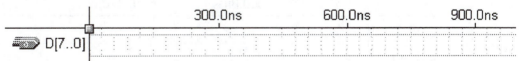

Figure 8

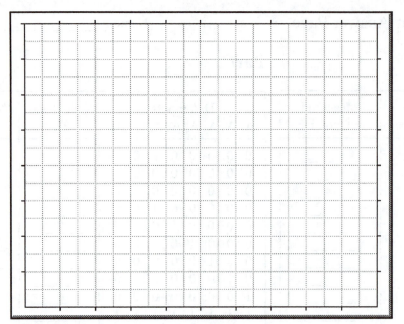

Figure 10

a. Show ground reference

b. $+E_{PEAK} = $ _____ v

c. $-E_{PEAK} = $ _____ v

d. Time for 1 cycle: _____

e. Frequency = _____

Time	(Step 1)	$\div E_{STEP}$ (Step 2)	Hex equivalent	Binary hgfedcba
0	_____ V	_____	_____	_____
1	_____ V	_____	_____	_____
2	_____ V	_____	_____	_____
3	_____ V	_____	_____	_____
4	_____ V	_____	_____	_____
5	_____ V	_____	_____	_____
6	_____ V	_____	_____	_____
7	_____ V	_____	_____	_____
8	_____ V	_____	_____	_____
9	_____ V	_____	_____	_____
10	_____ V	_____	_____	_____
11	_____ V	_____	_____	_____
12	_____ V	_____	_____	_____
13	_____ V	_____	_____	_____
14	_____ V	_____	_____	_____
15	_____ V	_____	_____	_____

Table 4

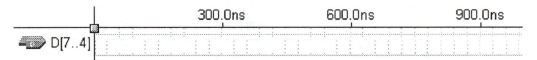

Figure 14

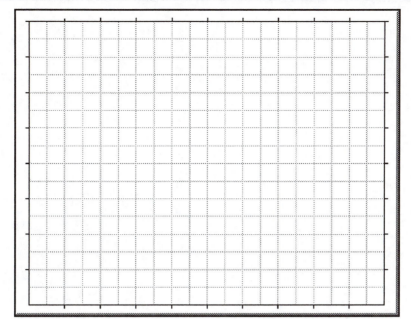

a. Show ground reference

b. $+E_{PEAK}$ = _____V

c. $-E_{PEAK}$ = _____V

d. Time for 1 cycle: _____

e. Frequency = _____

Figure 16

Demonstrated to: _____   Date: _____

Grade: _____

Lab 22: The A/D Convertor

Objectives:

1. Construct and demonstrate the operation of an A/D convertor in free running mode
2. Convert temperature variations to a digital pattern
3. Construct and test a network containing both D/A and A/D convertors

Materials List:

◆ Signal generator	◆ (1) 0.1 µF capacitor
◆ Power supply	◆ (1) 0.001 µF capacitor
◆ Dual trace oscilloscope	◆ (9) 1 KΩ resistors
◆ ADC0804 A/D convertor	◆ (3) 4.7 KΩ resistors
◆ (1) 10 KΩ potentiometer	◆ (1) 10 KΩ resistor
◆ (1) Thermistor	◆ (5) 100 KΩ resistors
◆ (1) 741 op-amp	◆ (1) Pushbutton switch
◆ (8) Light emitting diodes	◆ (8) SPDT switches

Discussion:

The analog-to-digital (A/D) convertor converts analog quantities to digital values. The 8-bit convertor shown in Figure 1 may be used as an I/O port on a microprocessor or as a stand alone unit. The A/D has three active-LOW inputs and one active-LOW output control signals.

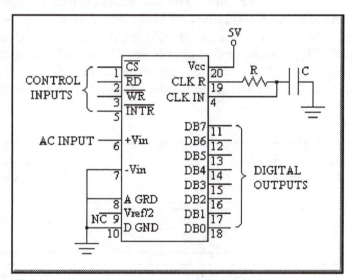

Figure 1

An internal successive approximation register (SAR) is *reset* when both the chip select, CS, and Write, WR, inputs are a logic-LOW. *Start of conversion* takes place from 1 to 8 clock cycles after either CS or WR go to a logic-HIGH. Once conversion starts, the internal SAR and a comparator will convert the analog input to a digital quantity in 64 clock pulses. The contents of the SAR will then be transferred to output tristate latches and cause an interrupt, INTR, to become active. Figure 2 shows the timing diagram of the A/D Convertor for the write cycle.

To read the data in the tristate output latches, both CS and RD must be a logic-LOW. Figrue 3 shows a typical read cycle based on an interrupt occurring on a microprocessor pin. Based on the interrupt, the microprocessor addresses the A/D convertor, then sends a read command, RD. Data is valid on the output pins during the time segment while both CS and RD are logic-LOW.

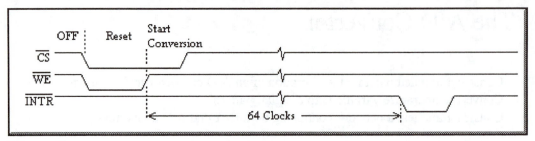

Figure 2

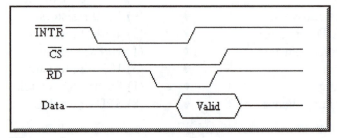

Figure 3

The A/D convertor may be operated in *free running mode* by connecting the INTR output to the WR input. Initially, WR will need to be forced to a logic-LOW to initiate the free running mode, but once started, the response of INTR will cause triggering of the next conversion time. Figure 4 shows the typical response of the A/D convertor in free running mode. Initially, the A/D is turned off by the WR input at a logic-HIGH. When WR drops to a logic-LOW, the A/D is reset. When WR goes to a logic-HIGH, the A/D starts its conversion of the analog input signal. After 64 clocks, the INTR goes low, forcing reset (when CS and WR are logic-LOW) and causes the output latches to latch onto the new sample. The new output data is the result of the conversion (after 64 clock cycles). Since CS and RD are tied low, the INTR is automatically returned to a logic-HIGH, hence starting the next conversion cycle.

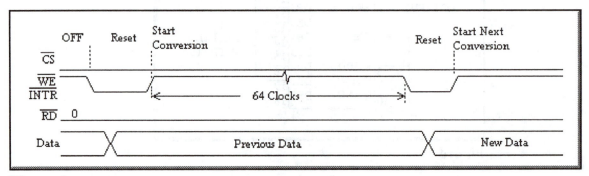

Figure 4

Part 1   Procedure

1.   Construct the circuit shown in Figure 5. Use 1-KΩ resistors in series with all light emitting diodes.

2.   Set the voltage at the wiper arm of the potentiometer to each value listed in Table 1, then record the binary equivalent as shown by the LEDs.

3.   Convert each 8-bit binary entry in Table 1 to its decimal equivalent. Record the equivalents in the third column in Table 1.

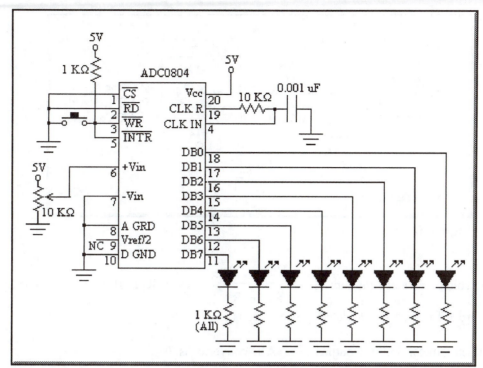

Figure 5

Input voltage (DCV)	Output H G F E D C B A	Decimal Equivalent of Binary Value	Multiply Decimal Equivalent by E_{STEP}
0 V	_____	_____10	_____
0.5 V	_____	_____10	_____
1.0 V	_____	_____10	_____
1.5 V	_____	_____10	_____
2.0 V	_____	_____10	_____
2.5 V	_____	_____10	_____
3 V	_____	_____10	_____
3.5 V	_____	_____10	_____
4 V	_____	_____10	_____
4.5 V	_____	_____10	_____
5 V	_____	_____10	_____

Table 1

4. Multiply the decimal equivalents of the binary numbers by the step voltage (19.5 mV) for the 8-bit A/D convertor. Record your answers in the fourth column in Table 1.

5. The frequency of the internal clock may be calculated by : $= \dfrac{1}{1.1RC}$ (see Figure 1)

Based on this equation and the parts shown in Figure 5, the oscillator frequency is: _____Hz

6. Disconnect the 10-KΩ potentiometer, replacing the potentiometer with the following circuit. Wire the E_{ERROR} output of the circuit shown in Figure 6 to the +V_{IN} input of the A/D convertor.

7. Resistance of the thermistor (out of circuit): _____ Ω.

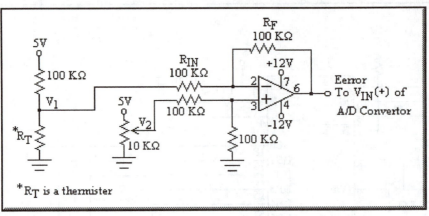

Figure 6

8. Using the voltage divider equation: $1 = \dfrac{Vcc \times R_T}{R_1 + R_T}$ where R_1 is 100 KΩ and R_T is the measured value recorded for Step 7, calculate V_1 when Vcc is 5 V. $V_1 = $ _____

9. Set the potentiometer until the output of the A/D convertor is 70_H.

10. Measure and record the voltages at
    - the potentiometer wiper arm: $V_2 = $ _____ V.
    - the junction of the thermistor and the two 100-KΩ resistors: $V_1 = $ _____ V.
    - the output of the operational amplifier: $E_{ERROR} = $ _____ V.

11. Was the measured value of V_1 recorded for Step 10 very close to the calculated value recorded for Step 8? (Yes/No)

12. The voltage at the output of the difference amplifier of Figure 6 may be calculated using the following equation: ERROR = $A_V(V_2 - V_1)$, where $A_V = R_F / R_{IN}$. Based on the recorded voltages in Step 10, calculate the error voltage when $R_F = R_{IN}$. $E_{ERROR} = $ _____ V

13. Was the calculated error voltage (Step 12) very close to the measured value? (Yes/No)

14. Place a voltmeter at the output of the operational amplifier to monitor the voltage.

15. Squeeze the thermistor, being careful not to short the thermistor wires to each other. Record the highest binary number seen at the output of the A/D convertor and highest voltage measured at the output of the operational amplifier.

    Binary number: _____ 2

    Highest DCV on operational amplifier output: _____ V

16. The circuit is not the best or most accurate temperature measuring device but it does show how temperature may be converted to a digital value. If the digital output of the A/D convertor is read by a microprocessor, the software controlling the microprocessor may equate different digital values read to an equivalent temperature. The microprocessor may take a temperature reading once an hour or more often as desired to monitor temperature, tabulate the results maybe once a week, and send the data to a central office to be included in monthly reports. Use your imagination for other applications of such a circuit.

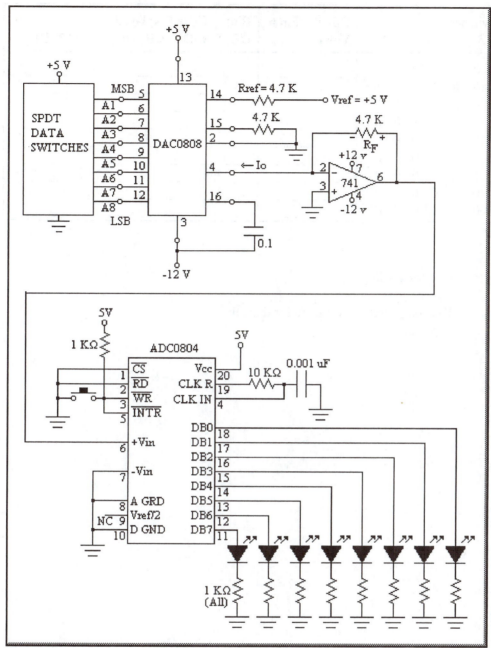

Figure 7

Part 2 Procedure

1. Construct the circuit shown in Figure 7.

2. For various values of switch settings listed in Table 2, measure the voltage at the output of the operational amplifier and record the pattern displayed by the LEDs.

3. Demonstrate your operational circuit (Figure 7) to your instructor. Obtain the signature of approval directly on the answer page for this lab.

4. Write a 1 to 2 page summary pertaining to this lab. Include embedded graphics of the schematic used for Part 2 of this lab.

Set Switches A_1 A_2 A_3 A_4 A_5 A_6 A_7 A_8	Op-amp Pin 6 Voltage	Binary Code Displayed DB_7 DB_6 DB_5 DB_4 DB_3 DB_2 DB_1 DB_0
0 0 0 0 0 0 0 0	_____	__ __ __ __ __ __ __ __
0 0 0 0 0 0 0 1	_____	__ __ __ __ __ __ __ __
0 0 0 0 0 0 1 0	_____	__ __ __ __ __ __ __ __
0 0 0 0 0 1 0 0	_____	__ __ __ __ __ __ __ __
0 0 0 0 1 0 0 0	_____	__ __ __ __ __ __ __ __
0 0 0 1 0 0 0 0	_____	__ __ __ __ __ __ __ __
0 0 1 0 0 0 0 0	_____	__ __ __ __ __ __ __ __
0 1 0 0 0 0 0 0	_____	__ __ __ __ __ __ __ __
1 0 0 0 0 0 0 0	_____	__ __ __ __ __ __ __ __

Table 2

5.   Submit the following for grading:
- Cover page
- The completed answer page for this lab
- Typed summary

Lab 22: The A/D Convertor Answer Page

Name: _____

Part 1

Input Voltage (DCV)	Output H G F E D C B A	Decimal Equivalent of Binary Value	Multiply Decimal Equivalent by E_{STEP}
0 V	__ __ __ __ __ __ __ __	_____$_{10}$	_____
0.5 V	__ __ __ __ __ __ __ __	_____$_{10}$	_____
1.0 V	__ __ __ __ __ __ __ __	_____$_{10}$	_____
1.5 V	__ __ __ __ __ __ __ __	_____$_{10}$	_____
2.0 V	__ __ __ __ __ __ __ __	_____$_{10}$	_____
2.5 V	__ __ __ __ __ __ __ __	_____$_{10}$	_____
3 V	__ __ __ __ __ __ __ __	_____$_{10}$	_____
3.5 V	__ __ __ __ __ __ __ __	_____$_{10}$	_____
4 V	__ __ __ __ __ __ __ __	_____$_{10}$	_____
4.5 V	__ __ __ __ __ __ __ __	_____$_{10}$	_____
5 V	__ __ __ __ __ __ __ __	_____$_{10}$	_____

Table 1

5. $F =$ _____ 7. _____ Ω 8. $V_1 =$ _____

10. $V_2 =$ _____ V $V_1 =$ _____ V $E_{ERROR} =$ _____ V

11. Yes/No 12. $E_{ERROR} =$ _____ V 13. Yes/No

15. _____$_2$ _____ V

Part 2

Set Switches A_1 A_2 A_3 A_4 A_5 A_6 A_7 A_8	Op-amp Pin 6 voltage	Binary Code Displayed DB_7 DB_6 DB_5 DB_4 DB_3 DB_2 DB_1 DB_0
0 0 0 0 0 0 0 0	_____	__ __ __ __ __ __ __ __
0 0 0 0 0 0 0 1	_____	__ __ __ __ __ __ __ __
0 0 0 0 0 0 1 0	_____	__ __ __ __ __ __ __ __
0 0 0 0 0 1 0 0	_____	__ __ __ __ __ __ __ __
0 0 0 0 1 0 0 0	_____	__ __ __ __ __ __ __ __
0 0 0 1 0 0 0 0	_____	__ __ __ __ __ __ __ __
0 0 1 0 0 0 0 0	_____	__ __ __ __ __ __ __ __
0 1 0 0 0 0 0 0	_____	__ __ __ __ __ __ __ __
1 0 0 0 0 0 0 0	_____	__ __ __ __ __ __ __ __

Table 2

3. Demonstrated to: _____ Date: _____

Grade: _____

Lab 23: Analog Storage

Objectives:

1. Using the Max+Plus II software, design digital control circuitry to control the sampling of an analog signal by an A/D convertor and the read/write cycles of a memory chip shown in Figure 1 according to the following criteria.

   B. The 7128S will contain a 12-bit binary counter with outputs A0 to A10 used to address memory from 000_H to $7FF_H$.

   C. Upon reset, the 7128S will turn ON the A/D convertor, turn ON memory, and write the first analog sample converted to digital at address 000_H in memory.

   D. As the counter counts up to $7FF_H$, the analog samples converted to digital will be stored in sequential memory addresses.

   E. Once the counter overflows (goes beyond $7FF_H$), the A/D convertor shuts off and the memory switches to a continuous read mode until the next manual reset pulse.

   F. The analog output of the D/A convertor is continuous.

2. Construct and demonstrate the circuit illustrated in Figure 1.

Materials Required:

- Max+Plus II software
- Computer requirements:
  Minimum 486/66 with 8 MB RAM
- ISP circuit card with the Altera EPM7128SEC84 chip

- Signal generator
- Power supply
- Dual trace oscilloscope
- Parts to successfully construct Figure 1

Discussion:

This lab is loosely defined so as not to stifle your creativity. Many years ago, analog oscilloscopes were called oscilloscopes because there were only one type . . . analog. Once digital scopes hit the market, the terms analog and digital were necessary to describe the type of oscilloscope in use. As digital oscilloscopes advanced, someone decided that we can store the digital information to memory, and later recall the stored signal.

Figure 1 shows the basic concept for a digital storage oscilloscope, an input signal is applied, it is converted to digital, and stored to memory in digital form. If or when necessary, the digital pattern in memory can reproduce the analog signal. How much storage is dependent on the size of memory.

This circuit works well to convert low frequency sine waves, pulse waves, or triangular waves to digital.

Part 1   Procedure

3. Open the Max+Plus II software. Assign the project name **lab23** and MAX7000S as the device family.

4. Open the Graphic Editor and design control circuitry and a 12-bit UP counter that will satisfy the criteria stated in the objectives.

5. Open the Waveform Editor and create a set of waveforms to demonstrate your design produces the desired output control signals. You may want to use bit 3 of the counter instead of bit 11 to trigger your control circuitry into a memory read mode. Once the circuit is functional, reassign the proper trigger bit before programming the device.

6. Connect the circuit card with the EPM7128SLC84 chip to the computer's printer port. If the computer has a software key attached to LPT1, connect the card to the parallel port, LPT2. See your instructor to determine the correct connection port.

7. Select Programmer in the Max+Plus II menu item (left of the File option).

8. Proceed to program the EPM7128SLC84 chip following the instructions in Appendix C or refer to the circuit board manufactures programming instructions.

8. Save all files to your disk in Drive A as **lab23**, then exit the Graphic and Waveform Editors.

9. Assume the board was successfully programmed, construct the circuit shown in Fig 1. Refer to the **lab23.rpt** file on your disk that was created during compilation for pin assignments of the EPM7128SLC84 IC.

10. Connect LEDs with series resistors on the address/control/data lines for visual signs that the circuit indeed is writing and reading data to/from memory and that the A/D convertor was shut off during memory read cycle time.

11. Demonstrate the functional circuit to your instructor. Obtain the signature of approval directly on your cover page for this lab.

    During the demonstration, you will disconnect the signal source once your circuit is in the memory read cycle. The output should then be a continuous wave without the input.

12. Obtain a hard copy of the Graphic and Waveform Editor files of your final design.

13. Write a 1 to 2 page summary explaining your circuit design. Provide an embedded schematic and waveforms obtained from the Graphic and Waveform Editor files.

14. Submit the following

    - Cover page
    - Typed summary
    - Hard copy of your control circuit (Graphic Editor file)
    - Hard copy of the Waveform Editor file

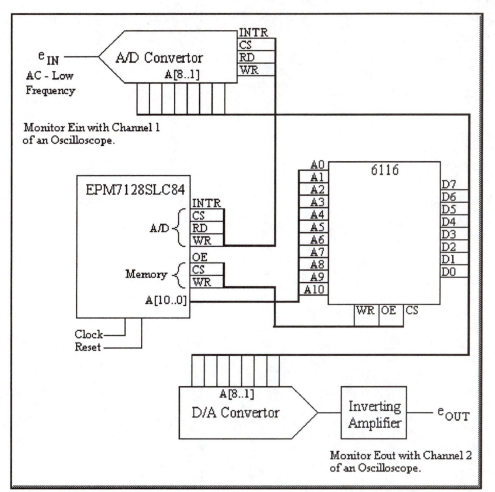

Figure 1

Lab 24: LPM_COMPARE

Objectives:

    1.   Use the LPM _COMPARE symbol in a functional circuit

    2.   Write a technical report with embedded graphics

Materials List:

- Max+plus II software by Altera Corporation
- University Board by Altera Corporation (optional)
- Computer requirements:
  - Minimum 486/66 with 8 MB RAM
- Floppy diskette
- Word processor

Discussion:

Standard TTL integrated circuits have physical limitations due to their fixed data widths and circuit functions. The OR gate in Figure 1 combines two output functions of the 7485 4-bit magnitude comparator to give a logic-HIGH output when input A is greater than or equal to input B. Additional logic gates are required to obtain functions such as less than or equal to and not equal to. Using a High Level Descriptive Language, VHDL, engineers can create their own logic circuit symbols with added features such as the LPM_COMPARE symbol (Figure 2).

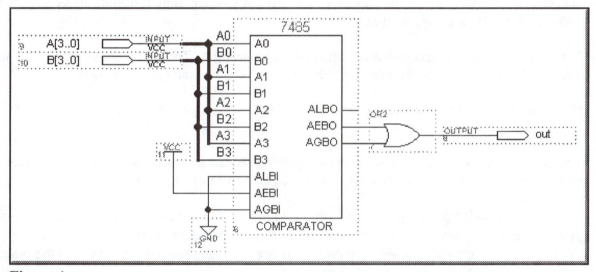

Figure 1

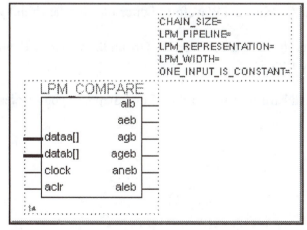

Figure 2

Added control lines such as clock and aclr make the comparator more functional. Also note that cascade inputs are no longer necessary since the data width becomes software controlled, LPM_WIDTH, not hardware based.

Ports dataa[ ], datab[ ], and at least one output are required and the LPM_WIDTH must be defined for normal comparison. Read the Help screen available in the Edit Ports/Parameters dialog box for pin usage and assignments. To open the Edit screen, double click on the Parameter box, upper-right corner of the LPM_COMPARE symbol. Click on the Help on LPM_COMPARE button for detailed descriptions of each port.

Part 1 Procedure

1. Create an asynchronous circuit using the LPM_COMPARE symbol to compare a 4-bit number (variable) to number 5 (constant). The output will be a logic-HIGH if the variable is equal to or greater than the constant, otherwise the output will be a logic-LOW.

2. Create a set of waveforms showing all possible combinations of the variable demonstrating the output satisfies the conditions as stated above.

3. Using a word processor, create a lab cover page and write a technical summary explaining your circuit and accompanying waveforms. Identify abnormal conditions that may occur in the output signal, time delays, parameter settings, and pin assignments. Include the following acronyms and identify their proper name and function: aeb, agb, ageb, alb, aleb, and aneb. The waveforms, circuit, and pin assignments are to be embedded in (not attached to) your summary. All pages of your report must include the footer, LPM_COMPARE, and page number.

4. Modify your circuit for synchronous operation with a latency of 1. The rising edge of the clock should occur at the same rate of the changing variable. Be sure the clock starts at a logic-LOW.

5. Obtain hard copies of the circuit modification and waveforms verifying that the circuit operates in synchronous mode.

6. Compare the waveforms for asynchronous and synchronous modes of operation. Update your summary to include advantages of using synchronous mode on the LPM_COMPARE symbol.

7. Construct a circuit that compares the output of a 4-bit binary counter to the output of a 4-bit Johnson counter. Both counters are to be asynchronously cleared in the first 5 ns. As the counters count, determine when each counter is greater than, equal to, or less than the other counter. Use LPM functions for all parts.

8. Obtain hard copies of the Graphic and Waveform Editor files for the circuit you designed.

9. Demonstrate the circuit designed to the instructor. Obtain the signature of approval directly on the hard copy of the Graphic Editor file.

10. Submit your summary and hard copies from Step 5 and Step 8 to your professor for review.

Lab 25: LPM_ADD_SUB

Objectives:

1. Use the LPM _ADD_SUB symbol in a functional circuit
2. Write a technical report with embedded graphics

Materials Required:

♦ Max+plus II software by Altera Corporation
♦ University Board by Altera Corporation (optional)
♦ Computer requirements:
    Minimum 486/66 with 8 MB RAM
♦ Floppy diskette
♦ Word processor

Discussion:

The LPM_ADD_SUB symbol shown in Figure 1 may be used for signed or unsigned addition or subtraction. Synchronous operation may be implemented by using the clock input.

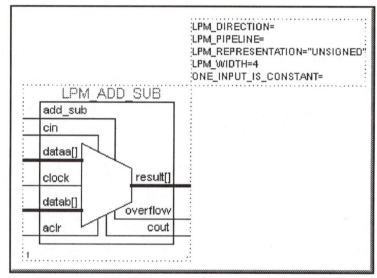

Figure 1

The dataa[ ], datab[ ], and results[ ] ports are required and LPM_WIDTH must be defined for basic summation. All other input and output ports are optional. Read the Help screen available in the Edit Ports/Parameters dialog box for pin usage and assignments. To open the Edit screen, double click on the Parameter box, upper-right corner of the LPM_ADD_SUB symbol. Click on the Help on LPM_ADD_SUB button for detailed descriptions of each port.

Part 1 Procedure

1. Create an asynchronous unsigned 4-bit adder with sum and carry outputs using the LPM_ADD_SUB symbol.

2. Create Waveform A[3..0], starting at 0, incrementing by 6 at a frequency of 10 MHz.

3. Create Waveform B[3..0], starting at 5, incrementing by 11 at a frequency of 10 MHz.

4. Using a word processor, create a lab cover page and write a technical summary explaining your circuit and accompanying waveforms. Embed the **LPM_ADD_SUB** symbol in your report and write a descriptive paragraph for each of these ports: add_sub, cin, dataa[ ], clock, datab[ ] aclr, result[ ], overflow, and count. The waveforms, circuit, and pin assignments are to be embedded in (not attached to) your summary. All pages of your report must include a footer showing LPM_ADD_SUB and the page number as shown in the footer at the bottom of this page.

5. Modify your circuit for synchronous operation with a latency of 1. Set the clock frequency to 20 MHz.

6. Obtain hard copies of the circuit modification and waveforms verifying the circuit operates in synchronous mode.

7. Compare the waveforms for asynchronous and synchronous modes of operation. Update your summary to include advantages of using synchronous mode on the LPM_ADD_SUB symbol.

8. Demonstrate the circuit designed to the instructor. Obtain the signature of approval directly on the hard copy of the Graphic Editor file.

9. Submit your summary and hard copies from Step 6 to your professor for review.

Lab 26: LPM_Counter

Objective:

    1.   This lab will step you through the process of creating a 4-bit binary up/down counter. There are many program options, but this lab will focus on the clock, counter enable, and the clear outputs. The synchronous load input will be selected but will never be active.

Materials List:

    ♦   Max+plus II software by Altera Corporation
    ♦   University Board by Altera Corporation (optional)
    ♦   Computer requirements:
                Minimum 486/66 with 8 MB RAM
    ♦   Floppy disk

Discussion:

If you need a 4-bit binary or BCD counter, select a chip and use it in your circuit design. However, at times larger counters are required, which can be constructed using basic integrated circuits, but having a macro design available simplifies the design considerably. The LPM_COUNTER function has all the standard synchronous and asynchronous inputs available that may be selected to customize a counter design. A dialog box appears when the LPM_COUNTER is selected, allowing one to select from a wide range of inputs by marking them as used or unused. The designer may assign either active-HIGH or active-LOW status to any one or more inputs or outputs.

It is assumed that students have a firm understanding of counters and know the differences between, advantages of, disadvantages of, and purpose of each asynchronous and synchronous input.

Part 1   Procedure

1.   Open the Graphic and Waveform Editors. Assign the project name **binupctr**.

2.   Select Symbol, then Enter Symbol. Double click on the **\Max2lib\mega_lpm** symbol library. Scroll down Symbol Files and select the **lpm_counter** then press OK.

3.   An Edit Ports/Parameters dialog box should appear on the screen. Set the ports according to the table below.

Name	Status
clock	used
cnt_en	used
q[LPM_WIDTH 1..0]	used
sload	used
all other ports	unused

4.   Set Parameters as shown in the table on the next page, then press OK.

Name	Value
LPM_AVALUE	\<none\>
LPM_DIRECTION	up
LPM_MODULUS	16
LPM_SVALUE	\<none\>
LPM_WIDTH	4

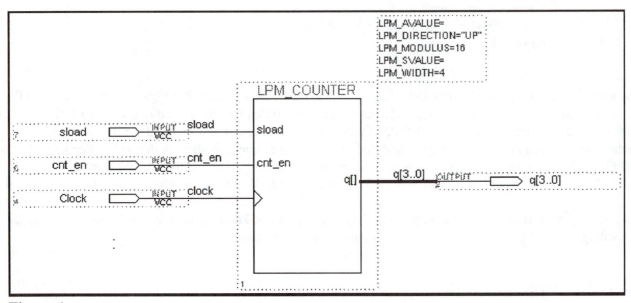

Figure 1

5.   Complete the circuit wiring as shown in Figure 1.

6.   Press the Compiler button. When finished, the Compiler Project Compilation window should show zero errors and one warning. Press OK.

7.   Double click on the **RPT** icon that appears below the Fitter box in the Compiler window and answer the following questions.

Questions	Responses
How many logic cells were used for this circuit?	a. _____
How many input pins were used?	b. _____
How many output pins were used?	c. _____
What percentage of the IC was used for this circuit?	d. _____
What was the total compilation time for this circuit?	e. _____
How many flip-flops were used for this IC?	f. _____
What name is assigned to unused pins?	g. _____

8.   Identify the pin numbers assigned to the following pins.

Pin Name	Pin Number
clock	h. _____
sload	i. _____
aclr	j. _____
q[0]	k. _____
q[1]	l. _____
q[2]	m. _____
q[3]	n. _____

9.   Answer the following questions.

What pin number is VCCIN?   o. _____

Identify all VCCIO pins.   p. _____

Identify all the ground pins.   q. _____

10.   Open the Waveform Editor and create the waveforms shown in Figure 2.

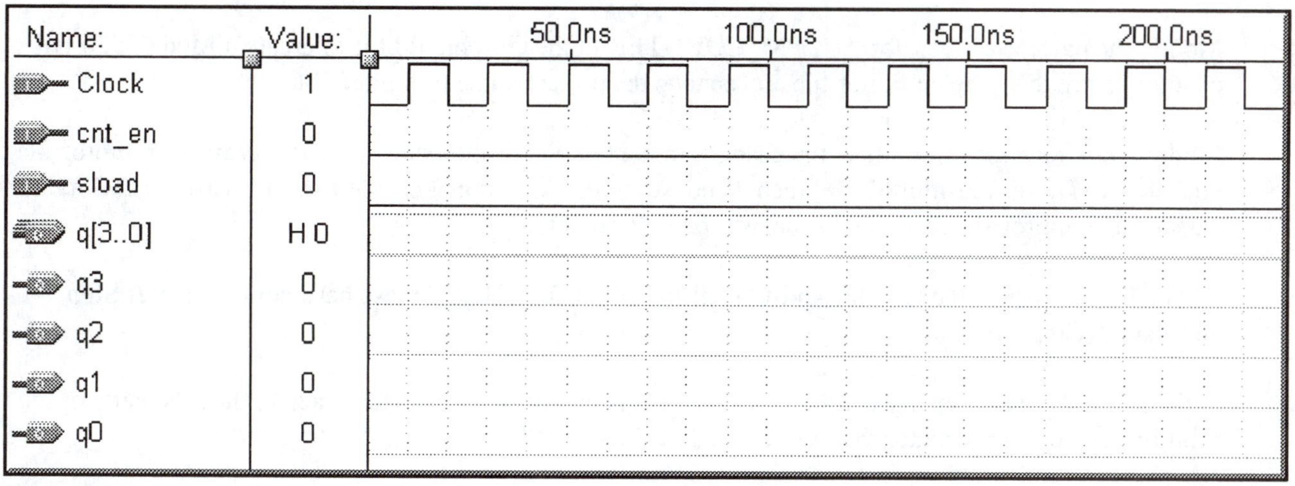

Figure 2

11.   Press the Simulator button. Correct all errors before continuing.

12. Answer the following questions.

What is the frequency of the clock?   r. _____

What direction does the counter count?   s. Up/Down

The counter advances on the _?_ edge.   t. Positive/negative

What is the count sequence?   u. _____

13. Select Max+plus II then Timing Analyzer. Press the Start button then press OK.

14. The Timing Analyzer shows the propagation delay time of the outputs with respect to the clock input. Record the delay: _____. Close the Timing Analyzer screen.

15. Save all files to Drive A as **binupctr**, then exit the Graphic and Waveform Editors.

Part 2   Procedure

1. Open the Max+plus II software.   Assign the project name **updnctr**.

2. Using the LPM_COUNTER in the Max+plus II software, create an 8-bit up/down counter.

3. Open the Waveform Editor, create clock pulses with a 10 ns period (5 ns pulse width), then verify the counter counts up or down as determined by LPM_DIRECTION designator. (You will not see the entire count sequence.)

4. Save all files to Drive A as **updnctr**, but do not exit the Graphic and Waveform Editors.

5. Modify the parameters box for the LPM_COUNTER in the Graphic Editor to create a Mod 65536 UP counter. Save the Graphic Editor file and change the project name to **mod65536**.

6. Modify your waveforms to reflect the changes in the Graphic Editor file. Save the Waveform Editor file to your disk in Drive A as **mod65536**, then demonstrate the operational circuit to your instructor. Obtain the signature of approval directly on the answer page for this lab.

7. Obtain hard copies of the Graphic and Waveform Editor files. Label these hard copies **Part 2, Step 7A** and **Part 2, Step 7B**.

8. Write a 1 to 2 page summary pertaining to the results obtained for this lab. Include the schematic of the 8-bit binary up/down counter that was created for Step 2 of Part 2.

9. Submit the following for grading:
   - Cover page
   - Typed summary with embedded graphics
   - The completed answer page for this lab
   - Hard copy of the Graphic and Waveform Editor files from **Part 2, Step 7A** and **Part 2, Step 7B**, respectively.

Name: _____

Part 1

7.

8.

9.

Numeric response

Pin Number

o. _____

a. _____

h. _____

p. _____

b. _____

i. _____

q. _____

c. _____

j. _____

d. _____

k. _____

e. _____

l. _____

f. _____

m. _____

g. _____

n. _____

12.

r. _____

s.   Up/Down

t.   Positive/negative

u. _____

14.   _____

Part 2

6.   Demonstrated to: _____ Date _____

Grade: _____

Appendix A: How do I ...

Assign a Project Name

From the main menu, select **File - Project - Name...** Complete the **Project Name** dialog box (Figure 1).

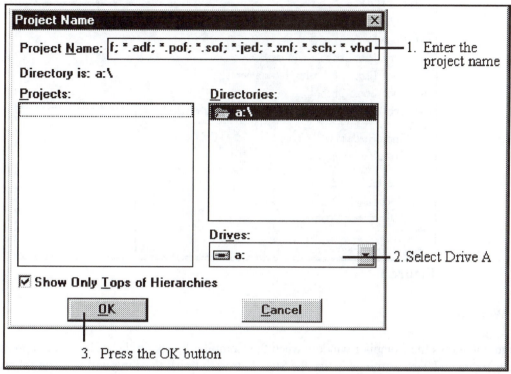

Figure 1

Open New Graphic or Waveform Editor

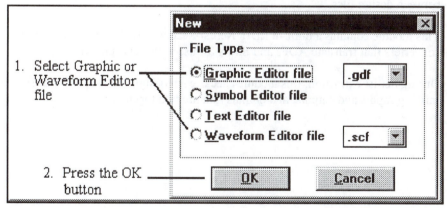

Figure 2

From the main menu, select **File - New...**. Complete the **New** dialog box (Figure 2).

Change the Font or Line Style

From the main menu, select **Option - Font** or **Option - Text Size** (Figure 3). Select the font or line type desired. The Graphic Editor must be in the foreground for this option.

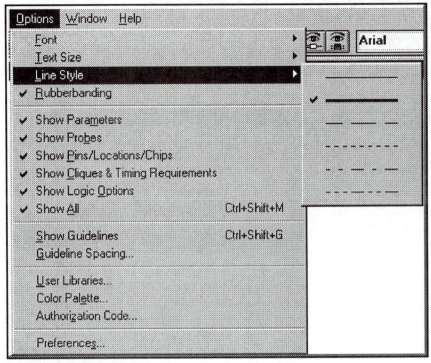

Figure 3

Compiler Window

Figure 4 shows the Compiler window when the Compiler button in the main menu is pressed. Assuming zero errors and zero warnings, press the Start button to finish the compilation. The following tasks are completed by the compiler[2].

The Compiler module converts each design file in a project into a separate binary CNF. The file names of the CNF(s) are based on the project name.

The Compiler Netlist Extractor also creates a single HIF that documents the hierarchical connections between design files.

This module contains a built-in EDIF Netlist Reader, VHDL Netlist Reader, and XNF Netlist Reader and converters that translate ADFs and SMFs for use with Max+plus II.

During netlist extraction, this module checks each design file for problems such as duplicate node names, missing inputs and outputs, and outputs that are tied together.

---

2   Max+plus II Help window for the Compiler Netlist Extractor.

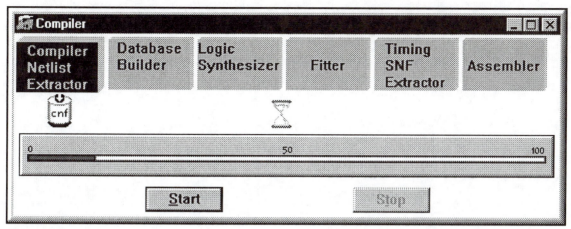

Figure 4

Appendix B: Error Messages

I cannot predict nor provide solutions to all possible errors students will make when using the Max+plus II software but here are a few common errors/solutions that my students have encountered.

Error #1:   **Cannot find the SCF file.**
                      Occurs when trying to simulate the file.
Solution: Save the Waveform Editor file to your disk in Drive A. Also, be sure both Graphic and Waveform Editor files **AND** the Project Name have been assigned to Drive A (Figure 1). You must have a current copy of the Waveform Editor opened (and on disk).

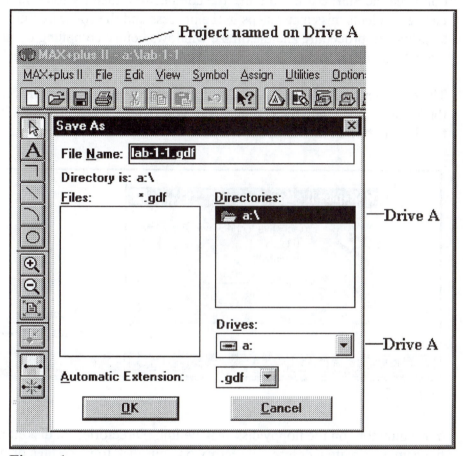

Figure 1

Error #2:   **Cannot Simulate – No SCF is loaded for the project.**
                      You forgot to save the Waveform Editor file.
Solution: Bring the Waveform Editor to the foreground and save the file.

Error #3:   **The software won't let you save files or assign a project name to Drive A.**
                      Bad disk in Drive A or the disk is full.
Solution: Use the Windows Explorer to verify disk space, read/write ability, or replace disk.

Error #4: **The software displays an internal error message.**

Max+plus II had a problem with the operating system.

Solution: Exit Max+plus II and re-open the software. Hopefully, your file was saved to the disk so you may reopen it. If you have to recreate your file, then this is a good practice session.

Error #5: **The software automatically boots you right out of the working area, you're now looking at the Windows[R] desktop screen.**

Oops, this typically is an "Operator Error" that causes the software to behave irrationally.

Solution #1: Many times, I have noticed that students like to minimize each screen instead of reducing the work area size to see what is in the background. As a result, when you compile, you don't see the Start button to finish the compilation, then try to continue to simulate. Hence, students miss many steps in the process and the software "gives up." Follow the step-by-step procedure and maximize windows before compiling or simulating. You miss the details of each screen left in minimize form, and hence, skip steps in the process.

The compiler box (Figure 2) will disappear when you press the OK button and you may think you're done with the compiler, but you're not. Maximize the Compiler icon to press the Start button in the Compiler window.

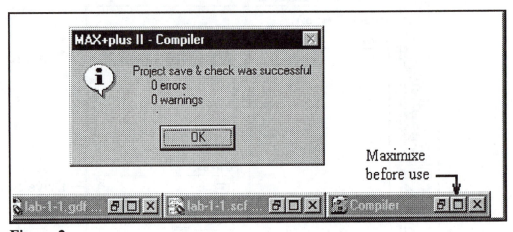

Figure 2

Solution #2: Your directory on the floppy disk may be full. Directories on diskettes are limited to 125 file names. Create a different directory on your disk to place files or obtain a new diskette.

Error #6: **Compiled, simulated, and the output waveform did not change at all.**

You assigned the output as an input in the Waveform Editor.

Solution: Double click on the waveform and reassign the wave as an output. Then re-simulate the circuit. Pay particular attention to the And2 labels in Figure 3.

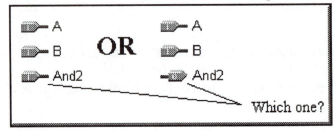

Figure 3

Error #7: **Programmer cannot detect hardware.**
Unrecognized device or socket is empty. (Figrue 4)

Solution 1: Select the proper Parallel Port under Hardware Setup in the Options menu.

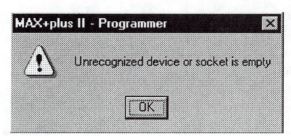

Figure 4

Solution 2: Be sure the interface cable between the circuit card containing the EPM7128SLC84 and the computer printer port is connected.

Solution 3: If this is an NT station, be sure the Byte Blaster driver (located on the Max+plus II CD-ROM) was installed. Installation of the drive will require administrative rights if this is a networked machine.

Solution 4: Download the self extracting **univers.exe** file from Altera's university support page at http://www.altera.com. Place this file on the Maxplus2 directory, then execute the file.

Error #8: **Unrecognized device or socket is empty.**
ByteBlaster is not present - - check power and cables. (Figure 5)

Solution: Connect the ByteBlaster (or interface cable) to the computer and board containing the EPM7128SLC84 chip.

Apply 7- to 12-VDC to the board containing the EPM7128SLC84 chip.

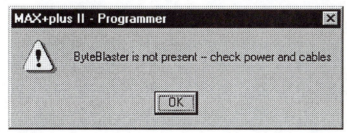

Figure 5

Error #9   JTAG chain information specified in this dialog box does not match.

Solution: Apply power to the circuit card containing the EPM7128LCM84 chip.

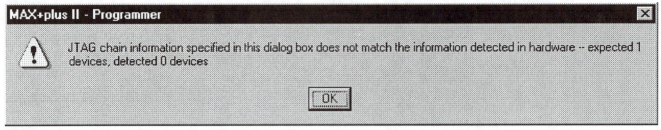

Figure 6

Error #10:   Not in Multi-device chain mode.

Solution: Press the OK button in the error window. (Figure 7)

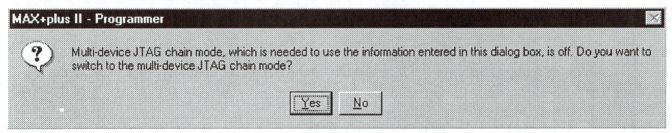

Figure 7

Appendix C: Programming the 7128S

1. Apply 7- to 12-volts DC to the input of the 5-volt regulator on the board containing the EPM7128SLC84 chip.

2. Connect the cable between the hardware Centronics interface to the parallel printer port on the computer, LPT1. If you are using the Byte Blaster from Altera, connect the Byte Blaster in the JTAG port on the circuit board to the printer port on the computer.

3. Open the Max+plus II software.

4. Open the Graphic (.gdf) and Waveform (.scf) files of the circuit you want to program to the hardware.

5. Run the compiler and simulator. Correct all errors before continuing.

6. Select the Max+plus II option in the main menu (the left side of "File").

7. Select the **Programmer** option in the Max+plus II drop-down menu (Figure 1). The Programmer dialog box (Figure 2) will appear on the screen.

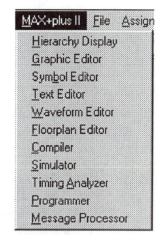

Figure 1

Figure 2

Figure 3

8. Select "Hardware Setup" in the Options menu. (Figure 3)

9. Select the ByteBlaster as the Hardwave Type (Figure 4) and choose the correct Parallel Port that your device is plugged into. See your instructor to identify the proper port used to program the EPM7128SLC84 chip. The example shown shows LPT1: as the port selected.

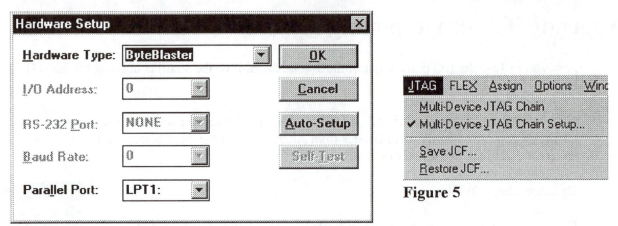

Figure 4

Figure 5

10.   Select the **Multi-device JTAG Chain Setup** option in the **JTAG** main menu (Figure 5). The Multi-Device JTAG Chain Setup dialog box (Figure 6) will appear.

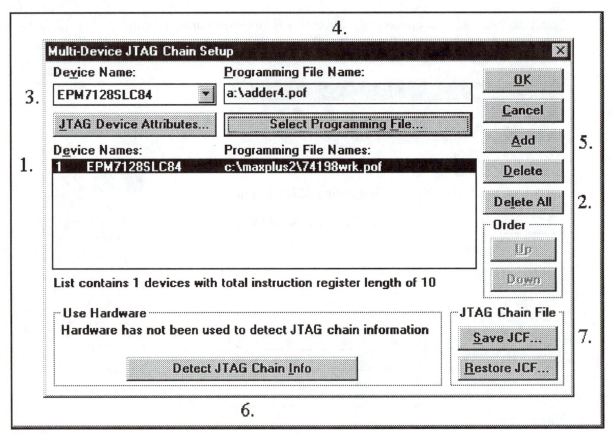

Figure 6

11.   Highlight any device name previously shown in the Device Names window (1) shown in Figure 6 and press the Delete or Delete All button (2).

12.   Select Device Name **EPM7128SLC84** (3) and the select the **.POF** file of the file you wish to program (4).

13.   Press the **Add** button (5) shown in Figure 6. Note: The window (1) now contains the device and file name you selected to program into the EPM7218LC84 chip.

14. Press **Detect JTAG Chain Info** (6) at the bottom of the window in Figure 6. Press the OK button in the 'JTAG Chain information confirmed by the hardware check" window (Figure 7).

Figure 7

15. Press the **Save JCF** button (7) in the Multi-Device JTAG Setup window (Figure 6).

16. Press the **OK** button.

17. Press the **OK** button to exit the Multi-Device Chain Setup window.

18. Press the **Program** button in the Programmer window (Figure 8).

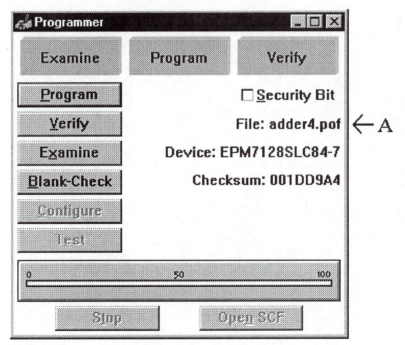

Figure 8

19. The Examine, Program, and Verify boxes should scan relatively fast. Your chip has been programmed if no errors appear. Press the OK button when the software displays the **Programming Complete** message.

Appendix D: The 555 Timer

Objectives:

1. Construct an oscillator using the 555 timer
2. Design an oscillator with a specific duty cycle

Materials List:

- Power supply
- Oscilloscope
- 555 timer IC
- 4.7-KΩ resistor

- 47-KΩ resistor
- 0.001 μF capacitor
- 0.01 μF capacitor

Discussion:

There are three types of multivibrators: the astable, bistable, and monostable. The bistable multivibrator, or flip-flop, has two stable states. When set, the flip-flop will remain set until a condition on the input forces the output to change. The same is true if the flip-flop is in reset mode. A monostable (one-shot) multivibrator has a single stable state. An input condition forces the multivibrator to become unstable for a period of time as determined by an external resistor and capacitor, then automatically reverts back to its stable state. The astable multivibrator doesn't have a stable state, it oscillates.

The TTL compatable 555 timer may be used as an astable multivibrator (oscillator) or as a monostable multivibrator (one shot). Illustrated in Figure 1, the 555 timer has three resistors in series to provide two reference voltages, V_{REF1} and V_{REF2}. The output of Comparator 1 becomes +Vcc when the threshold voltage at Pin 6 becomes more positive than V_{REF1}, causing the latch to reset. When the negated Q output is a logic-HIGH, the transistor is saturated causing the collector-to-emitter voltage to be approximately 0.2 V. When the Trigger voltage at Pin 2 becomes less positive than V_{REF2}, Set occurs causing the negated Q output to go to a logic-LOW. This in turn shut off the transistor.

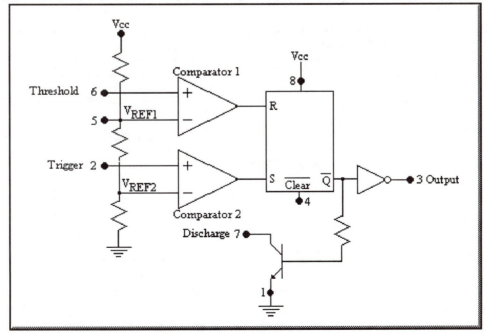

Figure 1

External components needed to cause the 555 timer IC to become a *free running* oscillator are shown in Figure 2. Capacitor C1 charges through R2 and R1 towards Vcc. When E_{C1} reaches the threshold, V_{REF1}, voltage required on Pin 6, the internal transistor saturates, effectively shorting Pin 7, allowing capacitor C1 to discharge. Once E_{C1} drops below the trigger voltage, V_{REF2}, on Pin 2, the internal transistor turns off, allowing C1 to charge again.

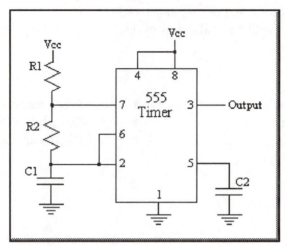

Figure 2

The charge time for C1 is determined by: $\qquad \text{HARGE} = .7(R_1 + R_2)C_1 \qquad$ (1)

The discharge time for C1 is determined by: $\qquad \text{ISCHARGE} = .7(R_2)C_1 \qquad$ (2)

The period of a complete cycle of the output frequency is the sum of the charge and discharge rates of capacitor C1. The period, T, may be calculated by : $\qquad = .7(R_1 + 2R_2)C_1 \qquad$ (3)

The output frequency, f, may be determined by taking the reciprocol of the period, T.

$$= \frac{1}{.7(R_1 + 2R_2)C_1} \qquad (4)$$

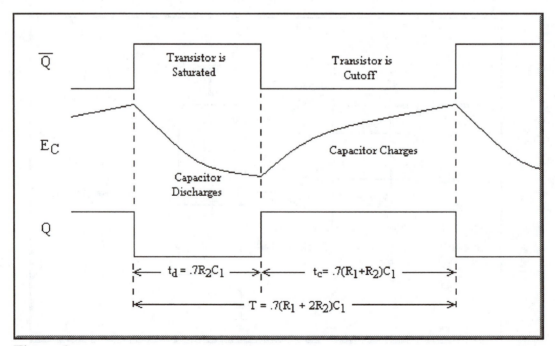

Figure 3

The waveforms in Figure 3 show the relationship of output Q with respect to the charge/discharge of capacitor C1. The pulse width (or space width) may be controlled by selecting different values of R1 and R2. As per equations 1 and 2, changing R1 only affects the charge time but changing R2 affects both charge and discharge times.

To ensure proper operation as an oscillator, R1 should always be greater than 1 KΩ, R1 + R2 should be less than 6.6 MΩ, and C1 should be greater than 50 pFd.

Part 1   Procedure

1.   Construct the circuit shown in Figure 2 using the values listed below.

- Vcc = 5 V DC
- R1 = 4.7 KΩ
- R2 = 47 KΩ
- C1 = 0.001 µFd
- C2 = 0.01 µFd

2.   Based on the component values given and Equations 1 through 4, calculate the following:
Show all work!
▸   Charge time for C1

▸   Discharge time for C1

▸   Frequency of the output signal

▸   Duty cycle (pulse width/period) of the output signal

3.   Use an oscilloscope to measure the frequency at the output (Pin 3) of the circuit constructed.

$$F_{Measured} = \underline{\hspace{3cm}}$$

4.   Accurately read the time for each segment of the output waveform displayed on the oscilloscope and record the results for the designated areas on the waveform shown in Figure 4.

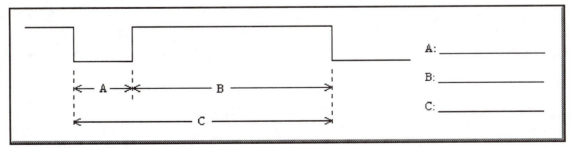

Figure 4

5.   Based on the recorded time measurements, for the pulse width and period, calculate the duty cycle for the waveform displayed on the oscilloscope.

DC = PW/T = _____ / _____ = _____

%DC = DC × 100 = _____ %

Part 2   Procedure

1.   Assume you want to create a 25-KHz pulse waveform with a 67% duty cycle. Assume C1 is 0.001 μFd and C2 is 0.01 μFd, calculate values of R1 and R2 that will produce the desired waveform. Remember that R1 must be greater than 1 KΩ.

2.   Construct the circuit shown in Figure 2 based on your calculated values from Part 2, Step 1. Use potentiometers for R1 and R2, set to the calculated resistances.

3.　Use an oscilloscope to measure the frequency at the output (Pin 3) of the circuit constructed.

$$F_{Measured} = \underline{\hspace{3cm}}$$

4.　Accurately read the time for each segment of the output waveform displayed on the oscilloscope and record the results for the designated areas on the waveform shown in Fig 5.

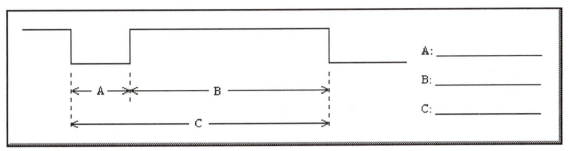

A: _____

B: _____

C: _____

Figure 5

5.　Based on the recorded time measurements, for the pulse width and period, calculate the duty cycle for the waveform displayed on the oscilloscope.

$$DC = PW/T = \underline{\hspace{1.5cm}} / \underline{\hspace{1.5cm}} = \underline{\hspace{2cm}}$$

$$\%DC = DC \times 100 = \underline{\hspace{2.5cm}}\%$$

6.　Demonstrate the circuit and displayed waveforms confirming the 25 KHz with 67% duty cycle to your instructor. Obtain the signature of approval directly on the answer page for this lab.

7.　Write a 1 to 2 page summary pertaining to the results obtained for this lab. Include embedded graphics of the circuit constructed for Part 2 and the computer drawn output waveform showing the pulse width, space width, and period similar to Figure 5.

8.　Submit the following for grading:

▸　Cover page
▸　Typed summary
▸　Completed answer page for this lab

Name _____

Part 1

2.

> ▸   Charge time for C1

> ▸   Discharge time for C1

> ▸   Frequency of the output signal

> ▸   Duty cycle (pulse width/period) of the output signal

3. $F_{Measured}$ = _____

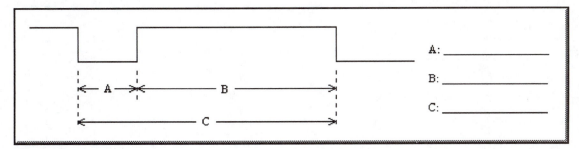

Figure 4

5.   DC = PW/T = _____ / _____ = _____

         %DC = DC × 100 = _____ %

Part 2

1.

3. $F_{Measured} =$ _____

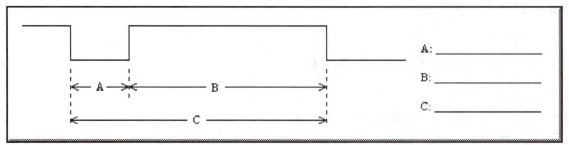

Figure 5

5.   DC = PW/T = _____ / _____ = _____

        %DC = DC × 100 = _____%

6.   Demonstrated to: _____   Date: _____

Grade: _____